# The Story of Paul

## *From Tarsus to Rome*

To Cyndi,
with appreciation for
your friendship and teaching
ministry. Hope to see you
in the Land soon!
Best, Carl
Phil. 4:13

## J. Carl Laney

*J. Carl Laney*

"Laney has taught on the Apostle Paul for years. Now he synthesizes the story of Paul into a precise outline of his life and ministry. People will find a readable history and timeline of Paul's story. Both new and old readers of Paul will find treasures in these pages. It is a great resource that will serve many as an introduction to the Pharisee turned Apostle to the Gentiles."

**Patrick Schreiner,** Associate Professor of New Testament and Biblical Theology, Midwestern Baptist Theological Seminary. Author of *The Kingdom of God; The Ascension of Christ; Matthew, Disciple and Scribe; The Body of Christ: A Spatial Analysis of the Kingdom of God in Matthew*

"The very first class that I took on the campus of Western Seminary was "Apostolic History" from Dr. J. Carl Laney. It was a captivating experience as Carl chronicled the life of Paul juxtaposed onto the biblical Book of Acts. I profited greatly from studying the life of Christianity's most influential missionary-theologian. My confidence in the Scriptures increased as I saw how the writings of Paul's New Testament letters came about during his missionary travels. My understanding of Paul's theology grew as I delved into the context of his inspired writings. Now Dr. Laney has gathered all the insights of that class and made them accessible to the church in this book. By all means, read this book! I have no doubt that if you do, you will be, as I was, blessed and enriched by Dr. Laney's teaching."

**Todd L. Miles,** Professor of Theology, Western Seminary, Portland, OR. Author of *A God of Many Understandings? The Gospel and a Theology of Religions; Superheroes Can't Save You: Epic Examples of Historic Heresies;* and *Cannabis and the Christian: What the Bible Says about Marijuana*

"It's my pleasure to recommend J. Carl Laney's newest book, *The Story of Paul: From Tarsus to Rome*. Drawing upon his decades of teaching the Bible and the life of Paul, Carl leads the reader first to an overview of the life of Paul, from his early life in Tarsus to his martyrdom in Rome in AD 68. The first half of the book is like an exciting travelogue where Carl combines the record of the book of Acts, history, archaeology, and current events. He draws much from his personal visits to many of the places where Paul ministered. The second half is a short course in systematic theology—adequate for a broad, basic introduction to Paul's teaching, yet deep enough and fruitful for the thoughtful reader. It has already enlarged my own understanding and appreciation for the Apostle Paul and his Master, the Lord Jesus Christ.

> **James B. De Young**, Senior Professor, Western Seminary. Author of *Burning Down the Shack* (2010) and *The Apocalypse Is Coming* (2020). Host of podcast, "Apocalypse Is Coming."

"We can learn to understand Jesus by viewing the life of one of his earliest followers, the Apostle Paul. And what a life that was jam-packed with opportunities, challenges, blessings and threats, as he faithfully carried the good news of Jesus into a complex and vibrant world. Carl Laney helps us along the way, by placing the life of Paul within its historical, geographical and cultural framework. By journeying with him through the book of Acts, we can perceive many of the ways that the Apostle connected the teachings of Jesus with the real needs of his day. In the process, we become better equipped to know how to live the Gospel in our own world today."

> **Paul H. Wright**, President, Jerusalem University College. Author of *Understanding the New Testament*; *Understanding Biblical Archaeology*; *Understanding Great People of the Bible*; *Heart of the Holy Land*; and Illustrated Guide to Biblical Geography.

"If you enjoy walking through your Bible, you will love walking beside Dr. Carl Laney as he tells the story of Paul and the early church. This is someone who knows Paul's life, how Paul thinks, the roads he traveled, and the places he visited. But behind this well-told story are the wonderful insights Paul delivered-insights that take us to the very mind and heart of God. The second portion of this book is a preacher and teacher's treasure trove. Here, Laney indexes and organizes the writings of Paul under subject headings. It really is two wonderful books in one."

> **John A. Beck**, Ph.D. Author of *The Basic Bible Atlas*, *The Holy Land for Christian Travelers*, and host of the film series, *The Holy Land-Connecting the Land with Its Stories*.

To my grandchildren:

May you get to know Jesus better
through the travels and teachings of the Apostle Paul.
(3 John 4)


*Acknowledgments*

I owe a debt of gratitude to my students at Western Seminary who listened attentively to my lectures on the Apostle Paul and stimulated my further study through their probing questions and insightful comments. I am deeply grateful to Dr. Barry Beitzel, editor of the *Lexham Geographic Commentary on Acts Through Revelation*, and my colleagues at the Jerusalem University College who contributed their research for this exciting new commentary. Your many geographical observations and insights are embedded (and referenced!) throughout my book. I extend my appreciation to Dr. Carl Rasmussen for the use of his fine photographs and for the geographical research and images he continues to add to his website, *www.holylandphotos.org*. I also wish to thank the friends who have read and corrected the typos and errors in my manuscript, including Kay Dillner, Cindy Ludeman and my wife, Nancy Laney. A big thanks to my friend and colleague, Jon Raibley, who has been so helpful with creating my recent book covers and formatting the manuscripts for publication. Finally, many thanks to my friends Dr. Patrick Schreiner, Dr. Todd L. Miles, Dr. James B. De Young, Dr. Paul Wright and Dr. John Beck, who have kindly endorsed this book.

# Table of Contents

# Preface

What does a seminary prof do after he officially "retires" from forty years of teaching the Bible? This is a question I asked myself during the summer of 2018 after I submitted my last semester's grades, spoke at my last commencement and turned in the key to my Western Seminary campus office.

After taking a ten-day vacation trip with my wife and completing some long delayed house projects, I turned on my computer and began doing what I have been doing for most of my career. I started writing another book. Although writing is one of the hardest things I do, it is also one of the most fulfilling. Writing enables me to take the material that I have researched and taught, and then put it into a form where it can be helpful for a broader audience than my seminary students. Writing enables me to create resources which will be available to students of Scripture long after I have finished my earthly ministry and have joined family and friends who are already in heaven.

Soon after retiring, I drew on my biblical studies and travels in Israel to write, *The Story of Israel: A Short History of the Land and Its People*. I self-published the book using CreateSpace, now Kindle Direct Publishing, an Amazon affiliate. After completing my book on Israel, I turned to my lectures on the Gospels and began writing *The Life of Christ: Past, Present and Future*. I was thrilled to be asked by Western Seminary to create an online "Life of Christ" class based on my new book.

Having spent many years teaching an elective class on the book of Acts, I decided that my next writing project would be the life and teachings of the Apostle Paul. Hence, the present volume, *The Story of Paul: From Tarsus to Rome*. It has been my privilege over the past year to deepen my own study and gain new insights into Paul's travels and teachings.

One of the nicest things anyone has said about my books was expressed by a friend who traveled and studied with me in Israel. She later commented, "Reading Dr. Laney's books are just like sitting in his classroom and hearing him teach." I hope this book will provide you with an experience like that. You are invited into my *virtual* classroom as you read and reflect on *The Story of the Apostle Paul*.

J. Carl Laney, Epiphany 2021

# Part 1  The Travels of Paul

## Chapter 1
## Saul's Early Years

If someone made a list of the top ten most influential people of the last two millennia, I am confident that the Apostle Paul would be included among them. His life, travels and writings were providently used by God to spread the good news of the coming of Israel's promised Messiah and the expansion of Christianity throughout the first-century Roman world.

Although we don't have a lot of details about Saul's early life, before he assumed the name "Paul," there are sufficient biblical references to provide us with some helpful background. Saul was at home in the Mediterranean region of the first-century Roman world. He was a Jew of the diaspora, which means that he was born and raised outside of the geographic region of his ancestry, the land of Israel. As he explained to the Roman commander who had arrested him in the temple court, "I am a Jew of Tarsus in Cilicia, a citizen of no insignificant city" (Acts 21:39; 22:3).

Tarsus, located today in south-central Turkey about 12 miles inland from the Mediterranean seacoast, was the capital of the Roman province of Cilicia. The city was situated at the junction of the land and sea routes connecting central Anatolia (Asia Minor) with the Mediterranean Sea.

Tarsus, Saul's home town, has a long and storied history. Alexander the Great passed through Tarsus with his army in 333 BC on his way to conquer Persia. Strabo, the Greek geographer, praised the city for its intellectual and literary reputation as a community of poets, linguists and philosophers. It was said that the schools of Tarsus rivaled those of Athens and Alexandria. Antiochus IV Epiphanes put down a revolt in Tarsus in 171 BC and renamed the city Antiochia on the Cyndus, but confusion with the Antioch of Syria resulted in the name reverting back to Tarsus (2 Maccabees 4:30). The region of Cilicia was dominated by pirates until 67 BC when Pompey eliminated them and brought Tarsus under Roman rule. It was at Tarsus in 41 BC that Mark Antony and Cleopatra met to solidify their alliance and fan the flames of their famous romance. During the Roman period, Tarsus continued as an important intellectual center, with educational academies, grand temples, palaces, agoras, baths, fountains, a gymnasium and a stadium. No wonder Paul could refer to his home town of Tarsus as "no insignificant city" (Acts 21:39).

Figure 1  Paul's Home Town of Tarsus

Little remains of first century Tarsus except a Roman road and a gate named for the Egyptian queen, Cleopatra VII, made famous by her love affair with Julius Caesar and later as wife of Mark Antony. In the heart of the city is a historic district where guides will direct tourists to "St. Paul's house" and well. The site doesn't create a strong impression of what Paul might have experienced during his early life in Tarsus. If you are offered the opportunity to drink from Paul's well, politely decline. The experience is not worth the inconvenience you will likely experience for the rest of your trip! The Church of Saint Paul, dating from the 11th century, but rebuilt in 1862, honors Paul's memory. Sadly, the church no longer serves an active congregation and has been officially designated a museum.

Figure 2  Cleopatra's Gate in Tarsus (www.Holylandphotos.org)

Saul was probably born early in the first century, perhaps around AD 10. He traced his ancestry to the tribe of Benjamin (Phil. 3:5), thus a descendant of Jacob and his beloved Rachel (Gen. 35:16-20). Israel's first king, Saul, was of the tribe of Benjamin and may account for the Apostle's Hebrew name, "Saul." He would later assume the Greek name "Paul" (Acts 13:9) during his ministry on Cyprus. Later Paul would explain to the Philippians that he was brought up under strict Jewish tradition, "circumcised on the eighth day…a Hebrew of Hebrews" (Phil. 3:5). Paul's description of himself as a "Hebrew of Hebrews" is a superlative, like other expressions found in the Hebrew Bible, "Lord of Lords," "King of Kings," and "Holy of Holies." Not only was Saul a Hebrew, but he was asserting that before his life changing encounter with Jesus on the way to Damascus, he was the *most* Hebrew of the Hebrews.

The only physical description of Saul is found in a second century AD non-canonical document in Greek, *The Acts of Paul*, recounting Paul's travels and teachings. The unknown author describes the apostle as "a man of middling size, and his hair was scanty, and his legs were a little crooked, and his knees were far apart; he had large eyes, and his eyebrows met, and his nose was somewhat large." Not exactly a flattering description! Although written more than a century after Paul died, it is not inconsistent with the words of his first century critics who said, "His letters are weighty and strong, but his personal presence is unimpressive" (2 Cor. 10:10).

Figure 3  Early portrait of Apostle Paul from 5/6 century AD; located in the Grotto of Saint Paul near Ephesus (www.holylandphotos.org)

Saul's standing in Judaism is further emphasized as someone who embraced Israel's law as an observant Pharisee (Phil. 3:5). While the Pharisees tend to get a "bad rap" because of the words of Jesus (Matt. 23:13-33), not all of them were "hypocrites." In contrast to the other Jewish sects of the first-century (the Sadducees and Essenes), Josephus describes the Pharisees as "the most accurate interpreters of the laws," "affectionate to each other," and cultivating "harmonious relations with the community" (*Jewish War* II.162-168). Unlike the priestly Sadducees, the Pharisees embraced the biblical doctrines of the resurrection, rewards and eternal punishment (Josephus *Antiquities* XVIII.12-15). The Pharisees emphasized ethics over theology and stressed individual fulfillment of the Mosaic law and oral tradition. Like many Christians today, the Pharisees were good people who loved and obeyed God, but their beliefs and practices were not always a perfect match. Yet Saul was clearly an observant and zealous Pharisee. As to "the righteousness which is in the law," he claimed to be "found blameless" (Phil. 3:6).

It was the responsibility of a Jewish father to teach his son a trade. The second century AD Rabbi Yehuda ha-Nasi, editor of the Mishnah, said, "He that teaches not his son a trade is as if he taught him to be a thief." Although we know nothing about Saul's father, sometime during his early life in Tarsus young Saul learned the trade of tent making. During his time in Corinth, Saul stayed with Aquila and Priscilla and worked with them as a "tentmaker" (Acts 18:1-3). The ancient craft of tent making consisted of weaving goat's hair into long strips, sewing them together, and attaching loops and ropes. Having learned this trade as a young man, Saul was later able to travel from city to city, knowing that he could always find work. This enabled the apostle to minister the gospel without being dependent on financial gifts from the newly established congregations of believers.

Although Saul was born in Tarsus, his parents, being devout Jews, arranged for their son to study in Jerusalem. Since he had a sister living in Jerusalem (Acts 23:16), it may be that Saul lived with her while receiving his training. One can imagine Saul as a young man, living far away from his home in Tarsus, exploring the streets and markets of Jerusalem, visiting the Holy Temple, and climbing to the summit of the Mount of Olives to enjoy the spectacular view. Unlike the Jews living in remote regions of the Roman Empire, Saul would have been able to regularly visit the colonnaded temple courts where he could listen to the rabbis expound the Torah and ask them engaging questions. Living and studying in Jerusalem must have been a dream come true for such a seriously minded young man as Saul.

Later in life, he told the riotous crowd seeking his arrest at temple court that he received his theological education in Jerusalem as a student of the famous rabbi, Gamaliel (Acts 22:3). Rabbi Gamaliel I (sometimes referred to as Gamaliel the Elder) was a member of the Sanhedrin and the grandson of the celebrated Rabbi Hillel, who is often quoted in the Mishnah and Talmud. Like his famed grandfather, Gamaliel is known for taking a more lenient view of the law than his more stringent contemporary, Rabbi Shammai. Luke records that in addition to being a Pharisee, Gamaliel was "a teacher of the law, respected by all the people" (Acts 5:34). The Jewish Talmud characterizes the importance of Gamaliel with these words, "when he died, the honor of the Torah ceased and purity and piety became extinct" (*Sotah* xv:18).

When the apostles John and Peter were arrested in Jerusalem for proclaiming the messiahship of Jesus and brought before the Sanhedrin, it was Gamaliel who brought wisdom and reason to the proceedings. He warned his fellow members of the Jewish court to "take care what you propose to do with these men" (Acts 5:35). He reminded them of previous messianic movements whose followers disbanded after their leaders perished. He cautioned the Sanhedrin saying, "Stay away from these men and let them alone, for if this plan or action is of men, it will be overthrown, but if it is of God, you will not be able to overthrow them; or else you may even be found fighting against God" (Acts 5:38-39).

Figure 4  Roman Road and Gate leading to Tarsus
(www.holylandphotos.org)

It was under this wise and learned teacher that Saul of Tarsus studied the Hebrew Bible, including the many prophecies about

God's future kingdom and Israel's coming Messiah. Like the rabbinical students studying in Jerusalem's Jewish yeshivas today, Saul would "sit and study," reading the Torah, memorizing important texts and debating their interpretations with his fellow students. Rabbi Gamaliel had no idea, as he mentored and taught his young scholars, that Saul of Tarsus would become his most famous and influential student.

*Note:* I will continue to use the name "Saul" throughout the early chapters of the book and switch to "Paul" in Chapter 8 when the apostle assumes this name during his first missionary journey (Acts 13:13).

# Chapter 2
# Saul's Persecution of the Church

Instead of returning to his home and family in Tarsus after completing his theological education, young Saul appears to have remained in Jerusalem. Perhaps he continued there as a disciple of Gamaliel or assumed a position as an instructor in one of Jerusalem's academies. But during this period of his life, Saul would have no doubt become aware of a growing messianic movement led by Jesus' disciples. The key leaders in this grass roots movement included Peter, James and John.

Research by Harold Hoehner (*Chronological Aspect of the Life of Christ,* Zondervan Publishing House: Grand Rapids, 1977) indicates that Jesus began His public ministry in the summer or fall of AD 29 and was crucified on April 3, AD 33. Since His crucifixion and resurrection, the followers of Jesus had grown from a handful of faithful believers to a noticeably significant community. Although the man they had proclaimed as Israel's Messiah had died, His apostles were busy proclaiming His resurrection! One of Jesus' closest followers, the Apostle Peter, had preached on the day of Pentecost, "This Jesus God raised up again, to which we are all witnesses" (Acts 2:32). He quoted passages from the Hebrew Bible (Psalms 16 and 110) as proof of the Messiah's resurrection, leading three thousand to believe Peter's message and identify themselves as Jesus' followers through the ritual of water immersion (Acts 2:41).

Saul must have heard the rumors circulating in Jerusalem about a miracle which had taken place by the Beautiful Gate in the temple court where Peter and John had healed a lame man "in the name of Messiah Jesus" (Acts 3:6). It is quite likely that Saul had heard with his own ears the apostles' preaching that the resurrected Jesus was Israel's promised Messiah. The words of Paul's later testimony, "I cast my vote against them" (Acts 26:10), may indicate that he was an official member of the Sanhedrin and voted with this judicial body to condemn Jesus' followers to death. If so, Saul would have been present in the Jewish court when Peter and John were commanded "not to speak or teach at all in the name of Jesus" (Acts 4:18). One can imagine how angry Saul would have been by the defiant words of the apostles, "We cannot stop speaking about what we have seen and heard" (Acts 4:20). When the Sanhedrin's warnings were not heeded, Saul may have witnessed the flogging of the apostles who persisted in teaching and preaching that Jesus was the Messiah (Acts 5:40-42).

We don't know what was going on in Saul's mind as he watched the growth of this first century messianic movement from a dozen "Jesus followers" to three thousand, then five thousand, and more. But the words of Jesus to Saul on the Damascus road, "It's hard to kick against the goad" (Acts 26:14) suggest that the Holy Spirit was prodding Saul, like a farmer goading some recalcitrant oxen to get moving. How would he respond to God's goading? Could these crazy Jesus followers be right? Although as a Pharisee, Saul would have had no kind regard for the Sadducees who dominated the Jerusalem temple, it must have really galled him to learn that "a great many of the priests were becoming obedient to the faith" (Acts 6:7).

Then there was Stephen. As the early congregation of Jesus' followers grew, the leaders established new ministries in response to the specific needs of the people. One of those needs was to care for certain widows who came from a Hellenistic (Greek) cultural background (Acts 6:1). They were Jews who spoke Greek instead of Aramaic and didn't observe all the cultural traditions of Jewish families. Some of the new Jewish believers were probably thinking that these widows weren't "Jewish enough." They were similar to some Orthodox Jews today who don't think fellow Jews of the Reformed tradition are "real" Jews because they don't strictly observe the kosher food restrictions and other rabbinic traditions. In distributing food to believers in need, these widows were being neglected, probably due to prejudice against their Hellenistic background. The apostles took action in response to this need by selecting seven men who could make sure that these widows received proper and necessary care. With the approval of the congregation, seven men were selected including Stephen, a man described by Luke as "full of faith and of the Holy Spirit" (Acts 6:5). The seven were brought before the apostles who commissioned them through the laying on of hands and sent them out to serve.

It wasn't long before Stephen advanced from ministering to the widows to preaching the Word of God. Not only was his street preaching powerful and convincing, but Stephen was authenticating his message with "great wonders and signs" (Acts 6:8). Since the

Jewish leaders could not silence Stephen in public debate (Acts 6:10), they brought false charges against him before the Sanhedrin. Stephen was charged with "blasphemy" for challenging the abiding validity of the Mosaic Law and the Jewish temple (Acts 6:11-14). These charges were probably a misrepresentation of Stephen's message that Jesus had fulfilled the law and had offered Himself as the final sacrifice for sins. Stephen was preaching that Jesus' work on the cross came in fulfillment of all that the sacrificial system of the temple had long anticipated.

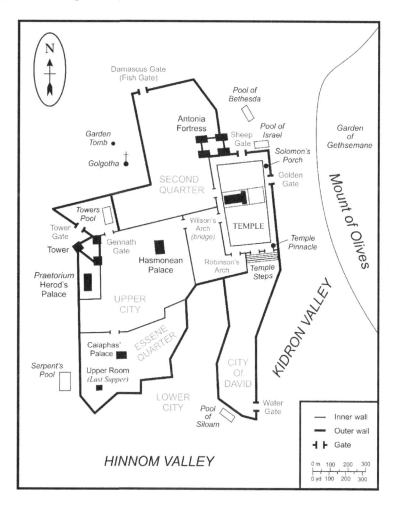

Figure 5 First Century Jerusalem.
(Reprinted from "The Synoptic Gospel" © 2009 by Smart Publishing Ltd.)

Stephen was hauled before the Sanhedrin authorities where the high priest demanded an explanation. "Are these things so?" he queried. Saul of Tarsus was probably present as a member of the Sanhedrin and heard Stephen's challenging reply. Stephen's so-called "defense" before the Jewish court was not designed to secure his acquittal but to confront the Jewish leaders with their rejection of Jesus, Israel's promised Messiah. His message was a summary of Israel's history emphasizing God's promise to Abraham and its ultimate fulfillment in Jesus (Acts 7:2-53). After rehearsing the great privileges of the nation of Israel, Stephen rebuked the nation's leaders for rejecting God's prophetic messengers. Stephen's message climaxed with words that must have stung the listeners' ears, "You men who are stiff-necked and uncircumcised in heart and ears are always resisting the Holy Spirit; you are doing just as your fathers did" (Acts 7:51). Stephen concluded his rebuke with an indictment, "You who received the law as ordained by angels, and yet *did not keep it*" (Acts 7:53).

For someone like Saul, a law abiding Pharisee, a "Hebrew of Hebrews," who believed himself to be "blameless" according to the righteous requirements of the Mosaic law (Phil. 3:6), Stephen's words must have triggered a volcanic eruption of hatred and hostility. Stephen was condemned by the enraged members of the Sanhedrin and driven out of the city for execution.

Stoning was the traditional method of execution by Jewish law. Jewish tradition records that this was done not by throwing many stones, but by dropping a heavy stone on the victim's chest (*Sanhedrin* 6:3). If the victim didn't die immediately, the process was repeated. Only after this initial step would the crowd pick up stones to finish the job.

There is some question as to whether the stoning of Stephen was legal or simply a mob action response to his soul searing message. Capital punishment was a closely guarded prerogative under Roman rule and only the prefects (or governors) had the authority to carry out an execution (Jn. 18:31). But there was one exception to this rule. According to Josephus, the first century Jewish historian, the Judeans were authorized to execute anyone who violated the sanctity of the Jewish temple (*The Jewish War* VI.126). Perhaps this was the "legal" justification which Jewish leaders appealed to in order to justify and carry out Stephen's execution.

Stephen was the first of Jesus' followers to be martyred. His death should not have surprised the apostles, for Jesus had warned them of coming hostility. In His final instructions to the apostles, Jesus said, "They will make you outcasts from the synagogue, but an hour is coming for everyone who kills you to think that he is offering service to God. These things they will do because they have not known the Father or Me" (Jn. 16:2-3).

In Christian tradition, the execution of Stephen took place just outside a gate that is named in his memory. The St. Stephen's Gate, also known as the Lion's Gate, gives access into the Old City of Jerusalem from the east, just north of the temple area. The four lions featured on the east side of the gate were placed there by the Ottoman sultan, Suleiman the Magnificent, to celebrate the Ottoman defeat of the Turks in 1517. In spite of the noise from the traffic entering the Old City through this gate, I usually pause with my students to read Luke's account of Stephen's martyrdom and how he died in a Christ-like manner, forgiving his executioners (Acts 7:60). Inside Stephen's Gate and to the left is an entrance to the Temple Mount, known to Moslems as Haram al Sharif (the Noble Sanctuary). Continuing straight from Stephen's Gate, visitors will find themselves on the Via Dolorosa (Latin for "Sorrowful Way"), the traditional route Jesus would have walked, carrying his cross from Pilate's Praetorium to Golgotha, the site of his crucifixion. The Via Dolorosa is lined with souvenir shops, packed with tourists and frequented by pick pockets. But no Christian visitor to Jerusalem wants to miss the opportunity to "walk in Jesus steps" on the Via Dolorosa.

In Luke's account of the execution of Stephen we find the first biblical reference to Saul of Tarsus. Luke reports, "When they had driven him out of the city they began stoning him; and the witnesses laid aside their robes at the feet of a young man named Saul" (Acts 6:58). Saul not only witnessed Stephen's execution, but gave it his approval. Luke comments that "Saul was in hearty agreement with putting him to death" (Acts 8:1). No one present at the stoning of Stephen could imagine that this young Jewish Pharisee was God's chosen instrument to carry the good news of salvation through Jesus throughout the Roman empire!

The stoning of Stephen marked the beginning of a "great persecution" against the followers of Jesus in Jerusalem (Acts 8:2). And Saul of Tarsus appears in Luke's account to be one of the chief instigators of this persecution. He apparently received authorization from the Jewish high priest to arrest and imprison others who, like Stephen, followed Jesus (Acts 9:1-2). Luke records that "Saul began ravaging the church, entering house after house, and dragging off men and women, he would put them in prison" (Acts 8:3).

As a result of the increasingly intense persecution, most of the believers left Jerusalem and scattered into the surrounding regions of Judea and Samaria. Only the apostles remained in Jerusalem (Acts 8:1), perhaps to provide leadership and stability for the mother church. Luke records how Philip, one of Stephen's associates assigned to serve tables (Acts 6:5), went north and began evangelizing the region of Samaria (Acts 8:4-25). Then the Lord directed him south on the road leading to Gaza where, by divine appointment, he encountered and evangelized an Ethiopian court official (Acts 8:26-40). Luke provides us with an exciting account of how the Ethiopian, a Gentile worshiper of the God of Israel, came to faith through the witness of Philip who explained how the prophecy of Isaiah 53 had been fulfilled by Jesus.

The church was growing in Judea and Samaria. But Saul of Tarsus was doing everything in his power to put a stop to it. Yet through the Holy Spirit, God was still prodding Saul's heart. He was a man who was thoroughly trained in the Scripture, yet his eyes were blinded to the good news that Israel's Messiah and Savior had come. What would it take to open the eyes of this zealous persecutor of the church to the truth? What would it take to turn Saul the persecutor into Paul, proclaimer of the gospel?

# Chapter 3
# Saul's Damascus Road Experience

Acts chapter 9 is a key turning point in the history of the early church. God had used Peter and John to bring the gospel to the Jewish people of Judea. God had used Philip to carry the message to the Samaritans. In Acts 9 we discover how God prepared a new witness to take the good news of the gospel to the Gentile nations of the first century Roman world. Saul's life defining experience on the road to Damascus took place about two years after Jesus' crucifixion, probably in the summer of A.D. 35.

Damascus, located in modern Syria, was about 150 miles north of Jerusalem. The journey would have taken about ten days if Saul was traveling by foot. Damascus has the reputation of being one of the oldest continually inhabited cities of the world. The name of the city appears on the list of cities conquered by Egypt's Pharaoh Thutmoses III in the 15th century BC. The reason for the city's importance and continuous occupation is that it was a desert oasis on the major caravan route from Mesopotamia to Egypt. While the city was repeatedly conquered during its long history, it was always rebuilt and reoccupied. Because of its strategic location along the northern segment of the international coastal highway, linking Africa and Asia, Damascus was indispensable for long-haul caravans and travelers. During the Roman Empire, the road from Jerusalem to Damascus would have been well traveled with roadside inns (caravanserais) available to accommodate travelers like Saul.

Although the Roman prefect (or governor) of Judea was the ultimate authority over the subjects of the province, the Sanhedrin was granted authority in matters of religion. Pursuing his policy of persecuting the followers of Jesus, a movement he regarded as a heretical cult, Saul procured letters from the Jewish high priest to arrest "any belonging to the Way" and bring them back to Jerusalem for trial. Luke records that "Saul, still breathing threats and murder against the disciples of the Lord, went to the high priest and asked for letters from him to the synagogues at Damascus, so that if he found any belonging to the Way, both men and women, he might bring them bound to Jerusalem" (Acts 9:1-2).

Notice that Luke doesn't refer to Jesus' followers as "Christians." This designation was not yet in use. The term "Christian" would eventually be adopted as a nickname for the followers of Jesus (Acts 11:26). Since Jesus had identified Himself as the only "way" to God the Father (Jn. 14:6), the earliest designation for the disciples of Jesus was simply those belonging to "the Way" (Acts 19:9, 23; 22:4; 24:14, 22). Saul had apparently heard that some of the believers who fled from his murderous intentions in Jerusalem had settled in Damascus. With the authority of the Sanhedrin, the Jews highest religious court, Saul set off for Damascus.

What route did Saul travel on his way to Damascus? In his article, "The Road from Jerusalem to Damascus," Paul Wright considers four possible routes Saul might have used: the Mediterranean coastal route; the watershed route through the hill country; the Transjordan highlands route and the Jordan Valley route (*Lexham Geographic Commentary on Acts Through Revelation* [henceforth abbreviated *LGCATR*], pp. 224-227). Wright argues for the heavily populated and well-traveled Jordan Valley route. According to this view, Saul would have left Jerusalem, traveling east through the Judean wilderness to cross the Jordan River in the vicinity of Jericho. This eastern route would have enabled Saul to avoid both the dangers and uncleanness associated with traveling through Samaria. Saul would then have traveled north through Perea to Pella where he likely would have crossed the Jordan back into western Galilee and continued north around the Sea of Galilee. He might have continued north to Caesarea Philippi where he would turn northeast to skirt the lower slopes of Mt. Hermon and then continue northeast to Damascus. Or Saul might have taken a short cut, crossing the Jordan River at a ford north of the Sea of Galilee, to ascend the Golan Heights and continue northeast toward Damascus.

Saul had probably been on the road to Damascus more than a week and was approaching his destination. Luke records that his unexpected encounter took place as he "neared" or "came near" to Damascus (Acts 9:3; 22:6). Saul was no doubt weary from travel and hungry for a good meal when suddenly, about midday (Acts 22:6), "a light from heaven flashed around him" (Acts 9:3). Falling to the ground, the startled traveler heard words spoken in Aramaic (Acts 26:14), "Saul, Saul! Why are you persecuting Me?" (Acts 9:4).

Luke records that Paul's traveling companions heard the voice,

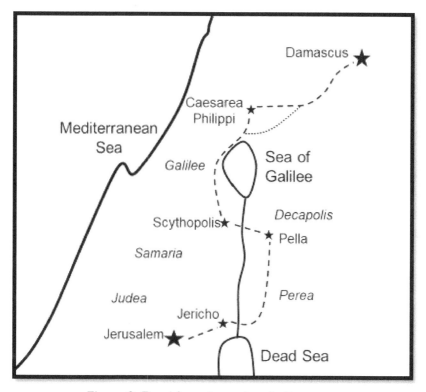

Figure 6  Road from Jerusalem to Damascus

but saw no one (Acts 9:7). This was probably true for Saul as well. He probably looked around wondering, "Who is speaking to me?" As a learned Jew, Saul could not have been unfamiliar with the concept of a "voice from heaven" (Deut. 4:36; Dan. 4:31). Jesus had heard a voice from heaven three times during His ministry. The rabbis tell of God speaking at various times from heaven with an audible voice. Now Saul was hearing a voice from heaven. No doubt puzzled and troubled by the blinding light, Saul responded with a question, "Who are you, Lord" (Acts 9:5). The word "Lord" could be as well translated "Sir," as in Acts 16:30 and Matthew 21:29,30.

The heavenly voice answered Saul's question with the words, "I am Jesus whom you are persecuting" (Acts 9:5). What a shock this must have been for Saul of Tarsus! The voice from heaven was none other than the voice of Jesus whose followers Saul was persecuting! It was as if the resurrected Jesus was crying out from heaven on behalf of his body which was suffering on earth. In the seconds that followed, Saul must have come to a startling and life changing realization. It was as if God had switched on the light in Saul's mind, giving him new and conclusive spiritual insight. Somewhere along the road to Damascus, Saul of Tarsus came to believe that the God whom he had sought so fervently to serve was *Jesus* whose followers he was persecuting!

Some Greek manuscripts add the phrase at the end of Acts 9:4, "It is hard for you to kick against the goad." The phrase is part of the original text in Paul's later testimony before King Agrippa (Acts 26:14), and may have been inserted into verse 4. This is a proverbial statement picturing for us oxen kicking against a pointed prod which the farmer was using to hurry them along. Kicking against the goad doesn't make the load any lighter; it just causes more trouble. One way or another, the farmer will have his way. Jesus appears to be telling Saul something like this: "You have been kicking against the goad, Saul. I have been patiently prodding you to recognize my messiahship, but you have been resisting. Your kicking against Me has not done any good. Like the nation of Israel, I have chosen you for a special purpose. You are Mine, Saul, and I will accomplish My sovereign purposes in and through your life."

As Saul lay on the ground, silently contemplating Jesus' words, he received his first instructions from the One who would become his Master and Lord, "Get up and enter the city, and it will be told you what you must do" (Acts 9:6). Luke records that Saul was blinded as a result of the vision. "Saul got up from the ground, and though his eyes were open, he could see nothing; and leading him by the hand, they brought him into Damascus. And he was three days without sight, and neither ate nor drank" (Acts 9:8-9). It was this blinded enemy of the church that God had appointed to be a preacher and teacher of the gospel. What did Saul think about as he waited, sightless, for further instructions from Jesus? He may have been thinking of how this life changing-experience would impact his relationship with his family, friends and his leadership among the Jews in Jerusalem. "What will they say? What will they think? Will I be expelled from the Sanhedrin? Will I experience the hostility I have shown to others?" I am sure that Saul was beginning to realize that becoming a follower of Jesus would be very costly personally.

Living in Damascus at the time of Saul's vision was a trusted disciple of Jesus by the name of Ananias whom God used to minister to the blinded Saul. The Lord spoke to him saying, "Get up and go to the street called Straight, and inquire at the house of Judas for a man from Tarsus named Saul, for he is praying, and he has seen in a vision a man named Ananias come in and lay his hands on him, so that he might regain his sight" (Acts 9:11-12). The street called "Straight" (Acts 9:11) has been identified with the *decumanus maximus*, the main east-west Roman road through the walled city of Damascus. Not surprisingly, Ananias was reluctant to take on this assignment. He was well aware of Saul's reputation as a dangerous persecutor of God's people (Acts 9:13-14). Ananias may have been one of those who had fled from Jerusalem as a result of Saul's persecution after the stoning of Stephen. But he was reassured by the Lord's further instructions, "Go, for he is a chosen instrument of Mine, to bear My name before the Gentiles and kings and the sons of Israel; for I will show him how much he must suffer for My name's sake" (Acts 9:15-16).

God revealed to Ananias that Saul of Tarsus had been chosen for significant future ministry. By God's sovereign design, Saul the persecutor was about to become a proclaimer of the gospel! He was a "chosen vessel" to be filled with God's Spirit for the purpose of bringing the gospel message to Gentiles, rulers and the people of Israel. Acts 9:15 captures the essence and focus of Paul's future ministry. Saul will become the apostle to the Gentiles (Acts 22:21; 26:17; Rom. 1:5; 15:16; Gal. 1:16; Eph. 3:8; 1 Tim. 2:7). In his future ministry, Saul would be given the opportunity to share God's love with rulers, like the Roman governors Felix and Festus, and the last ruler of the Herodian dynasty, King Agrippa (Acts 24:10-17; 25:1-12; 26:21-32). But in spite of his focus as an "apostle to the Gentiles," Saul would never neglect his own kinsmen, the people of Israel. His pattern for ministry would be to go to the Jews first, and then to the Gentiles (Acts 13:46; Rom. 1:16).

As he had been instructed by the Lord, Ananias went to Saul for two purposes: (1) that Saul might receive his sight, and (2) that he might be filled with the Holy Spirit. Although Ananias had at first been hesitant to go to Saul and attend to his needs (Acts 9:13-14), he was an obedient servant of the Lord. By the time he reached the house of Judas "on the street called Straight" (Acts 9:11), his heart was changed. God removed the fear and replaced it with a heart of love and compassion. He was now ready to receive Saul as a brother in Christ and welcome him into the body of Christ. After Ananias laid his hands on Saul, he said, "Brother Saul, the Lord Jesus, who appeared to you on the road by which you were coming, has sent me so that you may regain your sight and be filled with the Holy Spirit" (Acts 9:17). Immediately, Saul regained his sight and was immersed (*baptized*) in water.

The ritual of water baptism was used in Jewish tradition by someone who wanted to convert to Judaism. They must undergo an immersion in water which symbolized a new birth into a new life of faith in the God of Abraham. The same ritual was used by early Christians to symbolize their new birth (Jn. 3:3) into a new life of faith in Jesus, Israel's Messiah and Savior. For Saul of Tarsus, this was a new beginning. No longer the persecutor of God's people, Saul was to become a proclaimer of the gospel. Paul would later pen the words to young Timothy, "I was formerly a blasphemer and persecutor and violent aggressor, and yet I was shown mercy…Christ Jesus came into the world to save sinners among whom I am the foremost of all" (1 Tim. 1:13-15).

Saul's life-changing experience on the road to Damascus is usually called his "conversion." The problem with this terminology is that Saul didn't *convert* from anything. He didn't convert from Judaism to Christianity since there was no such thing as "Christianity" at this time. Saul was Jewish. Though ignorant of the fulfillment of messianic prophecy in Jesus, he had worshipped and served the God of Abraham, Isaac and Jacob. Saul had been zealous for his ancestral faith. And he continued to live as a Jewish man after his Damascus road experience. He continued to attend the synagogue on the Sabbath. He continued to observe the Mosaic law. He continued going up to Jerusalem for the Jewish festivals. Saul of Tarsus lived and died as a Jewish man. As Marvin Wilson has pointed out, "at no point in his life did Paul leave Judaism; rather he understood his relationship to the Messiah as the full blooming of his Jewish faith." (*Our Father Abraham,* Eerdmans Publishing Co., 1989, p. 46). Krister Stendahl adds, "Here is not that change of 'religion' that we commonly associate with the word conversion. Serving the one and the same God, Paul receives a new and special calling in God's service. God's Messiah asks him as a Jew to bring God's message to the Gentiles" (*Paul Among Jews and Gentiles,* Philadelphia: Fortress Press, 1976, p. 7).

Instead of using the word "conversion" to describe what took place in Saul's life on the Damascus road, I believe it can be more correctly labeled as his "calling." God *called* Saul to embrace the messiahship of Jesus and to proclaim the good news of His offer of salvation to Jews, Gentiles and the whole Roman world. The Damascus road experience didn't convert Saul to a new religion or give him a new theology. Rather, it supplied the missing piece of the messianic puzzle which enabled him "to integrate the message of the Cross with his understanding of the Old Testament" (Timothy J. Ralston, "The Theological Significance of Paul's Conversion, *Bibliotheca Sacra,* April-June, 1990, p. 210).

Figure 7  Ancient gate of Damascus. Photo curtesy of Ian Cowe.

# Chapter 4
# Saul's Early Witness

Almost immediately after his Damascus road encounter with the risen Jesus, Saul the persecutor became a proclaimer of the gospel. Luke records that after spending several days with the followers of Jesus in Damascus, Saul began proclaiming in the synagogues, saying "He is the Son of God" (Acts 9:20). The other disciples were amazed at the 180-degree reversal of Saul's attitude toward the believers. One day he was intent on arresting those who had believed in Jesus. And a few days later Saul had joined the ranks of Jesus' followers and was confounding the Jews by his preaching of the gospel.

You can just imagine the rumors circulating in Damascus about the change that had taken place in Saul. Was this a 1st century man's "mid-life crisis?" Had Saul lost his sanity? Was he doing this to infiltrate the church for the purpose of identifying the leaders whom he intended to arrest? I am sure that all the believers were asking such questions and seeking to know more about Saul's Damascus road encounter with Jesus. Had Saul hallucinated or was this experience "for real"? The days and weeks that followed would demonstrate the genuineness of Saul's faith in Jesus as Israel's Messiah and the world's Savior.

Saul's message was exactly what Peter had said when Jesus asked, "Who do people say that I am?" (Matt. 16:15) Peter had answered, "You are the Messiah, the Son of the living God" (Matt. 16:16). This was the message Saul was proclaiming in the synagogues of Damascus! He was declaring that Jesus is God's Son (Acts 9:20) and Israel's promised Messiah (Acts 9:22). Luke records that Saul was *proving* the messiahship of Jesus. This indicates that Saul was appealing to the biblical texts which he had studied during his student days in Jerusalem to demonstrate that Jesus had fulfilled messianic prophecy. Reflecting on this astonishing about face in the life of Saul, A.T. Robertson commented that it seemed as though "the most powerful piece of artillery in the Jewish camp was suddenly turned against them" (*Acts*, p. 122).

Saul's letter to the Galatians reveals that immediately after his Damascus road encounter with Jesus, he spent three years in Arabia (Gal. 1:17). His sojourn in Arabia is not recorded in Acts, but may be alluded to by Luke's reference, "When many days had elapsed...." (Acts 9:23). Barry Beitzel has pointed out that ancient sources used the term "Arabia" with reference to several different geographical regions, including Egypt, the Sinai Peninsula, and the Arabian desert ("The Meaning of Arabia," *LGCATR*, pp. 520-536). He favors the view that Paul went into the Gentile regions south of Damascus, perhaps as far as Bostra, the northern capital of the Nabateans in southern Syria, or Pella, south of the Sea of Galilee near the Jordan Valley. But the term "Arabia" does have much broader geographical range and was used in the first century to refer to the vast desert region southeast of the land of Israel which was occupied by the Nabateans and ruled by Aretas IV (9 BC-AD 39). The Nabateans had developed a flourishing culture by establishing cities and trade routes through this region. Nabatean caravans traveled from Damascus through Petra to Gaza and back again, carrying exotic wares and spices.

There is no definitive statement in Scripture as to what Saul was doing during his three years in Arabia. It has been suggested that he was simply fulfilling his calling as an apostle, preaching to the Gentiles living in the region (Acts 9:15; Rom. 1:5). He may have spent time in some of the prominent cities of the Decapolis, such as Jerash, Pella and Philadelphia. Some have speculated that Saul may have spent at least part of the three years in Petra, the mountain encompassed capital of the Nabateans and regional trading center. As I walked through the narrow gorge (the *Siq*) into Jordan's most visited tourist site, I wondered if I was walking in the footsteps of Saul. The passageway eventually opens into a sandy plaza where Hollywood's most famous archaeologist, Indiana Jones, entered the rock carved "Treasury" in search of the Ark of the Covenant. Passing by the Treasury, the path continues through rose colored sandstone, past tombs, monuments and the theater, into the city of Petra. The name of the city means "stone" in Greek and is appropriate for a city surrounded by mountains which serve as a natural rock fortress. I made my way with a group of students up hundreds of steps to the lofty "high place" where pagan sacrifices were offered to the gods of antiquity. Viewing Petra and the surrounding region from this towering perspective, it was hard to imagine Saul spending three years in such a busy commercial center, home to pagan gods and their monumental temples. I could be wrong, but I imagine him at a quieter location.

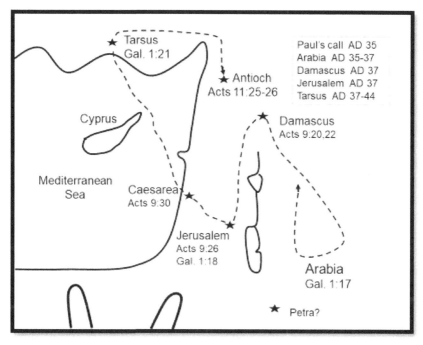

Figure 8  Paul's Early Ministry

Wherever Saul spent the three years in the region of Arabia/Nabatea, he probably used the time to process his new understanding of the messianic texts of the Hebrew Bible and how Jesus had fulfilled them by His life and ministry. You might say that Saul was reorienting his theology in light of his Damascus road experience, studying prophetic texts and coming to understand their fulfillment in the life and ministry of Jesus. Like my own sabbaticals from teaching at Western Seminary, Saul's time in Arabia may have been a combination of ministry and study.

Saul apparently returned to Damascus after his three-year sojourn in Arabia/Nabatea, but found himself to be an unwelcome visitor. Powerful Jewish leaders decided to put a stop to Saul's preaching and plotted to murder him (Acts 9:24). In a letter to the church at Corinth, Paul reports that the Nabatean ruler, Aretas, was the chief instigator of the plot. He and co-conspirators were watching the gates of Damascus day and night, looking for an opportunity to carry out their malicious plan (2 Cor. 11:32). Hearing of the death threats against him, the disciples helped Saul escape from Damascus through an opening in the city wall where he was lowered to the ground in a large basket (Acts 9:25). What a humiliating way to leave the city—sneaking away at night in a basket! This would not be the last of Saul's humbling experiences as a follower of Jesus.

After his escape from Damascus, Saul made his way back to Jerusalem. It was his first time to be back in Jerusalem since his life altering encounter with Jesus, "the Light of the world" (Jn. 8:12). I am sure that Saul wondered as he approached the city, "Will I be welcomed as a fellow-believer or rejected as a former enemy?" In his letter to the Galatians, the apostle makes it clear that his Jerusalem visit, three years after his Damascus road experience, wasn't for the purpose of being taught the gospel, but "to become acquainted with Cephas (Gal. 1:18).

After arriving in Jerusalem, Saul attempted to make contact and associate with the followers of Jesus. But, understandably, many had doubts as to the authenticity of Saul's profession of faith. They were afraid of him and didn't believe that Saul had become a true disciple (Acts 9:26).

Who did Saul see during his visit in Jerusalem? In Galatians 1:19, he wrote, "I did not see any other of the apostles except James, the Lord's brother." However, according to Luke's account, Saul *did* see the apostles (Acts 9:27). Had he forgotten the details of his visit? Another possible rendering of Galatians 1:19 is, "Other than the apostles, I saw no one but James" (Trudinger, *Novem Testamentum* (July 1975, p. 201). Saul interacted with the leaders of the Jerusalem church during his visit, but not members of the congregation.

There was one man among the church leaders in Jerusalem who believed that Saul should be given a chance. Barnabas, whose generosity was noted earlier in Acts (4:36-37), was from a Levitical family that had migrated to Cyprus. His name was "Joseph," but he had been given the nickname, "Barnabas," which means "son of encouragement" (Acts 4:36) or "Encourager." And he lived up to his nickname in the way he helped the former persecutor, Saul. Barnabas risked his own reputation by taking Saul before the apostles in Jerusalem and "described to them how he had seen the Lord on the road, and that He had talked to him, and how at Damascus he had spoken out boldly in the name of Jesus" (Acts 9:27). Luke reports that Saul was doing the same thing during his visit to Jerusalem (Acts 9:28).

Saul was able to spend 15 days in Jerusalem, preaching to the Jews who had known him so well as a zealous Pharisee and prosecutor against Jesus' followers. He would have undoubtedly visited the beautiful Jerusalem temple and perhaps contemplated how the sacrifices presented to God under the Mosaic law pointed to Jesus as the full and final sacrifice for humanity's sin. Little did he realize at the time that in a little more than thirty years, the sacrifices would cease and the magnificent temple would be destroyed by the Roman army (A.D. 70). It wasn't until the Hellenistic, Greek speaking Jews, organized a conspiracy against him that Saul was forced to flee from Jerusalem (Acts 9:29). When the plot was discovered, some of disciples escorted Saul to the port of Caesarea and sent him, probably by ship, to his home town, Tarsus (Acts 9:30). Saul would return to Caesarea on several occasions in the future and eventually spend two years there awaiting the outcome of charges that he had violated the sanctity of the Jewish temple (Acts 21:28).

# Chapter 5
# Preparation for Saul's Gentile Mission

In an amazing turn of events, Saul, the persecutor of Christians, had become a follower of Jesus. Even more, the Lord had chosen him to carry the message of salvation through Jesus to "Gentiles and kings and the sons of Israel" (Acts 9:15). There would be no objection to presenting this messianic message to Jewish kings and the people of Israel. But was this message appropriate for Gentiles? For many Jewish believers in Jesus, this was going to be a problem.

In the first century there was a huge gulf of culture and tradition which separated Jews and Gentiles. Because Gentiles didn't observe the Jewish food restrictions mandated in Leviticus 11, they were regarded as "unclean." The unclean state of Gentiles was compounded by the fact that they did not follow the mosaic regulations regarding contact with dead bodies (Lev. 11:24-40), sexual relations (Lev. 15:16-18) or menstrual purity (Lev. 15:19-30). The unclean state of a Gentile couldn't be removed by soap and water. This meant that Gentiles were living in a continual state of ritual impurity that was intrinsic to their personhood. Because they were regarded as "unclean," Gentiles could not pass beyond the barrier which restricted them to the outer court of the Jerusalem temple, the "court of the Gentiles."

How could a holy Jewish Messiah have any contact or relationship with the non-Jewish, ritually impure Gentiles? Something would have to change for Saul to fulfill his appointed mission as a messenger to the Gentiles. And a major change in the Jewish attitude toward Gentiles would be necessary before they were allowed to be included as full members of the messianic community that was blossoming in Jerusalem.

As God had been preparing Saul's heart to embrace Jesus, God was also preparing Peter's heart to embrace Gentiles. Following the instructions of Jesus (Acts 1:7), the Apostle Peter had taken the initiative to expand the witness of the early church into the Judean coastal plain. His ministry took him to Lydda, the location of Israel's Ben Gurion International Airport. There Peter preached the gospel and authenticated his witness by healing a paralyzed man who had been disabled for eight years (Acts 9:32-34). The miraculous healing resulted in many turning to the Lord.

Next, we find Peter at the city of Joppa, the Mediterranean port from which Jonah set sail, fleeing God's commission to go to Nineveh. There he interrupted a funeral by raising Tabitha ("Dorcus" in the Greek language) from the dead (Acts 9:36-41). The miracle became known all over Joppa and "many believed in the Lord" (Acts 9:42). Joppa was a Jewish city. All these new believers were Jewish people who had come to believe in a Jewish messiah. But this was about to change.

In Luke's account of the growth and expansion of the church, the scene shifts twenty-seven miles north to Caesarea, a major Mediterranean seaport and the seat of Roman government in Judea. As Joppa was a Jewish port city, Caesarea was a Gentile city with a culture that, in the words of Paul Wright, "exuded the stigma of an intrusive civilization" ("The Geography of Caesarea Maritima" *LGCATR*, p. 218). Caesarea was also the home of a Roman centurion who had been stationed there as an officer in Rome's army. His name was Cornelius, and as a centurion he was responsible for training soldiers and leading them in battle. He was also responsible to carry out daily duties such as posting guards, making inspections, maintaining the equipment of the hundred or so soldiers under his command. For further information about the Roman army and the duties of a centurion, see my article, "Peter and the Centurion Cornelius: Roman Soldiers in the New Testament" (*LGCATR*, pp. 246-268).

Although Cornelius was a Gentile, he had come to believe in the God of Israel! Luke reports that Cornelius was a man of piety and prayer, but he was not yet saved by faith in Jesus. Luke doesn't tell us how Cornelius, a Gentile Roman soldier, came to believe in the God of Israel. But the Bible does provide an explanation. It is encouraging to know that God has made Himself known through His creation. This is revealed by the

42

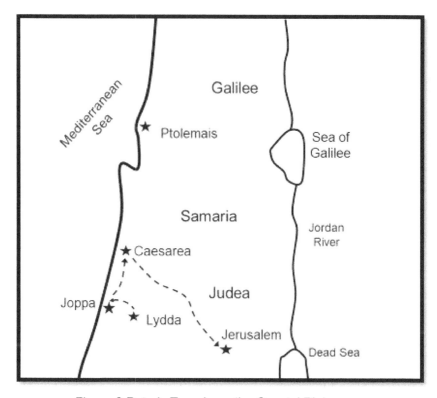

Figure 9 Peter's Travels on the Coastal Plain

words of David, "The heavens are telling of the glory of God; and their expanse is declaring the work of His hands. Day to day pours forth speech, and night to night reveals knowledge" (Ps. 19:1-2). David is saying that God has revealed Himself through the magnificence of His creation. There is a crystal clear, but unspoken message from the sun, moon and stars that declares "God exists!" In his letter to the Romans, Paul explains how God has made Himself known through what theologians call "general revelation." Paul wrote, "For since the creation of the world His invisible attributes, His eternal power and divine nature, have been clearly seen, being understood through what has been made" (Rom. 1:20). The heart of Cornelius had been touched by the beauty of the Mediterranean sunsets and the brilliant stars of the night sky. Through the revelation of nature, Cornelius, a

Gentile Roman soldier, had come believe in the Creator God--
the God of Abraham, Isaac and Jacob.

Luke's account continues to explain how God was preparing
the heart of Cornelius to take the next step in his spiritual journey
by coming to faith in Israel's messiah. One afternoon when he
was praying, an angel appeared to him, instructing Cornelius to
send for a man named Peter who was staying in Joppa at the
home of a tanner named Simon (Acts 10:1-6). It is significant to
observe that God heard and responded to the prayers of a
Gentile man who was seeking to know Him. Cornelius had
responded to the light which had been given to him through
creation (Rom. 2:7). Now God was providing Cornelius with
further light and directing him to a man who could present the
way of salvation.

As God had prepared Cornelius, so God was preparing
Peter. As the messengers sent by Cornelius were approaching
Joppa, Peter had a vision as he was praying on the rooftop of
the tanner's house. Around noon, Peter became hungry and
perhaps wondered what Simon was preparing for lunch.
Suddenly, the sky appeared to open up and Peter beheld a
vision. He saw "an object like a great sheet coming down" which
was filled with all kinds of animals, crawling creatures and birds"
(Acts 10;11-12). Then a voice said, "Get up, Peter, kill and eat!"
Seeing clearly that the creatures presented before him were
prohibited by Mosaic Law, Peter objected saying, "By no means,
Lord, for I have never eaten anything unholy or unclean" (Acts
10:14). Then the voice spoke again saying, "What God has
cleansed, no longer consider unholy" (Acts 10:15). These words
were repeated three times before the vision ended and the
menagerie of unclean animals disappeared.

While Peter was puzzling over the meaning of the vision, the
Gentile men who had been sent by Cornelius arrived at Simon's
gate. The Spirit of God then spoke to Peter saying, "Behold,
three men are looking for you. Get up and go downstairs and
accompany them without misgivings, for I have sent them
myself" (Acts 10:19-20). After inquiring as to their purpose, the
men explained that they had come as messengers from

Cornelius, "a centurion, a righteous and God-fearing man" who had been directed by an angel to send for Peter so he could "hear a message from you" (Acts 10:22). Perhaps it was at this point that Peter began to understand the meaning of the vision. The message God was communicating to Peter was not so much about food as it was about people! God was telling Peter that, contrary to Jewish tradition, the Gentiles should no longer be regarded as unclean. The Lord used Peter's vision to prepare him to go and preach to the Gentiles with the expectation that they could be saved and share in the same spiritual blessings which the Jewish believers in Jesus had received.

Peter graciously offered the messengers lodging for the night, and the next morning he set out with them for Caesarea (Acts 10:24). In view of the uniqueness of this mission, Peter wisely took six of the Jewish believers from Joppa with him (Acts 11:2). Peter wanted there to be witnesses of whatever might occur when he arrived in Caesarea.

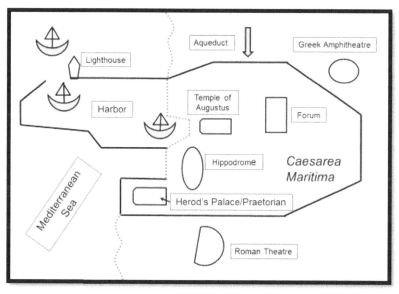

Figure 10  Sketch of Caesarea *Maritima* (on the sea)

When Peter entered the house of Cornelius, he explained that he had come because God had shown him that Gentiles were not to be regarded as ritually "unclean" (Acts 10:28). These

45

words reveal that Peter had understood the meaning of the vision. The point was not that Peter could change his diet and eat non-kosher food, but that God had removed the traditional distinction between Jews and Gentiles.

Having concluded his explanation for his presence in Caesarea, Peter asked Cornelius why he had sent for him. The centurion quickly related his own story of how a man "in shining garments" had instructed him to send messengers to Joppa with an invitation for Peter to come and explain all he had been "commanded by the Lord" (Acts 10:33). What did Cornelius want to know? Although he was a "God-fearing Gentile, whose devotion, prayers and almsgiving had pleased God, Cornelius wanted to know how to be *saved*. In Peter's report to the church leaders in Jerusalem, he quotes the angelic messenger as saying to Cornelius, "he will speak words to you by which you will be *saved*, you and all your household" (Acts 11:14). The Apostle Peter was quick to embrace this amazing evangelistic opportunity!

Luke records that Peter began his sermon by explaining that he now understood a biblical truth he had previously missed. Peter had come to realize "that God is not one to show partiality, but in every nation the man who fears Him and does what is right is welcome to Him" (Acts 10:34-35). Although the Mosaic law taught that "God does not show partiality" (Deut. 10:17), Peter now understood how this had application in relationship to Gentiles. Peter continued his message, presenting Cornelius with the essential facts about Jesus—His life, death and resurrection (Acts 10:36-43). When Peter announced to Cornelius and the other Gentile listeners that "everyone who believes in Him receives forgiveness of sins" (Acts 10:43), something astonishing happened. Peter was still speaking when "the Holy Spirit fell upon all those who were listening to the message" (Acts 10:44). God had opened the heart of Cornelius, along with his family and friends, to the good news of salvation. And the Holy Spirit authenticated their faith and salvation in the very same way He had done for the Jewish believers at Pentecost. Luke records that the new believers were "speaking with tongues and exalting God" (Acts 10:46). This was a sign to Peter and the believers who accompanied him that God was working among the Gentiles in the *very same way* He had worked among the Jews.

Since Cornelius and the other Gentiles listening to Peter had professed their faith in Israel's Messiah, Peter said, "Surely no one can refuse the water for these to be baptized who have received the Holy Spirit just as we did, can he?" (Acts 10:47). He then ordered that the new Gentile believers be identified with Christ and His church through the ritual of immersion in water (baptism). Peter remained in Caesarea for several days, perhaps answering questions and teaching the new Gentile believers more about the person and work of Jesus.

By the time Peter returned to Jerusalem, word about his ministry to the Gentiles had already reached the church leaders. What Peter had done was unprecedented. Some of the Jewish believers strongly objected to the fact that Peter had associated with "uncircumcised men" (i.e. Gentiles) and had eaten their food (Acts 11:3). Others were unhappy about the news that Gentiles had been saved and welcomed into the body of Christ without first becoming Jews. The Gentiles had accepted the Jewish Messiah. Shouldn't they have adopted the Jewish food laws, customs and other cherished traditions?

Peter patiently responded to these concerns by explaining in orderly sequence the events which he had witnessed in Joppa and among the Gentiles in Caesarea (Acts 11:5-16). He concluded by saying, "Therefore, if God gave to them the same gift as He gave to us also after believing in the Lord Jesus Christ, who was I that I could stand in God's way" (Acts 11:17). It was clear to Peter that what had happened in the heart of Cornelius and the other Gentiles was "a God thing." Surprised as he was, Peter couldn't object to what God was obviously doing. The church leaders in Jerusalem now understood. Having heard Peter's explanation, "they quieted down and glorified God, saying, 'Well then, God has granted to the *Gentiles* also the repentance that leads to life'" (Acts 11:18).

You may be wondering what the experience of Peter and Cornelius have to do with the story of the Apostle Paul. The fact is, this has everything to do with Saul's mission to the Gentiles. What God was doing through Peter and Cornelius was preparing the church leaders to recognize and embrace the Gentiles who would be coming into the church through Paul's ministry. Without Peter's ministry to the Gentiles and the church leaders' acceptance of the validity of Gentile salvation through Jesus, Saul's mission to the Gentiles would have been thwarted. He might have succeeded in seeing Gentiles accept a Jewish Messiah, but the new believers would likely have never been welcomed into a Jewish congregation. As a result, there may have been two churches—a congregation of Jewish followers of Jesus and a congregation of Gentile followers of Jesus. The body of Christ would have been divided by ethnic differences! What God did through Peter, while Paul was waiting in Tarsus for God's leading, was to prepare the church for the next phase of gospel outreach in which believing Gentiles would be fully integrated into the spiritual family of God's people. The Apostle Paul would later explain that Jesus "made both groups into one and broke down the barrier of the dividing wall" (Eph. 2:14).

There would still be challenges ahead and issues to be resolved, as we will see in Acts 15. But God was at work in the lives of the early church leaders to prepare them for the ministry of Paul, "the apostle to the Gentiles" (Rom. 11:13).

# Chapter 6
## Saul's Ministry in Antioch

What would it have been like for Saul to return to Tarsus, the city of his birth and childhood? Having been trained by the famous Rabbi Gamaliel and risen to the rank of a prominent Pharisee, one might imagine that he would have received a warm welcome by his family and friends. Here was a "home town boy who made good!" But the Saul who returned to Tarsus was not the same young man who had left home to study in Jerusalem some years ago. He had gained a reputation as a persecutor of a messianic movement known as followers of "the Way" (Acts 9:2; 19:9; 19:23; 24:14) or the "sect of the Nazarenes" (Acts 24:5). But the people of Tarsus had no doubt heard that the promising young man they so admired had experienced a puzzling vision and had joined the "heretical" group he had once so vehemently opposed! "How strange," they must of thought. "How disappointing!"

We don't really know what Saul experienced when he returned to Tarsus. According to Harold Hoehner's Dallas Seminary doctoral dissertation ("Chronology of the Apostolic Age," 1965), Saul was in Tarsus from AD 37 to AD 43. For such a long stay, he needed to earn a living and was probably thankful for his earlier training as a tentmaker. Perhaps Saul returned to this trade to support himself while he awaited further direction from the Lord. No doubt he attended synagogue services in Tarsus, but because of the scandal of his new association with a dissident Jewish sect, his speaking and teaching opportunities were probably limited.

Years passed slowly for Saul. Had God forgotten about him? What about his calling? Hadn't the Lord spoken to Ananias revealing that Saul was "a chosen instrument of Mine, to bear My name before the Gentiles and kings and sons of Israel" (Acts 9:15)? When and where would Saul have the opportunity to proclaim the name of Jesus as Israel's Messiah?

God had not forgotten about Saul. And neither had Barnabas! Just as years are required for the maturing of fine wine, so God may have been giving Saul time to mature and develop spiritually before assuming ministry and leadership in the growing messianic movement. During this time of waiting, God was at work in the congregation of Jesus' followers at Antioch.

The church at Antioch had been started by Jews who had fled from Jerusalem during the persecution connected with the martyrdom of Stephen (Acts 11:19). They came to Antioch announcing to other Jews the good news of Messiah Jesus and what His death and resurrection had accomplished for the people of Israel. But then some believers from the island of Cyprus and Cyrene, a Greek city in north Africa, came to Antioch and began speaking to Greeks about Jesus (Acts 11:20). The "Greeks" were people who were immersed in the Hellenistic culture and may have included both Jews and non-Jews (Gentiles). Luke reports that God blessed this outreach and, as a result, "a large number who believed turned to the Lord" (Acts 11:21).

It didn't take long for news of the rapid church growth at Antioch to reach the ears of the church leaders in Jerusalem. "Was this of the Lord?" they wondered. "Should people with a Greek cultural background be invited into the fellowship of the Jewish followers of Jesus?" They needed further information in order to answer these important questions. So the leaders of the church in Jerusalem decided to send Barnabas north to Antioch to investigate the matter (Acts 11:22).

Antioch, situated on the Orontes River, just fifteen miles from the Mediterranean Sea, was the capital of the Roman province of Syria and the third largest city in the Roman empire. The designation, "on the Orontes," served to distinguish this Antioch from five additional cities in Syria that had the same name (Elaine Philips, "The Geographic Importance of Antioch on the Orontes," *LGCATR*, p. 269). The Orontes River flowed west from Antioch, emptying into the Mediterranean Sea at Seleucia, which served as the city's seaport (Acts 13:4). Antioch was destined to become the new sending center for the advance of the gospel message throughout the Roman world. There is not much from Saul's day that can be seen by visitors to modern Antakya in south-central Turkey. Most of the ancient city lies under the alluvial deposits of the Orontes River. But still visible are remains of the massive fortification walls that surrounded the ancient city. A number of fine mosaics from the Roman period can be seen at the Hatay Archaeology Museum.

The most interesting Christian site in Antioch is the Church of St.

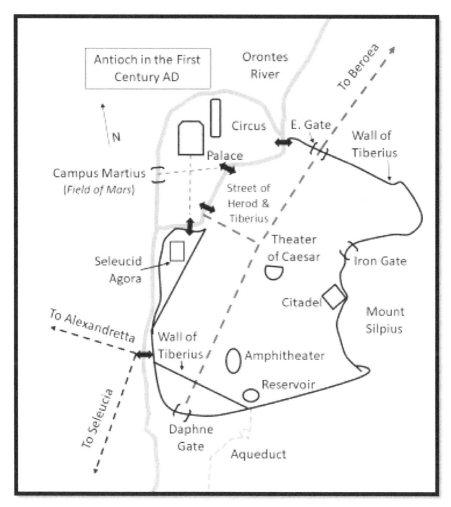

Figure 11  Ancient Antioch

Peter. The church is actually a cave carved into Mount Starius with a decorated façade. The earliest remains date from the 4th or 5th century with the façade dating from the Crusader period (AD 1100). Although the church no longer serves an active congregation, it is a reminder of the vibrant, mission-minded believers that launched Saul and Barnabas on their ministry of gospel outreach.

When Barnabas arrived at Antioch he rejoiced at what was clear evidence of the "grace of God" at work (Acts 11:23). The church at Antioch was growing exponentially! True to the meaning of his name, "Barnabas" (*son of encouragement*) encouraged the new believers to remain true to the Lord. But he knew that encouragement was not enough. New believers need to be taught God's Word. Where could he find someone who could instruct the young church at Antioch in the story of God's great plan of salvation through Israel's Messiah, Jesus? Barnabas had not forgotten the young man, Saul, who had come to Jerusalem after his Damascus road encounter with Jesus. In the sovereignty and perfect plan of God, Saul was about 120 miles away in Tarsus. Luke records that Barnabas immediately "left for Tarsus to look for Saul" (Acts 11:25).

After finding Saul in Tarsus, Barnabas shared with him the need and the opportunity for biblical teaching at the young church in Antioch. It must have been very encouraging for Saul to know that in spite of his history as a persecutor of Christ's church, there was an opportunity for him to serve. In response to this invitation, Saul left Tarsus and traveled with Barnabas to Antioch. Luke records that Barnabas and Saul spent a year together in Antioch, meeting with the church and teaching "considerable numbers" of new believers (Acts 11:26).

The citizens of Antioch couldn't help but notice that something unusual was happening in their city. There was a growing congregation of Jews and Gentiles who worshiped the God of the Hebrews and believed that a resurrected rabbi named Jesus was God's Son and Israel's promised Messiah. These people didn't seem to fit any of the traditional religious categories. Were they Jews? Were they Gentiles? Were they a blend of both? It didn't take long before the pagan Gentiles of Antioch began calling them "Christians" (Acts 11:26). This term is based on the Greek word, *Christos*, which means "anointed one" and refers in Scripture to Israel's promised Messiah (*meshiach*). The root meaning and cultural background suggest that *Christianos* would be better translated as "Messianics." Since these followers of Jesus believed that He was Israel's Messiah, the people of Antioch called them "Messianics." But the Greek word *Christianos* has been traditionally transliterated as "Christian." This may have been intended as a derogatory name used by outsiders, or perhaps an appellation used by Roman authorities to distinguish the new Jewish sect (Philips, p. 275). It is helpful to note that none of Jesus' apostles ever called themselves "Christians." Nor did Paul ever self-identify as a "Christian." Not until the end of the first century does this designation appear in the writings of Ignatius, bishop of Antioch.

It was the spring of AD 44 when the church at Antioch received some visitors from Jerusalem. Among them was a prophet by the name of Agabus who predicted a "great famine" which would impact the whole Roman world (Acts 11:28). Luke links this prophecy with the reign of the Emperor Claudius (AD 41-54). The Jewish historian, Josephus, actually reports that a great famine occurred about AD 46 (Josephus, *Antiquities* XX.51,101). The believers at Antioch recognized their responsibility to reach out and offer help to the needy brethren in Jerusalem who had suffered persecution and job loss as followers of Jesus. Responding with genuine sincerity to this need, the believers at Antioch gathered a contribution which they sent to the elders of the church in Jerusalem in the care of Barnabas and Saul (Acts 11:30).

We must pause in the "Story of Paul" for some reflections and comments about Barnabas. I believe there would not be a "story of Paul" had it not been for Barnabas who vouched for Saul in Jerusalem (Acts 9:26-27) and brought him to serve in the church at Antioch (Acts 11:25-25). Throughout the first half of the book of Acts we see Barnabas as a generous man (Acts 4:36-37) who encouraged and empowered others in their service for Christ (Acts 11:22-24). When people failed, as John Mark did on his first missionary journey (Acts 13:13; 15:38), Barnabas was willing to take a risk and give them a second chance. While some see people's failures and flaws, Barnabas saw people as God sees them, with spiritual potential. While he could have done all the teaching at Antioch himself, Barnabas was a man who was willing to share his ministry opportunities with others, mentoring them and encouraging them along the way. Helping others grow and excel can be one of life's greatest joys. Looking back on his life, I am confident that Barnabas was blessed and gratified knowing the significant part he had played in ministries of the Apostle Paul and the gospel writer, John Mark.

# Chapter 7
# Saul's Famine Relief Visit to Jerusalem

The famine relief visit was Saul's second visit to Jerusalem since his Damascus road encounter with the risen Jesus. Following Harold Hoehner's "Chronology of the Apostolic Age" (Dallas: Th.D. dissertation, 1965), Saul's famine relief visit to Jerusalem took place in the autumn of AD 47. Luke doesn't provide any details about this visit, but he does provide the background of why this relief was needed.

The church in Jerusalem was undergoing persecution. Although there was a lull in such hostility as a result of Saul's turning to the Lord (Acts 9:31), there was still a great deal of resentment among the Jewish leaders against the apostles for their preaching of Jesus as Israel's Messiah. Peter and John had been arrested for preaching in the court of the Jerusalem temple (Acts 4:1-3). Although the apostles were released, they were threatened with further consequences if they persisted in preaching about Jesus (Acts 4:21). When they violated the Sanhedrin's orders to stop their preaching, the apostles were arrested again and flogged (Acts 5:40). Stephen, who had originally been assigned to care for the needs of believing widows, was executed by stoning for preaching the gospel (Acts 7:2-60). It wasn't long afterward that the Apostle James was arrested by Herod Agrippa I (AD 37-44) and executed in an apparent attempt to gain political support from the Jewish leaders (Acts 12:1-3).

The "great persecution" against the followers of Jesus resulted in the scattering of many believers in search of a less hostile environment (Acts 8:1). But the early apostles remained in Jerusalem to provide leadership and support for those who couldn't afford to move. Many believers lost their jobs because of their faith and were in serious financial need. James, the half-brother of Jesus and author of the first New Testament letter (AD 45), reflects these conditions in his comments about suffering (Jms. 1:3), poverty (Jms. 1:9) and giving to those in need (Jms. 2:14-17).

In addition to the persecution that led to economic uncertainty and instability for the believers in Jerusalem, there was also a food shortage due to the famine that struck the Roman world during the reign of Claudius (AD 41-54). Famines are not uncommon in the Middle East due to drought, pestilence, crop destroying warfare and divine chastening (Paul Wright, "Famines in the Land" in *LGCATR*, pp. 280-84). People living on the edge of subsistence living are the most likely to suffer deprivation and hunger during famine. Josephus describes Jerusalem being gripped by famine in 37 BC, again in 25-24 BC and yet again during AD 70 when Jerusalem was under siege by Titus and his Roman troops (*Antiquities* 14.471; 15.299-316; *The Jewish War* 1.347; 6.193-213). Josephus also reports that during the reign of Claudius, Queen Helena of Adiabene visited Jerusalem and witnessed the famine conditions herself. According to Josephus, she found the city "hard pressed by famine, and many were perishing from want of money to purchase what they needed (*Antiquities* 20:51-53). In response to this need, she sent some of her attendants to Egypt and others to Cyprus to buy grain and figs to provide necessary food for the hungry Jerusalemites.

It was famine conditions like this that led the church in Antioch to reach out and bless the church in Jerusalem with financial assistance. The believers in Antioch recognized that the unity of the body of Christ bridges economic and geographical boundaries. In spite of the cultural and ethnic differences between the largely Jewish congregation in Jerusalem and the Hellenistic congregation in Antioch, the believers at Antioch knew that in Christ they were one. And when one suffers, all the believers suffer (1 Cor. 12:26).

Saul must have been excited, but also a bit nervous about returning once again to Jerusalem where he had been known as a persecutor of Jesus' followers and having played a significant role in Stephen's martyrdom (Acts 8:1). Perhaps he was hoping that Stephens dying words would be heeded, "Lord, do not hold this sin against them" (Acts 7:60). It was a beautiful gesture. But would it be applied in Saul's case?

Although Luke's account of the famine relief visit is brief, Saul, soon to be known as "Paul," had more to say about it in what appears to have been his first letter, the epistle to the Galatians. In Galatians 2:1-10, Paul wrote about a visit to Jerusalem. But which visit was he referring to? Was it the famine relief visit (Acts 11:27-30) in AD 47 or the Jerusalem Council visit (Acts 15) several years later? Paul's words in Galatians 2:2, "it was because of a revelation that I went up," suggest he is describing the famine relief visit that was initiated by the prophecy of Agabus who, by divine revelation, announced the coming famine (Acts 11:28). Ancient records attest to the fact that this prophecy was historically fulfilled during the reign of Claudius (AD 41-54).

Paul began his account of his famine relief visit to Jerusalem by telling the Galatians that it was fourteen years after his Damascus road experience (Gal. 2:1), which took place in AD 35. Some might object that fourteen added to thirty-five should give us the date of AD 49 instead of Hoehner's date of AD 47. But we must remember that for the purposes of chronological reckoning, the Jews regarded any portion of a year as the whole year. There were twelve complete years (AD 35-47) and a fraction of a year at the beginning and end of this period. Following the culture of his day, Paul included the partial years in this "fourteen-year" span.

Paul recounts in his letter to the Galatians that Titus, a Greek Gentile believer, accompanied him and Barnabas on the famine relief trip to Jerusalem (Acts 11:30; Gal. 2:3). Titus was in Antioch, apparently having joined Paul and Barnabas in their ministry there. Titus eventually became Paul's "partner and fellow worker" (2 Cor. 8:23) in the ministry and later served the church on the island of Crete (Tit. 1:5).

While he was in Jerusalem with Barnabas and Titus, Saul took the opportunity to meet with the church leaders and present the gospel which he was preaching to the Gentiles in Antioch. Saul explained that he did this "for fear that I might be running, or had run, in vain" (Gal. 2:2). Did Saul fear that he might be mistaken about the gospel? Not at all, for he had received his gospel message from Christ (Gal. 1:12). What Saul feared was that his ministry to the Gentiles would be hindered if his preaching was undercut by the church leaders in Jerusalem.

While some whom Saul calls "false brethren" wanted to impose Jewish markers, like circumcision, on the new Gentile believers, Saul refused to yield to their demands. The truth of the gospel was at stake and could not be compromised. He insisted that both Jews and Gentiles were justified (declared righteous) on the basis of faith, not through Jewish ritual and traditions like circumcision, food laws and Sabbath observances (Gal. 2:16).

As a result of the meeting with the leaders of the Jerusalem church, Saul's commission to the Gentiles was recognized and his gospel of grace was approved. Saul reported to the Galatians that James, Peter and John "contributed nothing" to his gospel message

(Gal. 2:6). They simply extended to Saul and Barnabas "the right hand of fellowship," recognizing their call to preach to the Gentiles as Jerusalem's church leaders had been called to preach to the Jews (Gal. 2:9).

Figure 12  Jerusalem in Paul's Day

The gift from Antioch to the Jerusalem church was no doubt greatly appreciated, but would not permanently relieve the poverty and distress of the Jerusalem believers. Saul reported in his letter to the Galatians that the church leaders had urged him to continue "to remember the poor," the very thing he was eager to do (Gal. 2:10).

During Saul's second visit to Jerusalem, following his encounter with Jesus on the Damascus road, the question of Gentile salvation "by grace alone," apart from Jewish markers and traditions, had been addressed. And while the church leaders had concluded from Peter's testimony that "God has granted to the Gentiles also the repentance that leads to life" (Acts 12:18), the issue had not been fully resolved. It was going to take a while for the early church leaders to embrace this truth. There was still some debate as to whether non-Jewish believers could experience compete salvation and the blessings of the New Covenant as Gentiles. Saul would return to Jerusalem after his first missionary journey for a more extensive discussion and debate with the apostles and church leaders over this critical question (Acts 15:6-29).

# Chapter 8
# Saul's First Journey

Luke has recorded how the early Christians spread the message of salvation through Jesus, Israel's Messiah, from Jerusalem to Antioch (Acts 1-12). Now, as his account continues, we read of how the early messianic movement extended from Antioch to Rome through the travels and preaching of Saul. Here Luke reports that Saul of Tarsus assumed a new name and became the Apostle Paul.

The church at Antioch gradually superseded the Jerusalem church, becoming the new center for gospel witness and world outreach. The largely Gentile congregation at Antioch was active and growing (Acts 13:1-3). There was a strong teaching ministry with many hungry students; and, it was a church led by the Spirit. Luke records that while they were praying and fasting, the Holy Spirit said, "Set apart for Me Barnabas and Saul for the work to which I have called them." (Acts 13:2). Under the Spirit's clear leading, Barnabas and Saul were appointed by the church to bring the good news of Jesus to the island of Cyprus, the home island of Barnabas (Acts 4:36). These gospel ambassadors were sent off with fasting, prayer and the laying on of hands. By this traditional means of identification, the church leaders were saying to Barnabas and Saul, "You will be our hands, feet and voices as you represent us and carry our gospel message to the people of Cyprus." John Mark, Barnabas' cousin (Col. 4:10) and the son of a certain Mary of Jerusalem (Acts 12:12), accompanied the team as "their helper" (Acts 13:5). Barnabas may have had plans to mentor John Mark as he had Saul.

## Ministry on Cyprus

Leaving Antioch in the spring of AD 48, the trio of travelers sailed from Seleucia, the port of Antioch, to Cyprus, the third largest island in the Mediterranean Sea, about eighty miles or a 24-hour journey from their point of embarkation. They landed at Salamis, the main port and commercial center of Cyprus (Acts 13:4-5). Not only was Salamis the main port of Cyprus, but it was a shopper's mecca, boasting the largest *agora* (market place) in the Roman colonial world. Zeus, patron deity of Salamis, was honored with a large temple located near the city's *agora.* Literary sources indicate that Cyprus had a sizable Jewish population (Mark Fairchild, "Barnabas, John Mark, and their Ministry on Cyprus," *LGCATR*, p. 312). Given the proximity of this island to the land of Israel, this should not be surprising. Anxious to share the good news with the Jewish people, the team of evangelists began visiting the synagogues of Salamis and proclaiming the message of salvation. While Paul is often regarded as "the apostle to the Gentiles" (Acts 9:15; Gal. 2:9), he and Barnabas went first to the people who had been anticipating the coming of Israel's Messiah. Living outside the land of Israel, the Jews might not have known that the promised Messiah had come, died for their sins, and risen again!

**Paul's First
Missionary Journey**

Figure 13  Paul's First Journey (*Baker's Concise Bible Atlas*, 1988. By permission of Baker Books, Baker Publishing Group)

Having traveled the length of the island, the missionary team came to Paphos, the capital of Cyprus in Roman times. Paphos was also the center for the worship of the legendary goddess of love, Aphrodite, who had been born from the foam of the sea and floated to shore on a scallop shell. It was here at Paphos, as the light of the gospel began to penetrate the spiritual darkness of Cyprus, that Saul

60

and Barnabas encountered opposition. When God's people are doing strategic work for His kingdom, you can be assured that Satan's agents will be there in opposition. Saul and Barnabas had been invited to the court of the Roman proconsul (or governor), Sergius Paulus, who was interested in their teaching. But one of Satan's agents attempted to dissuade the proconsul from believing (Acts 13:8). Paul harshly rebuked Elymas, the magician and advisor to the proconsul, and declared that he would be blind for a time. The miracle of blindness, which immediately followed Paul's pronouncement, authenticated the apostle's message and led Sergius Paulus to believe (Acts 13:12). The spiritual victory which took place at Paphos may be attributed in part to faithful prayers of the church at Antioch (Acts 13:3), who had sent the mission team to Cyprus.

## Saul Becomes Paul

An interesting thing happened during Paul's ministry on the island of Cyprus. Luke records that during his time at Paphos, Saul began to go by the name, "Paul" (*Paulos* in Greek). Luke doesn't elaborate, but simply referenced "Saul, who was also known as Paul" (Acts 13:9). The name "Paul," derived from the Latin *Paulus*, means "humble" or "small." It is possible that Saul had two names, as did Daniel and other biblical characters. The apostle may have been known by the Hebrew name "Saul" among Jews and "Paul" among the Greek-speaking Gentiles. It has also been suggested that Saul changed his name to Paul to distance himself from his past as a persecutor of the church (Phil. 3:6) or perhaps to commemorate the conversion of the proconsul, Sergius Paulus (Acts 13:7,12).

Saul's parents, being of the tribe of Benjamin, had given their son the name "Saul" in honor of Israel's first king, a Benjaminite. Knowing the history of King Saul's disobedience and spiritual failures, Saul may have wanted to mark his own obedience to the Lord by adopting a new name. Patrick Henry Reardon suggests a literary link between the two "Sauls" which may account for this decision (*Touchstone Magazine*, July/August, 2013). On the road to Damascus, Saul of Tarsus heard the words, "Saul, Saul, why are you persecuting me"? (Acts 9:4). Looking back to First Samuel, we find that King Saul was "persecuting" David, the Lord's anointed (1 Sam. 23:25,28; 24:14; 25:29; 26:18-20). Before Saul's Damascus road encounter with Jesus, he had imagined himself as God's faithful servant. But after meeting Jesus, the apostle realized that he had been "all along, just another Saul" (Reardon, *Touchstone*). Turning away from the spiritual blindness of his past, Saul "became" Paul for the remaining narrative of Acts.

## Ministry in Pisidian Antioch

Having completed their mission on Cyprus, the team left Cyprus and sailed from Paphos to Asia Minor. They apparently landed at Perga, a city about 12 miles inland, but with river access to the Mediterranean seaport of Attalia (Acts 14:25). At this point in their journey, John Mark separated and returned to Jerusalem. Luke doesn't record the reasons why John Mark returned home. Perhaps he was homesick, tired of travel or was fearful of the dangers that lay ahead (2 Cor. 11:26). Paul was so disappointed in him that he refused to allow John Mark to accompany him on a later journey. Luke records Paul's concern that Mark had "deserted" the team and "not gone with them to the work" (Acts 15:38).

Antioch of Pisidia was an important commercial and religious center on the main travel route from the port of Ephesus to the Euphrates. It was also the worship center for the supreme Anatolian god, Dionysus, the Greek god of wine. This city was strategically located as a springboard for the spread of the gospel into the surrounding regions (Acts 13:49). Interestingly, ancient inscriptions reveal that Antioch was actually in the province of Phrygia, not Pisidia. Some historians have accused Luke of making a geographical error. But Luke, and other ancient writers, associated the city with the better known, more prominent and *nearby* province of Pisidia. While Antioch was technically in the province of Phrygia, it was popularly known as Pisidian Antioch.

When the province of Galatia was established, Antioch became part of it and the believers there were among the recipients of the letter Paul later addressed to the Galatians. The Western Gate served as the main entrance into ancient Antioch and is the gate Paul would have used when he entered the city. Passing through the gate, visitors walk along the main east-west street, the Decumanus Maximus, where the paving stones from Paul's day display the grooves worn by ancient wheeled vehicles. I thought of Paul and Barnabas as I walked this route to the junction of the Cardo

Maximus, Antioch's main north-south street. Turning left, I proceeded about eighty yards to the 4th century remains of the Central Church, believed to have been built over the ruins of the synagogue in which Paul preached.

As was Paul's custom, he first went to the synagogue to preach and announce to the Jews of the diaspora that Israel's Messiah had come. It was here at Pisidian Antioch that Paul preached his longest recorded sermon (Acts 13:14-41). Like Stephen's defense before the Jewish Sanhedrin (Acts 7), Paul presented an outline of Hebrew history rehearsing the prophetic and historical background for the coming of the promised Messiah. As in his letter to the Corinthians, Paul set forth the basic elements of the gospel including Jesus' death, burial, resurrection and resurrection appearances (Acts 13:28-31; 1 Cor. 15:3-4). To prove his case for Jesus as Israel's Messiah, Paul appealed to prophetic Scripture (Acts 13:31-37). Paul applied his message to his listeners making the main point: Israel's Messiah, Jesus, has made forgiveness of sins and justification available apart from the law of Moses (Acts 13:38-39). This is a summary of what would become most prominent in Paul's preaching. The message of forgiveness and justification by faith is thoroughly expanded in Paul's letters to the Galatians and Romans.

David deSilva has pointed out that Paul's proclamation of the gospel in Antioch would have been heard as a challenge to the prevailing views surrounding the imperial cult, the worship of the deified emperor Augustus ("The Social and Geographical World of Pisidian Antioch," *LGCATR*, pp. 330-31). Having been deified after his death by the Roman senate, Augustus was regarded as a "son of a god" and a "savior" whose birth marked the beginning of "good news" (*euangelion*) for the whole world. A monumental temple, the *Augusteum*, dedicated to emperor worship, was a major feature of Antioch in Paul's day. Paul's preaching would have challenged his hearers' views about who is the *true* "Son of God" and "Savior" of the world.

The response to Paul's message was mixed. Some were "begging" that he might return the next Sabbath to speak more on the same subject. When Paul spoke again on the following Sabbath, some of the Jews became jealous of the attention the visitors were receiving and began contradicting Paul's message (Acts 13:45). Paul had given his Jewish kinsmen a chance to receive the good news, but now he would turn to the Gentiles who were delighted to learn that God's program of salvation included them (Acts 13:47-48; Isa. 49:6). Luke records that many believed and received God's gift of forgiveness and eternal life (Acts 13:48). In the face of increasing hostility, Paul and Barnabas were forced to leave Antioch, but not without the beginnings of a joyful and spirit-filled congregation (Acts 13:52).

## Ministry in Iconium

Forced to flee from Pisidian Antioch, Paul and Barnabas travelled 80 miles southeast to Iconium, identified today with modern Konya. There is very little to see in Konya today that connects us with Paul's visit. The Konya Archaeological Museum does feature exhibits from the Roman period, including a sarcophagus dating from around AD 250 depicting the seven labors of the mythical strong man, Hercules.

At Iconium, Paul followed his practice of going to the synagogue and proclaiming the gospel there. While there was a good response by both Jews and Greeks, there was also significant opposition. Luke records, "But the Jews who disbelieved stirred up the minds of the Gentiles and embittered them against the brethren" (Acts 14:2). Relying on the Lord, Paul and Barnabas continued to preach while God confirmed their message with "signs and wonders" (Acts 14:3). But when they became aware of plans of a threat against their lives, Paul and Barnabas fled from Iconium to Lystra, about eighteen miles to the southwest.

## Ministry in Lystra

Lystra is located in the Roman province of Galatia and had once been a military outpost for the Roman army. After the area became subdued, the city declined in population and importance. In fact, it was so far off the main routes of travel that Lystra's inhabitants didn't even speak Greek (Acts 14:11). This was probably a welcome change for Paul and Barnabas after the opposition they had experienced in Iconium. One day while preaching the gospel Paul observed a lame man who was very attentive to the message. Paul spoke to the man saying, "Stand up on your feet" (Acts 14:10) and the man, who had been lame from birth, was miraculously healed. While the miracle was intended to confirm the apostolic message, it was interpreted by the citizens of Lystra to indicate that Paul and Barnabas were gods visiting their city! They began calling Barnabas, "Zeus," the chief deity of the Greek pantheon. They called Paul, "Hermes," the Greek messenger god who symbolized the crossing of boundaries between Mt. Olympus, the realm of the gods, and humanity. When the priest of Zeus brought an ox as an offering to the visiting "gods," Paul and Barnabas were barely able to keep the citizens from sacrificing to them (Acts 14:13-14,18).

It is significant that Paul's message to the pagan audience at Lystra (Acts 14:14-18) makes no appeal to the Hebrew Bible or messianic prophesy. Instead, Paul wisely adapted his message to the needs and background of the people by pointing them to God's revelation in creation and His providential care for humanity. Paul declared that God "did not leave Himself without witness, in that He did good and gave you rains from heaven and fruitful seasons, satisfying your hearts with food and gladness" (Acts 14:17).

While there was a positive response to Paul's message, the citizens of Lystra were won over by agitators who arrived from Antioch and Iconium. Barnabas appears to have escaped unharmed, but Paul was stoned, dragged out of the city and left for dead (Acts 14:19). It is uncertain as to whether Paul was knocked unconscious or actually died (2 Cor. 12:1-5). Either way, by God's grace, Paul survived the experience. He must have shocked the citizens of Lystra when the man they had stoned got up and returned to the city!

## Ministry in Derbe

On the day following Paul's stoning at Lystra, he and Barnabas left for Derbe, a remote little city about seventy miles southeast of Lystra. Based on an inscription found in 1956, the site of Derbe has been identified with a yet to be excavated mound known as *Kerti Huyuk*. We hope that future exploration will disclose more about the site. Luke records that Paul preached the gospel at Derbe and "made many disciples" (Acts 14:21).

## Return to Antioch

Leaving Derbe, Paul and Barnabas retraced their steps to Antioch, strengthening the believers and appointing elders in the newly established congregations as they journeyed home (Acts 14:23). Before leaving the district of Pamphylia, Paul preached in Perga where extensive ruins can be seen today. While Luke doesn't provide details of Paul's visit at Perga, archaeologists have uncovered the city as it would have appeared in Paul's day, with streets, gates, a theater, stadium and marketplace (*agora*). Making their way to the picturesque port of Attalia, modern Antalya, Paul and Barnabas sailed for Antioch of Syria where they gathered the believers and reported "all that God had done with them and how He had opened a door of faith to the Gentiles" (Acts 14:27).

Paul and Barnabas had been gone for a year-and-a-half (AD 48-49) and had traveled by land and sea a distance of about 1,250 miles. It must have been thrilling to report to the believers at Antioch the good things God had accomplished through them on their journey. But they also were in need of some rest to recover from the stress and strain of travel. Luke might have been thinking about their physical needs for rest when he commented that having returned to beautiful Antioch, nestled below terraced Mt. Silpius, Paul and Barnabas "spent a long time with the disciples" (Acts 14:28).

Three significant things happened after Paul and Barnabas returned to Antioch. First, the Apostle Peter came to Antioch for a visit (Gal. 2:11-16). Second, Paul wrote a letter to the churches of Galatia, which he had just visited, emphasizing the importance of embracing the gospel of justification by faith apart from Jewish legalism (Gal. 2:16). Third, Paul and Barnabas traveled to Jerusalem to participate in the Jerusalem council to discuss whether faith alone, without practicing Jewish traditions, was sufficient for Gentile followers of Jesus to be fully justified members of the body of Christ (Acts 15).

# Chapter 9
# Paul at The Jerusalem Council

God chose Abraham and his descendants to be the family line through which the blessings of the Messiah and His provision of salvation would be brought to the world. But did people have to be members of the people of Israel in order to participate in these blessings? Did non-Jewish people (Gentiles) need to become Jews to be blessed as the people of God? These were important questions which concerned the early church and needed to be answered by the followers of Jesus.

After the Apostle Peter reported the conversion of the Gentile centurion Cornelius, the leaders of the church in Jerusalem initially concluded, "God has granted to the Gentiles also the repentance that leads to life" (Acts 11:18). On the basis of this recognition, Paul and Barnabas had been preaching to the Gentiles and many had trusted in the atoning work of Jesus and been saved (Acts 13-14). But now there arose some opposition to the practice of accepting believing Gentiles into the assembly on an equal basis with Jewish followers of Jesus.

The theological question facing the early church was, "Is a Gentile acceptable to God without becoming a Jew first?" This was not a question of "how" to be saved, but "who" could be saved. To answer this question, Paul and Barnabas went to Jerusalem to meet with the apostles and church leaders. This meeting took place in the fall of AD 49 and has become known as "the Jerusalem Council."

The catalyst for this meeting was a visit by Jewish believers who came to Antioch and began teaching the new Gentile believers. They were saying, "Unless you are circumcised according to the custom of Moses, you cannot be saved" (Acts 15:1). These *Judaizers*, as they are often called, had a difficult time integrating the salvation of Gentiles into God's redemptive program for Israel. They concluded from their study of the Hebrew Bible that God had a program of salvation for Israel and to participate in that program you had to become Jewish. This involved not only belief in the God of Israel, but also adopting the traditional ethnic and religious markers of the people of Israel, including circumcision, Sabbath observance and dietary restrictions. This was the very issue Paul had addressed in his letter to the Galatians where he argued at length that both Jews and Gentiles are justified (declared righteous) and saved on the basis of faith apart from Jewish laws and traditions (Gal. 2:16). Paul was clearly against the idea that Gentile believers needed to be *Judaized* by requiring that they adopt and practice the ceremonial traditions of the Jews (Gal. 2:14).

Luke records that there was a "great dissension and debate" over this issue in Antioch (Acts 15:2). You can imagine the heated arguments by those who may have declared, "How can a person who eats unclean food participate in the blessings God promised Israel?" An opponent may have shouted back, "But Jesus said that foods don't make a person clean or unclean! Whether or not Gentiles eat pork is irrelevant to the question of their salvation!"

Because the question of Gentile participation in the church family had such serious implications for the early believers, it was agreed that Paul and Barnabas, along with some other believers, should travel to Jerusalem to bring the question before the apostles and elders. When they arrived at their destination, Paul and Barnabas were warmly received by the church leaders in Jerusalem. But they soon discovered that certain Pharisees, who had come to faith, were teaching the same thing as the Judaizers in Antioch. Instead of welcoming new Gentile believers into the church, they were saying, "It is necessary to circumcise them and direct them to observe the Law of Moses" (Acts 15:5). Advocating strict adherence to the ceremonial laws of the Torah, they didn't believe that Gentiles could enter into God's family as Gentiles, but needed to adopt the traditional markers of the people of Israel.

I would have loved being there to watch the apostles and early church leaders debate this controversial issue. Was it like some annual church meetings where harmony and unity don't seem to be on the agenda? Did tempers flare? Did someone say, "Let's just agree to disagree?" We don't know all that was said and done at this critical juncture of early church history, but Luke provides a summary of the essential details (Acts 15:6-21). After considerable debate, the Apostle Peter addressed the council. He rehearsed his own experience of what God had done in bringing the gospel message to the Gentiles (Acts 10-11). He reminded those gathered that not even their fellow Jews, much less the Gentiles, could bear the heavy yoke of Jewish ceremonial law. Peter insisted that since Jewish people are saved only by the grace of the Lord Jesus, the same principle must apply to Gentiles since God "made no distinction between us and them" (Acts 15:9-11).

Paul and Barnabas spoke next (Acts 15:12), adding further evidence to support Peter's argument by reporting the "signs and wonders" that God had accomplished through them as they brought the gospel to the Gentiles of Galatia (Acts 13-14). Certainly these miracles were evidence of God's blessing on their gospel outreach to Gentiles.

James, the half-brother of Jesus (Matt. 13:55; Gal. 1:19), and author of the epistle known by his name, appears to have occupied a position of leadership among the leaders of the Jerusalem church (Acts 12:17, 21:8). Speaking next, James summarized the message of Peter (Act 15:14) and then appealed to Scripture as validation of what had happened. James recognized that regardless of what Peter, Paul and Barnabas had experienced, the ultimate authority for church practice and doctrine was the Word of God. James quoted Amos 9:11-12, a prophecy of God's future blessing on disobedient and unfaithful Israel. Amos predicted that God would one day restore the Davidic dynasty, making Israel a light and a blessing to the world, including "all the *Gentiles* who are called by My name" (Acts 15:17). The fact that Amos mentioned "Gentiles who are called by My name" was conclusive evidence that Gentiles could enter God's spiritual family and receive His blessings as Gentiles. James' point is that what God was doing in blessing the Gentiles through salvation by faith alone was in perfect harmony with His program for Israel's future!

Some have argued that James quoted Amos to show that the church was fulfilling the prophecies given to Israel. But carefully note how he introduces the quotation from Amos. James prefaced his quotation by saying, "With this the words of the Prophets *agree*" (Acts 15:15). James is not equating Israel with the church, but simply pointing out the consistency in God's redemptive program to bless Gentiles as Gentiles.

The verdict of James is clear. "It is my judgment," he said, "that we do not trouble those who are turning to God from among the Gentiles" (Acts 15:19). In other words, Gentiles who turn to Jesus need not be circumcised in order to enter into God's family through saving faith. This decision guarded the fundamental principle of justification by faith alone apart from Jewish ceremonial laws, rituals

69

or traditions. But in order to promote harmony and respectful relationships between Jewish and Gentile believers, James recommended that the council ask Gentiles to abstain from certain practices that were particularly abhorrent to Jewish followers of Jesus.

James mentioned four practices from which Gentile believers would be asked to abstain: (1) eating meat which had been offered to idols; (2) *porneia*, usually translated "fornication;" (3) eating meat from animals which had been strangled; and (4) from blood. These four regulations are all based on prohibited activities described in Leviticus 17-18. James did not present them as a basis for salvation, but as a means of promoting harmony between believers of different cultural backgrounds. Paul would later instruct two women at Philippi "to live in harmony in the Lord" (Phil. 4:2). James was advocating the same thing. He was encouraging the believing Jews and Gentiles to focus on the faith they share in common and "live in harmony in the Lord."

The recommendations proposed by James were accepted by the church leaders gathered at the council and it was decided to put them into a letter to be carried by representatives of the council, including Paul and Barnabas, to the churches (Acts 15:22). We should note that this was not just a decision by church leaders. The letter states, "It seemed good to *the Holy Spirit* and to us to lay upon you no greater burden than these essentials" (Acts 15:28).

It is significant that in the letter delivered to the churches, the order of the prohibitions was changed to follow the order as detailed in Leviticus 17-18. *Porneia*, which is mentioned *second* by James, is listed *fourth* in the official announcement to the churches.

The Order of Things Prohibited

| James' Proposal | The Council's Letter |
|---|---|
| Idol Sacrifices | Idol Sacrifices |
| *Leviticus 17:8-9* | *Leviticus 17:8-9* |
| Porneia | Blood |
| *Leviticus 18:6-18* | *Leviticus 17:10-12* |
| Things Strangled | Things Strangled |
| *Leviticus 17:13-14* | *Leviticus 17:13-14* |
| Blood | Porneia |
| *Leviticus 17:10-12* | *Leviticus 18:6-18* |

F.F. Bruce suggests that in this context, *porneia* must refer to something deemed acceptable to Gentiles, but was forbidden because it was offensive to Jews (*Apostle of the Heart Set Free*, p. 185). While there would be no question about the illegitimacy of illicit sex (fornication), marriage within the prohibited (incestuous) relationships described in Leviticus 18:6-18 was apparently a debated issue which Paul had to address in his letter to the Corinthians. Paul had to rebuke the believers at Corinth for tolerating incestuous marriage (*porneia*) in the church (1 Cor. 5:1).

When the letter from the Jerusalem council was read to the congregation at Antioch, it was joyously received (Acts 15:30-31). What a relief this must have been for Gentile believers in the church. Circumcision would not be required! They could still enjoy a slice of bacon with their eggs at breakfast! Gentile followers of Jesus wouldn't have to adopt the customs and traditions of the Jews. While the Jerusalem based members of the delegation returned home, Paul and Barnabas remained in Antioch during the winter of AD 49/50 teaching and preaching the Word of God (Acts 15:35).

What is the significance of the Jerusalem Council's decision for believers today? Although the need for these regulations arose out of the unique, first century context in which Jewish law and traditions were being observed by new, Jewish believers, there is some relevant application for today. Some churches have their own lists of what new believers can and cannot do in order to be recognized as members in good standing. The Jerusalem Council reminds us of the fact that all people, Jews and non-Jews, are all saved the same way—by grace, through faith, based on the atoning sacrifice of Jesus (Eph. 2:8-9). And while we may have different backgrounds and customs, we must be careful not to allow those traditions to damage the peace and harmony of the body of Christ.

The decision of the early church at the Jerusalem Council didn't compromise any essential biblical doctrines. There are doctrines, like the deity of Jesus and inspiration of Scripture, that believers should "fight and die for." But there are customs and traditions, like modes of baptism, which may be important to us and our Christian experience, but are not embraced by all believers. The Jerusalem Council teaches us that the non-essential differences of opinion and tradition should be accepted for the sake of spiritual unity and Christian harmony.

71

The story is told that when the English theologian and evangelist, John Wesley (1703-1791), arrived in heaven, he asked Saint Peter, "Where are the Methodists?" He was shocked to hear the reply, "There are no Methodists here, John" Then he asked, "Where are the Baptists?" Again, Saint Peter replied, "There are no Baptists here." Confused, the famous evangelist again asked, "Where are the Presbyterians?" To which Peter replied, "There are no Presbyterians here." "Then who *is* here?" asked the befuddled Wesley. Saint Peter answered, "The *Christians* are here, John, only the Christians."

# Chapter 10
## Paul's Return to Asia Minor

Paul and Barnabas spent the winter of AD 49/50 in Antioch, teaching and enjoying fellowship with the believers who had sent them on their journey to Cyprus and Asia Minor. Paul had followed up his preaching ministry in Galatia with a letter. In his Epistle to the Galatians, Paul refuted the idea that Jewish traditions and ritual observances were necessary for the complete salvation of non-Jewish believers in Jesus. I am sure that Paul prayed fervently for the churches that he and Barnabas had established on their journey, but he was also probably wondering if they were remaining true to his teaching. Were the new believers wavering in their understanding that justification resulted from faith in Jesus, apart from any meritorious obedience to the Mosaic law? In light of this concern, Paul proposed to Barnabas that they return to Asia Minor. Luke records his words, "Let us return and visit the brethren in every city in which we proclaimed the word of the Lord and see how they are" (Acts 15:36).

But there was a problem. While Barnabas was in agreement with Paul about the need for a return trip, he wanted to take his young relative, John Mark, with them on this mission. But Paul felt that John Mark's failure to complete the first journey (Acts 13:13) disqualified him from being included on this second mission. Paul used some pretty strong words in this dispute with his co-worker, Barnabas. Luke records that Paul "kept insisting that they should not take him along who had *deserted them* in Pamphylia and had *not gone with them* to the work" (Acts 15:38). It was such a "sharp disagreement," in Luke's words, that Paul and Barnabas "separated from one another" (Acts 15:39). The word "separated" (*apochorizo*) is the same Greek word for divorce! Paul may have felt that Barnabas was compromising his standards. Barnabas may have thought that Paul was unwilling to extend the grace that he himself had received. You can imagine the negative feelings and personal hurt that resulted from the rupture in their relationship.

It is encouraging to know that God was able to bring good out of the dispute between Paul and Barnabas. Two missionary teams left

Antioch instead of one. Barnabas took John Mark and they returned to Cyprus. Paul chose Silas to join him in returning to Asia Minor. It seems as though the church at Antioch supported Paul's mission as he was "committed by the brethren to the grace of the Lord" (Acts 15:40). No further mention is made by Luke regarding Barnabas and Mark heading back to Cyprus.

Luke's account of this dispute is the last we see of Barnabas in the Book of Acts. It was the end of the joint ministry of Paul and Barnabas, but not the end of their friendship (1 Cor. 9:6). Good people don't always agree, but God is bigger than our disagreements. And later Paul commended John Mark in his letter to Timothy as someone he has found "useful" for the ministry (2 Tim. 4:11).

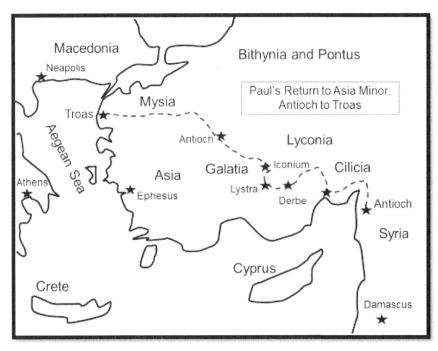

Figure 14  Paul's Second Journey: From Antioch to Troas

We don't know what happened to Mark as he traveled with Barnabas to Cyprus, but I am confident that it was a time of healing, nurturing and discipleship. Through his love and patience, Barnabas was able to salvage the life and ministry of a young man who would go on to accomplish great things for Christ and His kingdom. In fact,

74

without the discipleship ministry of Barnabas in the life of John Mark, he probably would have never written the book we know today as "The Gospel of Mark." Barnabas is one of my favorite biblical characters. I want to be like him in the way he thought the best of others and believed in their God-given potential. Barnabas extended to others the grace and understanding he himself had received from the Lord. So many broken lives have been restored, encouraged and blessed through people like Barnabas.

Paul and Silas left Antioch, but they didn't travel by sea as Paul had on his earlier journey. Instead, they traveled either by foot or by horseback on Roman roads north through Syria and Cilicia into Asia Minor. Mark Wilson has pointed out that travel by sea was preferred "because of speed, ease and cost" ("The Roman Road System Around the Mediterranean," *LGCATR*, p. 190). But the Mediterranean Sea was closed for travel during the stormy winter season and unpredictable in the late fall and early spring. The well-developed Roman road system, primarily constructed for the movement of Rome's legions to areas of conflict, provided a suitable alternative to sea travel.

Following Rome's network of roads north from Antioch, Luke records that Paul and Silas stopped at various cities along the way to encourage the believers and strengthen the churches (Acts 15:41). It must have taken some courage for Paul to return to the churches of Derbe and Lystra where there had been such hostile opposition to the gospel (Acts 14:19). It was probably at Lystra that Paul was greeted by a man who had apparently come to faith through Paul's ministry on his previous visit. The young man's name was Timothy. He was the son of a Jewish woman who had believed in Jesus, but his father was Greek. Paul was impressed by Timothy's "sincere faith" (2 Tim. 1:5) and wanted to have Timothy accompany him and Silas on their mission, but there was a problem. Timothy had not been circumcised. Because of this, it would be difficult for him to fully participate in the social life and ministry among the Jewish people they would meet on the journey. In Jewish communities and synagogues, Timothy would always be considered an outsider—a Greek Gentile.

While the Jerusalem Council had concluded that circumcision was not necessary for Gentiles (Acts 15:19), Paul recognized that this procedure would enlarge Timothy's usefulness, enabling him to travel freely with Paul into Jewish communities. F.F. Bruce comments that, in Timothy's case, circumcision was "a mere surgical operation, not a religious rite" (*Paul: Apostle of the Heart Set Free*, p.215). In Jewish tradition, the delicate procedure of ritual circumcision (*bris*) is done by a professional, called a *mohel*. But Paul must have had some training in this minor surgery, for Luke records that Paul took Timothy "and circumcised him" (Acts 16:3). Glancing at the razor sharp knife in Paul's hand, I am sure Timothy must have thought to himself, "I certainly hope he has done this before!"

As the missionary team continued through Asia Minor visiting the congregations which had been established on Paul's first journey, they reported the decision of the Jerusalem Council (Acts 16:4). As a result of this vital follow-up ministry, "the churches were being strengthened in the faith, and were increasing in number daily" (Acts 16:5).

Having passed through the provinces of Phrygia and Galatia, Paul, Silas and Timothy wanted to continue south to Asia. But the Holy Spirit didn't permit them to carry through with these plans. When they reached the region of Mysia, they were determined to go north to Bithynia, but with the same result (Acts 16:16-17). The Holy Spirit indicated, "No." They couldn't go north and they couldn't go south. So the trio of travelers continued west to Troas, a port city in western Turkey on the Mediterranean seacoast.

It is helpful to observe that while Paul exhibited strategic planning in his travel and mission endeavors, he remained sensitive to the leading of the Holy Spirit. He appears to have recognized that neither the *need* nor the *opportunity* constituted God's call to minister in a particular region or city. But God was still leading the mission. While Paul, Silas and Timothy were patiently waiting at the colorful seaport of Troas, near ancient Troy, a city made famous by the story of the Trojan horse, God directed the team to the next phase of their ministry.

# Chapter 11
# Paul's Ministry in Macedonia

There is wisdom in waiting for God's leading before making a major decision. Taking time to wait, pray and ponder such a decision can help avoid making a commitment and then having second thoughts or regrets. The Holy Spirit had prohibited Paul and his missionary colleagues from turning north to Bithynia or south to Asia, so they continued west until further travel by road was blocked by the Mediterranean Sea. Paul must have wondered, "Where should we go next?" He may have been praying about this decision late one night as they waited in Troas, known officially as Alexandria Troas in memory of Alexander the Great. It was there that Paul had a vision of a man appealing to him and saying, "Come over to Macedonia and help us" (Acts 16:9). The man in the vision is not identified, but Luke gives us a clue. In the very next verse, Luke switches from using the pronouns "he" and "they" to narrate the journey and begin using "we" (Acts 16:10). Perhaps Luke was the man in the vision which God used to direct Paul and his team to Macedonia, a region of northern Greece. In any case, God used the vision to lead Paul on the next step of his second missionary journey.

The very next day, Paul, Silas, Timothy and Luke, put out to sea from Troas, sailing across the Aegean Sea to Neapolis, a distance of about 175 miles. Neapolis was the port of Philippi and the terminus of a Roman road, the *Via Egnatia* (Egnatian Way), which ran through Macedonia to connect with the *Via Appia* (Appian Way) and Rome. As a missionary strategist, Paul was anxious to preach the gospel in places where his message could have the greatest impact. Because of the strategic plain it commanded, the Roman colony of Philippi was Paul's destination.

## In Philippi

Philippi was located on the Gangites River, about ten miles inland from the port of Neapolis. In light of its political and economic importance, Philippi was regarded as a "leading city" of Macedonia (Acts 16:12). There was no synagogue at Philippi, so devout Jews gathered at a nearby stream, the Gangites, for prayer and ritual purifications. Paul joined them there one Sabbath morning and began speaking to them about Israel's Messiah. His message would have included the coming of Jesus, His life, death and resurrection (1 Cor. 15:3-4).

Figure 15  Paul's Journey Through Macedonia

Among the listeners on that Sabbath morning was a devout woman named Lydia, a native of Thyatira (Rev. 1:11), famous for its purple dye and fabrics. Luke records that "the Lord opened her heart to respond to the things spoken by Paul" (Acts 16:14). God was no doubt at work in Lydia's heart before Paul came to Philippi. Perhaps she had heard prophecies about Israel's Messiah and was hungry to learn more. God was sovereignly preparing Lydia to respond to the gospel. Not only did Lydia believe, but her family joined her in trusting in the person and work of Jesus! Together with her family, Lydia identified herself as a follower of Jesus through immersion (*baptism*) in the chilly waters of the Gangites. Immersion in water was a Jewish tradition of cleansing and marking new beginnings which was required of pagans who were converting to Judaism. Following this

78

custom, immersion in water was a way to identify new believers as followers of Jesus. Lydia demonstrated the genuineness of her faith by extending Christian hospitality to out-of-town visitors. She invited the missionary team to be her house guests (Acts 16:15). Lydia epitomized the meaning of the Greek word for hospitality, literally rendered as "love of strangers." The Apostle Paul instructed believers to "practice hospitality" (Rom. 12:13) and listed this welcoming and generous spirit as a qualification for church leadership (1 Tim. 3:2).

Figure 16  The Gangites River in Philippi

Since there was no synagogue in Philippi, Paul took the opportunity to speak about the Lord Jesus in the *agora,* or market place. One day as he was going to the place of prayer, Paul encountered a slave girl who was possessed by "a spirit of divination" whose masters were profiting by her fortune telling.

The expression, "spirit of divination," can be literally translated, "a Pythian spirt." Pythia was the priestess of Apollo, the god of prophecy at Delphi, where she would sit on a tripod in the Temple of Apollo and prophesy. Pythia would respond to questions with ecstatic utterances which were translated by the temple priests and given to the temple visitors as a message from Apollo. Familiar with this background, Paul recognized that a demon was enabling the prophetic gift of the slave girl at Philippi. When the demon attempted to thwart the gospel message by discrediting the missionary team, Paul commanded the demon in the name of Jesus Christ, "Come out of her" (Acts 16:18), and the young woman was miraculously delivered.

Having cut off a source of income for the owners of the slave girl, Paul and Silas were arrested and dragged before the city magistrates who had them stripped, beaten with rods and jailed (Acts 16:22-23). Luke notes that they were locked in the "inner prison," something like a dungeon, and their feet fastened in stocks. Humanly speaking, there was no possible chance of escape!

As God had prepared the heart of Lydia, so He had prepared the heart of the Philippian jailer. While Paul and Silas witnessed to the other inmates by singing hymns of praise to God, an earthquake shook the prison to its foundations, opening the doors and miraculously unfastening the prisoner's chains (Acts 16:26).

Fearing that his prisoners had fled, the jailer was about to commit suicide when Paul cried out, "Do not harm yourself, for we are all here" (Acts 16:28). In response to the jailer's question, "What must I do to be saved?" Paul explained the gospel and both the jailer and his family believed. After tending to the wounds of Paul and Silas, the jailer identified himself as a follower of Jesus through immersion in water. He must have been pretty excited about his new life in Christ because he didn't even wait until the next day to be baptized!

In the morning, when the magistrates sent word to release the prisoners, Paul let it be known that he was a Roman citizen whose rights had been violated by the unlawful proceedings of the previous day. Fearful of the legal consequences of their actions, the magistrates released Paul and Silas, "begging them to leave the city" (Acts 16:39). Paul and the team left Philippi, but not before visiting Lydia and encouraging the newly established congregation of believers gathered at her house.

The Philippian church would continue to have a special place in the heart and memory of Paul (Phil. 1:3). This would not be Paul's last visit to the church he founded at Philippi. He would visit the church several more times during his ministry and write the believers at Philippi a joyful and encouraging epistle.

# In Thessalonica

Leaving Philippi, Paul and his mission team travelled one hundred miles west along a Roman road, the *Via Egnatia*, until they came to Thessalonica. The fact that Paul didn't stop to minister as he passed through the towns of Amphipolis and Apollonia reflects something of his mission strategy. Paul consistently focused his energy for ministry on places where his witness could impact the greatest number of people with the gospel message. Thessalonica was not only the capital of Macedonia in Paul's day, it was also the largest city with an estimated population of 200,000. Situated on the Thermaic Gulf with its excellent harbor, as well as being on the main east-west travel route, Thessalonica was regarded by the ancients as "the key" to the whole region.

Visitors to Thessalonica, modern Thessaloniki, can explore the Roman Forum where Paul no doubt walked during his ministry. At the harbor today stands an impressive statue of Alexander the Great who is depicted on his famous stallion, Bucephalus, riding east in 334 BC to conquer the Persians. The Archaeological Museum of Thessaloniki, in the center of the city, displays artifacts illustrating the Greek, Roman and Byzantine history of Thessalonica.

As usual, Paul spoke first to the Jews, telling them that Israel's long awaited Messiah had come. He presented this message in the Jewish synagogue for three Sabbaths, explaining and giving evidence from the prophetic Scriptures about the death and resurrection of King David's ultimate descendant, Jesus (Acts 17:3,7). Paul must have been encouraged by the positive response of some of the Jews, as well as a large number of the Gentiles ("God-fearers") who had embraced the God of the Hebrews.

But things turned against Paul quickly as some the city's Jewish residents became jealous over the attention the gospel message had received. As jealousy led to anger and tempers flared, violence erupted.

Luke records that "wicked men" formed a mob and attacked the home of Jason, Paul's host, dragging him and some of the believers before the city authorities saying, "These men who have upset the world have come here also" (Acts 17:6). They charged that Jason had welcomed these trouble makers who were teaching that there was a king other than Caesar, by the name of Jesus (Acts 17:7).

After receiving a "pledge" or guarantee from Jason that there would be no further trouble, those who had been charged were released.

## In Berea

Late that night, the believers at Thessalonica sent Paul and Silas to Berea, a small city which was about forty miles away and a few miles off the main highway, the *Via Egnatia*. Berea had no political or historical importance and was a good place to wait for the opposition and hostility in Thessalonica to subside. Most tour groups bypass Berea, modern Veria, and ours was no exception. Even though our guide insisted that "there is nothing there to see," I was able to persuade him to turn off the main highway for a short visit at a beautiful mosaic featuring the Apostle Paul's preaching at Berea. Veria had a Jewish population until World War II when the Nazi holocaust brought Jewish life in the city to an end. The restored synagogue is a mute witness to the existence of Veria's vibrant Jewish community of the past.

Figure 17  Restored Synagogue at Berea

Once again, Paul took the opportunity which was afforded a visiting rabbi to speak in the community synagogue (Acts 17:10).

Here Paul found a congregation more receptive to his message. Luke records that the Bereans "received the word with great eagerness, examining the Scriptures daily to see whether these things were so" (Acts 10:11). More than a few churches and Sunday School classes have been named "Bereans," sharing the eagerness of the first century Bereans for the study of Scripture.

Many of the citizens at Berea believed Paul's message and soon a messianic congregation was established. But it didn't take long for news about Paul's ministry in Berea to reach the ears to the Jewish agitators in Thessalonica. When they arrived, intent on causing trouble, Paul was forced to leave the city, although Silas and Timothy remained, no doubt to engage in follow-up ministry. Paul was escorted to the Thermaic Gulf in the northwestern region of the Mediterranean Sea, where he embarked on a ship sailing south to Piraeus, the port of Athens. His companions would later join Paul at Athens, a city named for Athena, the Greek goddess of wisdom and war (Acts 17:14-15).

# Chapter 12
# Paul's Ministry in Achaia

Paul left Macedonia and traveled by ship to the southern region of Greece known as Achaia. He arrived at the busy port of Pireaus, about five miles by road from the magnificent city of Athens, the intellectual, cultural and religious center of southern Greece. Athens was named for Athena, the goddess of war and wisdom, whose gleaming marble temple, the Parthenon, crowned the acropolis. The Parthenon, featuring a gold and ivory statue of Athena, was constructed in 438 BC and would have been easily visible by Paul as he made his way along the idol lined road to the city center.

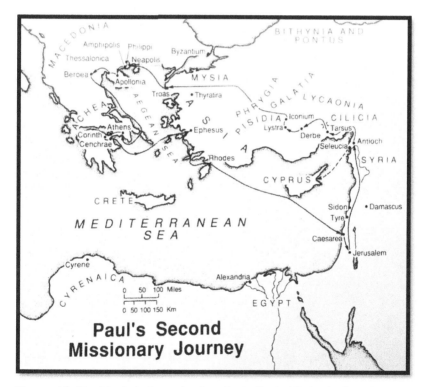

Figure 18  Paul in Achaia and return to Antioch (*Baker's Concise Bible Atlas*, 1988. Used by permission of Baker Books, Baker Publishing Group)

Paul's discussions with Jews in the synagogue and Gentiles in the *agora* soon attracted the attention of Athen's leading philosophers, the Epicureans and Stoics (Acts 17:18). The Epicureans believed that the avoidance of pain and the pursuit of pleasure was the chief end of life. Epicurus, the Greek founder of this philosophy (341-270 BC), believed that breaking the law or harming others was bad since the consequence of these activities would detract from your own happiness. The Stoics advocated self-denial as the basis for human self-sufficiency. This philosophy, founded by Zeno of Citium (336-265 BC), advocated indifference to pain and hardship and encouraged adherents to endure suffering without complaint. Zeno established the Stoic school of philosophy in which he taught in Athens. It was the custom of these teachers and philosophers to oversee matters pertaining to religion and culture in Athens, and to evaluate itinerate teachers such as Paul. To learn more about Paul's teaching, he was invited to meet with them on the Areopagus, a hill northwest of the Acropolis which was dedicated to Ares (Mars), the god of war.

Figure 19  Steps leading to the summit of Mars Hill

Visitors to Athens today can ascend the well-worn steps to the rocky summit of Mars Hill and stand where Paul did as they reflect on his message to the intellectual leaders of Athens. The Areopagus also offers a spectacular view of the Propylaea, the monumental entrance of the Acropolis, and the Temple of Winged Nike, the goddess of victory.

Paul's message before the members of the Areopagus is very different from a message he would have given in a Jewish synagogue. Instead of appealing to prophetic Scripture as a basis for his presentation about Israel's Messiah, Paul made a culturally sensitive connection with their own religious background by speaking to them about the "unknown God." The Athenians had many gods whom they honored with temples and altars. They even had an altar dedicated to an "unknown god," just in case they had missed one. You may be wondering how such an altar came into existence.

According to Diogenes Laertius (*Lives of Philosophers* 1.110), a terrible plague began in Athens around 600 BC. The Athenians prayed to their many futile gods for relief and healing. Some have said that in those days it was easier to find a god than a man in the city of Athens! But none of the Athenian's gods answered their prayers for relief from the plague. The leaders of Athens concluded that one of their gods had been offended and had sent the plague to their city. Sacrifices were offered to propitiate their deities, but the plague continued. Finally, Epimenides suggested that the Athenians had probably offended an "unknown god." He ordered that a number of sheep be released in Athens and that wherever they lay down, a sacrifice would be offered to an unknown god. Altars were built, sacrifices were offered, and the plague ended. Many years later when Paul visited Athens, one of these altars was still standing. Paul used the inscription on the altar to introduce the Athenians to a god they had honored, but didn't know.

Addressing the learned philosophers gathered on Mars Hill, Paul said, "What you worship in ignorance, this I proclaim to you" (Acts 17:23). The Apostle Paul went on to speak about the person and work of the true God, appealing to the facts of creation (Acts 17:24-25), divine providence (Acts 17:26-27), the fatherhood of God over the whole human family (Acts 17:28-29) and future judgment by a "man" who was raised from the dead (Acts 17:30-31). Adapting his message to the cultural context of his listeners, Paul quoted two Greek poets to emphasize God's relationship and personal involvement with the whole human family (Acts 17:28). Epimenides the Cretan wrote, "Oh holy one, you are not dead, you live and abide forever, *for in you we live and move and have our being.*" Paul also adapted a line from Aratus of Cilicia who wrote, "It is with Zeus that everyone of us in every way has to do, *for we are also his offspring.*"

With Paul's mention of the "resurrection," some of the members of the council began to sneer. Greeks believed that the spirit was liberated from the body at death and resurrection, if this were true, would involve a return to the limitations of material life on earth. Resurrection was not in their theology nor a hope that Greek philosophy embraced. While Paul's message was rejected by most of his listeners, several believed, including a man named Dionysius, who became the first bishop of Athens (Eusebius, *Ecclesiastical History* III.4,10; IV.23.3), and a woman named Damaris. Paul appears to have been denied the right to preach in Athens and there is no record of an early congregation being established there.

### In Corinth

Leaving Athens, Paul headed west to Corinth, strategically situated on the isthmus which links the Peloponnesus with the mainland of Greece. Corinth was an important trade center with two fine ports: Cenchreae gave access to the Saronic Gulf and the Aegean Sea and Lechaeum, to the west, provided access to the Corinthian Gulf and the Adriatic Sea. In times of danger, the citizens of Corinth could find a safe refuge on the 1,886 foot-high Acrocorinth which also served as a worship center for Aphrodite, the goddess of love. The Greek geographer and historian, Strabo (63 BC – AD 23), reports that there were a thousand temple prostitutes serving worshipers of Aphrodite at her magnificent temple (*Geography* 8.6.20). Some scholars question whether Strabo was describing first century Corinth or an earlier time in its history. Nevertheless, Corinth had a reputation that made it a popular destination for sailors, merchants and soldiers. Like so many urban centers today, Corinth was both a needy and challenging place to present the gospel.

Soon after arriving in Corinth, Paul met a Jewish couple from Italy who had been evicted from Rome under the edict of the emperor Claudius (10 BC–AD 54) in AD 49. Paul was able to find housing and a job with Aquila and Priscilla in their family business of making tents (Acts 18:2-3). When Silas and Timothy rejoined Paul after completing their follow-up work in Macedonia, he was able to devote himself completely to his preaching and teaching ministry. Among the first believers at Corinth was Crispus, leader of the synagogue (Acts 18:8). Luke records that Paul spent a year and six months sharing the good news of salvation through Jesus and founding the Corinthian church (Acts 18:11).

Today's visitors at Corinth can walk along Lechaeum road leading to the western harbor and see the remains of shops which lined the street. I wonder if one of these small shops served as the location of the tent making business of Aquila and Priscilla? Paul would have seen the Doric style Temple of Apollo, built in 540 BC, and no doubt frequented the Periene fountain, a water source and public gathering place for the Corinthians of antiquity. One of the most interesting archaeological discoveries at Corinth is an inscription mentioning the name of Erastus, the city treasurer of Corinth and one of Paul's associates (Rom. 16:23). Discovered near a paved area by the theater, the Latin inscription reads, "Erastus, in return for his civic office paved it at his own expense." Could this be the same Erastus? It is an interesting possibility.

Figure 20  Temple of Apollo in Corinth (540 BC)

During his stay in Corinth, Paul wrote two letters to the congregation which had been established in Thessalonica. Silas and Timothy brought an encouraging report about the believers and how they were persevering in faith, hope and love in spite of persecution by those hostile to the gospel. Having received this report, Paul sat down and wrote the letter we know as First Thessalonians (AD 51). He commended the believers for how they "turned to God from idols to serve a living and true God" (1 Thess. 1:9) and offered corrections about a misunderstanding regarding the return of Jesus and the resurrection of those who had died in Christ (1 Thess. 4:13-16).

Paul's second letter to the Thessalonians, probably written several months after the first, offered encouragement for the persecuted saints and further instruction regarding the prophetic events preceding the return of Jesus (2 Thess. 1:3-10; 2:1-12). While Paul taught that Jesus was coming again, he corrected the opinion of some that they should stop working and simply await His return. Paul embraced a strong work ethic. He declared, "If anyone is not willing to work, then he is not to eat, either" (2 Thess. 3:10).

Opposition from the Jewish community against Paul and his teaching led to his departure from Corinth. Paul was brought before the "judgment seat" (*bema*) of Junius Annaeus Gallio, proconsul of Achaia (AD 51-65), and accused of propagating an unauthorized religion (Acts 18:13). Gallio judged that the dispute was merely a religious squabble among the Jews. Since Judaism had legal sanction under Roman law, Gallio was unwilling to act on the charges brought against Paul (Acts 18:15-16).

Sensing that his ministry at Corinth was over for the time, Paul departed for Cenchrea, Corinth's seaport on the Saronic Gulf. His co-laborers, Priscilla and Aquila, accompanied him and they crossed the Aegean Sea to the magnificent port city of Ephesus (Acts 18:18-19), a city devoted to the worship of the goddess Artemis. Leaving Aquila and Priscilla in Ephesus to lay the groundwork for future ministry, Paul boarded a ship sailing to Caesarea. He promised his fellow-workers that he would return to Ephesus "if God wills" (Acts 18:21).

After landing at Caesarea, Paul went up to Jerusalem to greet the church leaders before heading north to report in with the church at Antioch. Paul arrived back in Antioch in the late fall of AD 52. He had been gone for two-years and six-months, during which he had traveled about 2,400 miles by foot and approximately one-thousand miles by sea. At Antioch, Paul took a well-deserved furlough before starting out on another journey.

In the meantime, back in Ephesus, the Lord was working through Aquila and Priscilla who were privileged to disciple a young Jewish believer by the name of Apollos. This young man was a Hellenized (Greek speaking and culturized) Jew from Alexandria, a seaport founded by Alexander the Great o Egypt's Nile delta. His parents named him for Apollo, the Greek god of prophecy, reknown for his oracle at Delphi. Luke's comment that Apollos was "mighty in the Scripture" (Acts 18:24) suggests that he had been educated in one of the famous schools of Alexandria.

It was here at Alexandria, according to the *Letter of Aristeas*, that the Torah was first translated by seventy-two Jewish scholars from Hebrew into Greek. Apollos probably studied this translation, known as the Septuagint (meaning "seventy"), and quoted from it as he expounded the scripture.

The city of Alexandria was famous for its monuments, academies and grain exports to Rome. Next to Rome, Alexandria was regarded as the second most important city of the Roman Empire and had the largest Jewish community living outside the land of Israel (Benjamin Foreman, "The Social and Geographical Significance of Alexandria," *LGCATR*, pp. 369-384).

Apollos had an excellent knowledge of Scripture and was an eloquent speaker. But his understanding about Jesus was limited to what John had announced about the coming of Israel's Messiah (Acts 18:25). After learning "the way of God more accurately" through the discipleship of Aquila and Priscilla, Apollos had an expanded ministry. Luke records that he powerfully refuted opponents of the gospel, "demonstrating by the Scriptures that Jesus was the Messiah" (Acts 18:28).

I admire Apollos as a young man who was well trained and immanently gifted, but was humble enough to receive instruction from a seasoned missionary couple like Aquila and Priscilla. A proud person might have thought of himself as quite sufficient and capable without their mentoring. But this kind of attitude would have deprived Apollos of the benefit of further training and would have limited his future ministry.

I will never forget the comment of Dr. John Walvoord, former President of Dallas Theological Seminary, after he attended a class I was teaching on the Gospel of Mark. He offered several helpful comments and suggestions about how I could improve my teaching. Then added that he had even "learned a few things" from my lecture! Even as a seasoned theologian and Bible teacher, Dr. Walvoord never stopped learning.

# Chapter 13
# Paul's Ministry in Ephesus

Paul spent the winter of AD 52/53 in Antioch of Syria. Although Luke provides no details regarding his activities, we can assume that Paul gave the church at Antioch a good report of his ministry in Macedonia and Achaia and took the opportunity to teach and preach to the congregation that had sent him on his earlier mission trips. But Paul was a traveling man and was anxious to get back on the road. In the spring of AD 53, Paul set out from Antioch for Asia Minor by the same route he and Silas had followed on the second journey. Paul wanted to make sure that the churches which he had established during his previous travels were spiritually healthy and maturing. Luke records that he passed through the regions of Galatia and Phrygia "strengthening all the disciples" (Acts 18:23).

On his earlier journey through this region, Paul and Silas had been "forbidden by the Holy Spirit" to go south to Asia or north to Bithynia (Acts 16:6). Instead, the Holy Spirit led them to Troas where they crossed the Aegean Sea to Macedonia. But Paul had recognized the strategic importance of Ephesus, Asia's most prominent city, for the spread of the gospel. He was anxious to return to this city where he had left Aquila and Priscilla six months earlier with the words, "I will return to you again if God wills" (Acts 18:21). Now would be his opportunity!

Ephesus, located on the Cayster River, a short distance inland from the Aegean Sea, was the port of a major caravan route that extended across Asia Minor to Mesopotamia. It was regarded as one of the most important cities of the ancient world with a population estimated at two hundred thousand. Ephesus was regarded as the foremost city of Asia, not only because of its fine harbor (the largest in Asia Minor) and commercial importance, but because it was the guardian city of the Temple of Artemis. According to legend, the sacred image of Artemis fell from heaven (Acts 19:25) and was honored in Ephesus by her magnificent temple.

The Temple of Artemis was four times the size of Athen's Parthenon and featured 127 marble columns, one of which still stands among the ruins of the city. Interestingly, you can see more of

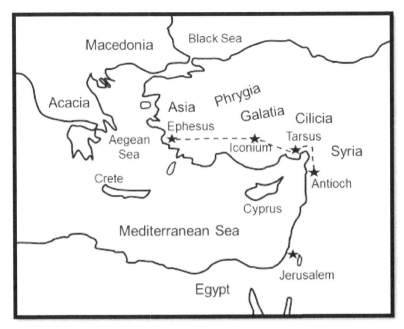

Figure 21  Paul's Return to Ephesus

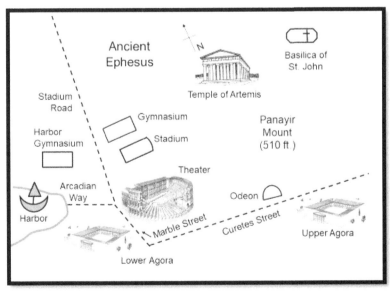

Figure 22  Ancient Ephesus

the Temple of Artemis in Istanbul, Turkey, than you can in Ephesus. Among the 140 monolithic columns in Istanbul's 5th century AD church (now a mosque), the Hagia Sophia, stand eight columns taken from the famous temple Paul would have seen at Ephesus. Artemis was the goddess of hunting, wild animals, childbirth and nature. Images of Artemis were crafted by silversmiths and sold to visitors who traveled from the surrounding province of Asia to worship the "magnificent" goddess.

When Paul arrived at Ephesus he discovered a rather unique group of twelve believers who had come to faith through the ministry of John the Baptizer (Acts 19:3). They were Jews who had welcomed John's message about the coming of Israel's Messiah (Matt. 3:1-6, Jn. 1:29-36), but they were Old Covenant believers who had not embraced Jesus as the resurrected Sin-bearer and Savior. They were ignorant of the coming of the Holy Spirit at Pentecost (Acts 19:2; cf. 2:1-21) and how God's Spirit would indwell and empower believers through the New Covenant (Jer. 31:31-34; Ezek. 36:25-28). After receiving Paul's instruction, these messianic Jews entered by faith into the blessings of the New Covenant and identified themselves as followers of Jesus through the ritual immersion in water (*baptism*).

Following his customary strategy for ministry, Paul went to the synagogue and preached to the Jews regarding God's kingdom program and the promised coming of Israel's messianic King (Acts 19:8; 2 Sam. 7:12-16). But after three months of presenting and defending the case for Jesus as Israel's Messiah, Paul found his Jewish kinsmen to be hardened and unaccepting of his message. Paul was forced to withdraw from his focus on Jewish outreach, but continued teaching and mentoring his disciples "in the school of Tyrannus" (Acts 19:9-10). It appears that Paul rented a lecture hall as a classroom for his students. According to one Greek manuscript, he used the school facilities "from the 5th hour to the 10th" hour (11 AM to 4 PM) while the Greeks took their customary rest during the heat of the day.

Not only did Paul teach at Ephesus, but the disciples he mentored had a significant ministry as well. Luke reports that while Paul ministered in Ephesus, "all who lived in Asia heard the word of the Lord, both Jews and Greeks" (Acts 19:10). This ministry was very likely carried out by Paul's students as is suggested by Paul's comment about the believers in this region "who have not personally seen my face" (Col. 2:1). It was during these years of Paul's ministry at Ephesus that the churches in the Lycus Valley (Colossae, Hierapolis and Laodicea) were founded (Col. 2:1; 4:13).

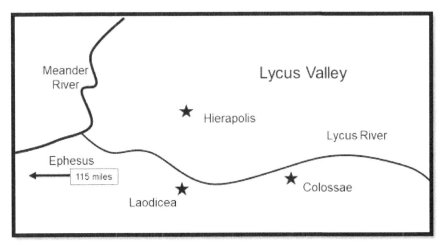

Figure 23  Lycus Valley Churches

God continued to work in Ephesus, confirming Paul's preaching through extraordinary signs and miracles (Acts 19:11; 2 Cor. 12:12). But where God is at work, His enemy Satan is also at work, endeavoring to thwart the advance of God's kingdom. This was true in Paul's day as well as ours. Luke records how some Jewish exorcists attempted to use the name of Jesus to exercise authority over demons. They superstitiously believed that there was magic in the name "Jesus." But their attempts to cast out demons with this formula backfired. The Jewish exorcists were overpowered by the demons so that they fled "naked and wounded" (Acts 19:16). Claiming the name and power of Jesus to do gospel centered ministry is a powerful weapon in spiritual warfare. But it is not a magical formula to be used by unbelieving amateurs.

When news spread of how the Jewish exorcists had been beaten up and chased away by the demons, many of the Ephesians repented of their involvement in the occult and became followers of Jesus. In demonstration of the genuineness of their faith, these new believers burned the books that had held them captive to the dark world of the magic arts (Acts 19:19). The strength of their commitment is evidenced by the sacrifice they made. Luke records that the value of the books they burned was an astonishing "fifty thousand pieces of silver."

When Paul sensed that his ministry in Ephesus was drawing to a close, he began making plans for the future (Acts 19:21-22). Luke records that he planned to return to Macedonia and Achaia where he and Silas had preached on the second journey. Moving ahead with these plans, Paul sent his two co-workers, Timothy and Erastus, ahead to Macedonia. From there Paul planned to travel on to Jerusalem. But he wasn't going to be content to sit back and enjoy the fruits of what had already been accomplished. In the back of his mind, Paul was longing to preach in the heart and capital of the Roman empire. Luke quoted Paul as saying, "After I have been there, I must also see Rome" (Acts 19:21).

Paul's departure from Ephesus came about as a result of what Luke calls "no small disturbance concerning the Way" (Acts 19:23). The silversmiths of Ephesus had a thriving business of selling small silver images of the fertility goddess Artemis to worshipers who visited her temple. The images could be donated to the temple as a votive offering or taken home as a reminder of one's visit to the magnificent temple. But business had fallen off significantly as many of the Ephesians had turned their backs on Artemis and become believers in Jesus, the resurrected Jewish Messiah and Savior. A silversmith by the name of Demetrius gathered the city's tradesmen together and complained of the damage Paul's preaching was doing to the honor of Artemis and the business loss that had resulted. He asserted, "Not only is there danger that this trade of ours fall into disrepute, but also that the temple of the great goddess Artemis be regarded as worthless and that she whom all of Asia and the world worship will even be dethroned from her magnificence" (Acts 19:27).

Hearing this, the frantic craftsmen poured into the streets and began crying out, "Great is Artemis of the Ephesians!" Soon the citizens of Ephesus heard the shouting and rushed into the theater, dragging with them two of Paul's co-workers, Gaius and Aristarchus (Acts 19:29). Paul wanted to enter the theater to speak to the crowd; but sensing the danger of the riotous situation, he was warned against this. Luke records that the impassioned crowd in the theater shouted for about two hours, "Great is Artemis of the Ephesians" (19:34). Finally, the town clerk was able to quiet the mob and remind them that the law courts were in session and were available to deal with any legitimate charges against Paul and his companions. He

Figure 24  Artemis of Ephesus (www.holylandphotos.org)

then dismissed the assembly (Acts 19:41).

The riot over Artemis being "dethroned from her magnificence" marked the end of Paul's three years of ministry in Ephesus. But he would continue his teaching and discipleship of the believers through a future letter (Eph. 1:1) and would eventually return to Ephesus with Timothy for further ministry (1 Tim. 1:1-3).

# Chapter 14
## Paul's Return to Jerusalem

Paul left Ephesus in the Spring of AD 56 to begin his journey back to Jerusalem. He traveled north from Ephesus to Troas where Paul expected to meet Titus (Acts 10:1-2; 2 Cor. 2:12-13), but he couldn't be found there. So Paul crossed the Aegean Sea and continued his journey into Macedonia, the province of northern Greece and location of the churches at Philippi, Thessalonica and Berea.

It was somewhere in Macedonia that he met up with Titus and was encouraged to receive a positive report regarding the situation in Corinth (2 Cor. 7:6 ff.). It was at that time, about six months after leaving Ephesus, that Paul sat down and penned the letter we know as Second Corinthians in anticipation of his plans to revisit Corinth. "Second Corinthians" might be better known as "Third Corinthians" since Paul had already written to the church twice (1 Cor. 5:9). Second Corinthians, written around AD 56, is a very personal letter and reveals a great deal about Paul's own heart and feelings. The letter was intended to reconcile Paul's relationship with the Corinthians which had been damaged by his change in travel plans (chaps. 1-7); to encourage the Corinthians to fulfill their promise of sending a gift to needy believers in Jerusalem (chaps. 8-9); and to vindicate Paul's apostolic authority which was being questioned (chaps. 10-13).

Leaving Macedonia, Paul may have traveled directly south to Achaia to spend the winter in Corinth. Alternatively, Eckhard Schnabel suggests that Paul may have traveled west on the *Via Egnatia* to the Adriatic coast to Illyricum ("Paul's Missionary Work in Asia and Illyricum," *LGCATR,* pp. 391-393). This is indicated in his letter to the Romans, "from Jerusalem and round about as far as Illyricum, I have fully preached the gospel of Christ" (Rom. 15:19). Illyricum was the first Roman province on the eastern Adriatic coast and a visit there would have provided Paul with another opportunity to engage in pioneer missionary work.

Paul eventually made his way south, by land (from Macedonia) or by sea (from Illyricum), to Achaia where he spent the winter of AD

56/57 (Acts 20:3a,5). Most of this time was probably spent at Corinth, teaching and encouraging the believers there.

Figure 25  Paul's Return to Jerusalem (*Baker's Concise Bible Atlas*, 1988. Used by permission of Baker Books, Baker Publishing Group)

Sometime during his winter in Corinth, Paul wrote what is known as his longest and most theological epistle, his epistle to the Romans. But the book of Romans is more than a theological treatise. Paul presented his gospel of justification by faith not only to inform his Roman readers theologically, but to enlist their support for his plans to carry this message to Spain. Paul spent the first chapters of Romans detailing the great truths of salvation (chaps. 1-8). This is followed by a lengthy discussion of Israel's election, rejection of the Messiah, and future salvation (chaps. 9-11). The last section of

Romans focuses on the practical living out of the gospel in the lives of believers (chaps. 12-16). Paul's prayer for the believers in Rome is a fitting conclusion to the doctrinal section of his letter: "Now may the God of hope fill you with all joy and peace in believing, so that you will abound in hope by the power of the Holy Spirit" (Rom. 15:13).

Learning of a conspiracy against him, Paul decided to return north through Macedonia instead of sailing directly east from Corinth (Acts 20:3). Luke reports that Paul traveled with some co-workers from Berea, Thessalonica and Derbe, and others who were waiting for Paul at Troas (Acts 20:4-5). We might wonder why Paul needed so many traveling companions. Although Luke doesn't tell us, I imagine that Paul was mentoring these believers in preparation for their future leadership and ministry. Discipleship can be defined as "companionship in preparation for spiritual leadership." As Barnabas had discipled Paul through companionship and partnership in ministry (Acts 11:25-26), the apostle was now discipling others.

Continuing east along the *Via Ignatia*, a road he had previously traveled (Acts 17:1), Paul and his companions came to Philippi for a brief visit before taking a boat downstream to the port of Neapolis and sailing to Troas (Acts 20:6) where Paul had received his call to "come over to Macedonia (Acts 16:8-9). Luke records that Paul and his companions stayed for a short time at the Mediterranean port of Troas before continuing their journey.

During the evening before their departure from Troas, Paul preached late into the evening. A young man named Eutychus, who was sitting on a window sill, was overcome with sleep and fell three stories to the ground below (Acts 20:7-9). Although thought to be dead, Paul embraced him and said, "Do not be troubled, for his life is in him" (Acts 20:10). Did Paul raise him from the dead? From Luke's brief account of the incident, it is difficult to answer this question with certainty. But the fact that Eutychus survived the fall from a three story building certainly reflects God's providential protection and care. This story may serve as a subtle reminder of the risks of falling asleep during a sermon!

Leaving Troas, Paul may have felt that he needed some time alone with the Lord and perhaps some exercise. He decided to walk the twenty miles to Assos while Luke and the other travelers went by ship (Acts 20:13). At Assos, Paul joined the others and they sailed for Miletus, a port at the mouth of the Meander River, about thirty miles south of Ephesus. We wonder why Paul didn't stop at Ephesus where he had spent the first three years of his third missionary journey. It appears that Paul wanted to reach Jerusalem by the feast of Pentecost (Acts 20:16) and didn't want to be delayed by a prolonged visit with his many friends in Ephesus. In addition, his ministry at Ephesus ended with a riot which had been instigated over Paul's preaching regarding the goddess Artemis (Acts 19:23-34). A return to the scene of that encounter could lead to further controversy and possible delay.

While staying for a short time at Miletus, Paul sent for the elders of the church at Ephesus and spoke to them about their ministry responsibilities. Having recounted his own ministry among the believers at Ephesus, Paul shared an important principle that was the essential key to his own successful ministry. Paul declared, "I do not consider my life of any account as dear to myself, so that I may finish my course and the ministry which I received from the Lord Jesus, to testify solemnly of the gospel of the grace of God" (Acts 20:24). Paul considered himself an *expendable* instrument in his service for Christ. Like Jesus, Paul was willing to lose his life for the cause of Christ. His humble attitude enabled Paul to serve others with a total disregard for himself in fulfillment of the mission for which he had been called.

The focus of Paul's message to the elders of Ephesus was their responsibility as "shepherds" to care for the "flock" of God's people which had been entrusted to them (Acts 20:28-32). Paul referred to the church leaders as "elders," a word which reflects their spiritual *maturity*, and as "overseers," a word which reflects the responsibility of spiritual *oversight* (Acts 20:17,28). But the word that best describes their ministry as elders is the verb "to shepherd" (*poimaino*). As a shepherd cares for his sheep, so the elder/overseers are to feed, lead and protect the congregation of believers which God has committed to their care (cf. 1 Pet. 5:1-3).

Paul concluded his words to the Ephesian elders by vindicating the integrity of his ministry. During his ministry in Ephesus, Paul did not take advantage of the opportunity for personal gain. He didn't covet material or financial resources, but worked with his own hands to meet his personal needs so that he would not be a burden on the church. Paul's quotation from the words of Jesus, "It is more blessed to give than to receive," is not found in the gospels, but the substance of this truth appears in Luke 6:38 and 11:9.

Bidding a tearful farewell to the Ephesian elders (Acts 20:36-38), Paul set sail from Miletus and journeyed on to the ancient port of Tyre (Acts 21:1-3), a flourishing commercial center in the Roman province of Syria. While the ship was being unloaded Paul and his companions spent time with the believers who were concerned about his safety. Luke records, "They kept telling Paul through the Spirit not to set foot in Jerusalem" (Acts 20:4). In spite of these warnings, Paul said farewell, boarded the ship and continued his journey.

Paul's next stop was Ptolemais, the port city known previously as Acco, but renamed Ptolemais not long after Alexander the Great's conquest of the region. Under Roman rule, the city expanded and the harbor, became a major port on Israel's northern coastal plain. Ancient walls built on Crusader foundations still surround the Old City of Acco. From the southern sea wall, visitors have a splendid view of the harbor and, on a clear day, can see Mount Carmel in the distance across the Bay of Haifa.

Paul spent a day at Ptolemais before continuing the next day to Caesarea, the city King Herod had built and named for the Roman emperor, Augustus. Caesarea was the governmental center for Roman rule over the province of Judaea. It was a grand city with a massive breakwater and harbor, a splendid theater and a hippodrome (chariot race track) to entertain visitors. The temple dedicated to the worship of the deified Augustus was situated on a hill overlooking the harbor for all to see as they arrived at Caesarea. Ancient Caesarea has been thoroughly excavated and beautifully restored to the amazement of modern visitors. Can you imagine stepping onto the grounds of Herod's palace, viewing his swimming pool, and walking through the hippodrome where Judea's most infamous king watched chariot races? And did I mention the Mediterranean sunsets over the ancient harbor? Simply spectacular!

Paul stayed with the evangelist Philip (Acts 6:5; 8:5-40) for several days before beginning his journey by land up to Jerusalem. During that visit, Agabus, the prophet who had predicted the great famine (Acts 11:28) arrived in Caesarea and prophesied that Paul would be delivered "into the hands of the Gentiles" if he continued his journey to Jerusalem (Acts 21:11). Hearing this, Paul's traveling companions, along with the believers at Caesarea, began begging him not to proceed to Jerusalem. But Paul responded, "I am ready not only to be bound, but even to die at Jerusalem, for the name of the Lord Jesus" (Acts 21:13).

Some have suggested that returning to Jerusalem was a serious mistake since Paul had been warned several times of pain and imprisonment if he continued his journey (Acts 20:22-24; 21:4,11-14). His arrest in Jerusalem and two-year imprisonment in Caesarea is thought to be God's chastening of the disobedient apostle. On the other hand, these warnings only predicted suffering and there was never a clear word from God, "Don't go to Jerusalem!" Paul was never rebuked by the Lord for going to Jerusalem and he never refers to his imprisonment in Caesarea as the consequence of disobedience. I suggest that Paul was simply fulfilling his calling to bring the name of Jesus "before Gentiles, kings and the sons of Israel" (Acts 9:15-16). He was willing to do so in spite of the personal cost (Acts 20:24).

Several days after his arrival in Caesarea, Paul and his companions traveled the fifty-five miles up to Jerusalem, the ancient capital and worship center for the Jewish people. Paul arrived in Jerusalem in the spring of AD 57. It had been four years since he had begun this journey from Antioch in the spring of AD 53. During this time Paul had traveled approximately 2,700 miles.

When Paul arrived in Jerusalem, he was welcomed gladly by the believers. But trouble was brewing. The leaders of the Jerusalem church were concerned about rumors that Paul was teaching the Jews of the Diasporea that they should "forsake Moses and not circumcise their children" (Acts 21:21). Did this mean that Paul was no longer Jewish? Had he rejected the Mosaic law? What should be done to assure the leaders of the Jerusalem church that the Apostle Paul was still a *Jewish* follower of Jesus?

# Chapter 15
# Paul's Arrest in the Temple

Paul arrived in Jerusalem on the eve of the Feast of Pentecost (May 27, AD 58), bringing his third missionary journey to a close. It had been twenty-five years since Peter's preaching on the Day of Pentecost when the church had received the ministry of the Holy Spirit (Acts 2:1-41). This was Paul's fifth visit to Jerusalem since his life altering experience on the road to Damascus. During the years since becoming a follower of Jesus, Paul had been preaching in the synagogues and market places in Galatia, Macedonia, Achaea and Asia. He was fulfilling his calling as an apostle to the Gentiles and had seen many people, both Jews and Gentiles, come to faith through his ministry. God was powerfully at work in Jerusalem as well. The Jerusalem church leaders reported that there were "many thousands" among the Jews of Jerusalem who had believed (Acts 21:20).

While the Jerusalem church leaders rejoiced in Paul's service for Christ, there was a major concern over the interpretation of his ministry to the Gentiles. A rumor was circulating that Paul was against the Mosaic law and was teaching the Jews of the Diaspora "to forsake Moses, telling them not to circumcise their children nor to walk according to the customs" (Acts 21:21). It was as if Paul was saying, "It is wrong for Jesus' followers to be Jewish." This implied that there was something wrong with Jewish culture and traditions, and that Jews had to renounce their customs and live like Gentiles in order to please God. Of course these reports were not true. Paul affirmed the Mosaic law as "holy, righteous and good" (Rom. 7:12), but argued that the law was never intended as a basis for justification, which could take place only by faith (Gal. 2:16).

What could be done to correct this rumor and demonstrate that Paul was not teaching that Jewish believers couldn't be Jewish? The Jerusalem church leaders had an idea. There were four Jewish believers who were preparing to complete what appears to be a Nazirite vow (Num. 5:13-21). They had taken upon themselves a commitment for a designated period not eat or drink anything produced from grapes, cut their hair, or go near a dead body.

Concluding this period of separation would require cutting their hair and offering a sacrifice in the temple. The church leaders proposed that Paul join the four believers in the traditional purification ritual and pay the expenses for their temple offering (Acts 21:23-24). It was hoped that these actions would demonstrate that Paul himself was a law abiding Jew and was not requiring Jewish followers of Jesus to disregard Jewish law, customs and traditions. And Paul agreed to this plan! He saw no problem with Jewish people being Jewish, as long as they did not look to the law and Jewish ritual as a means of justification.

On the next day, Paul joined the four men in the Jewish tradition of ritual immersion in a *mikveh*, a ritual bath. Adjacent to the steps leading to the southern entrances of the temple, archaeologist have discovered about forty ritual baths that would have been used by the Jews of Paul's day. Worshipers would enter the bathhouse, remove their clothing and completely immerse themselves in a ritual pool. After drying themselves and dressing, worshipers would proceed up the steps and into the colonnaded court of the temple (Todd Bolen, "The Jerusalem Temple in the Book of Acts," *LGCATR*, pp. 115-123). Following this purification ritual, Paul accompanied these messianic believers into the temple, paying the expenses to conclude their

Figure 26 Model of Jerusalem's Temple and Antonia Fortress

106

Nazirite vow with a "peace offering" (Num. 6:18), signifying the peace they enjoyed in their relationship with God. Like all the sacrifices of the Old Covenant, the peace offering pointed to Jesus who ultimately fulfills its purpose and significance by providing peace with God (Rom. 5:1) through what He accomplished on the cross.

Paul and the leaders of the Jerusalem church were well intended. They had expected that Paul's participation in a Nazirite ritual would quell the rumors that Paul had turned against the Jewish law. But things don't always go as planned. What happened next determined the course of Paul's life for the next four years!

Luke reports that some Jews who had traveled from Asia for the Feast of Pentecost recognized Paul in the temple court and jumped to the unwarranted conclusion that he had brought one of his Gentile co-workers into a restricted area of the Jerusalem temple. Josephus reports that there was a wall, a waist high barrier, that separated the court of the Gentiles from the more sacred courts of the temple with warnings posted in Hebrew, Latin and Greek that any Gentile who is caught going beyond the barrier "will have himself to blame for his ensuing death" (Josephus, *The Jewish War* V.193-194). An inscription containing this warning was discovered in 1871 just outside one of the gates to the temple mount and can be seen today in the Istanbul Archaeology Museum. A fragment of an inscription with the same warning was found just outside the Lion's gate and is displayed in the Israel Museum. Assuming that Paul had disregarded and defied the warning against Gentiles entering the restricted area of the temple, they shouted, "Men of Israel, come to our aid! This is the man who preaches to all men everywhere against our people and the law and this place; and besides he has even brought Greeks into the temple and has defiled this holy place" (Acts 22:28).

Believing the "fake news" of his accusers, the crowd of worshipers took hold of Paul, dragged him out of the temple area which was reserved for Jewish worshipers, and were "seeking to kill him" (Acts 22:31). The Jews of the first century were fanatical about the sanctity of Jerusalem's temple. In the hands of an angry mob, Paul's life was in serious danger.

The disturbance quickly came to the attention of the commander of the Roman cohort stationed in the Antonia Fortress which overlooked the temple area. The fortress had been built by King Herod and named in honor of his friend, Mark Antony (Josephus, *The Jewish War* V.238-245). It served as an outpost for Roman soldiers in order to watch the crowds of Jewish worshipers and intervene in case of a disturbance or riot. While it served as a fortress, Josephus wrote that "the interior "resembled a palace in its spaciousness and appointments" (*The Jewish War* 5.241). The Antonia palace/fortress is traditionally believed to be the *praetorium* where Pilate was residing when the Jewish leaders brought their charges against Jesus (Jn. 19:28-29). This location marks the beginning of the *Via Dolorosa* and the "way of the cross" leading through the streets of Jerusalem to the Church of the Resurrection (the Holy Sepulchre).

Figure 27  Steps of The Antonia Fortress

Breaking through the crowd surrounding Paul, Lysias, the Roman commander (Acts 24:7), arrested the apostle and bound him with chains (Acts 21:33). This intervention probably saved Paul's life! Lysias then began asking about Paul's identity and what he had done (Acts 21:33). But the shouting of the mob and general uproar prohibited him from getting any information. The commander could see that the situation was becoming violent as the crowd began shouting, "Away with him!" Seeking to protect their detainee from harm, the soldiers began carrying Paul up the steps of the Antonia Fortress! (Acts 21:35). But just before he was to be taken into the

Fortress, Paul spoke to Lysias, identifying himself as "a Jew of Tarsus in Cilicia, a citizen of no insignificant city" (Acts 21:39) and asked permission to speak to his accusers. Realizing that Paul was not the leader of the "Assassins" (*Sicarii*), bitter enemies of the Romans who mingled with crowds and stabbed their opponents with hidden daggers (Acts 21:38), the Roman commander granted Paul permission to address the crowd. Standing on the stairs leading to the entrance of the fortress, Paul raised his hand and speaking in what Luke termed "the Hebrew dialect," referring to Aramaic, a Semitic language similar to Hebrew which the Judeans adopted during their seventy years in Babylon. Luke records that there was "a great hush" (Acts 21:40) as the people quieted and began listening to what Paul had to say.

# Chapter 16
# Paul's Defense before the Jews

In his defense before the Jewish people gathered in the court of the temple, Paul testified that he was an observant Jew whose life had been dramatically and irreversibly changed through a personal encounter with Israel's resurrected Messiah, "Jesus the Nazarene" (Acts 22:8). This is a first person account of Paul's Damascus road experience, whereas in Acts 9:1-20, the story is told by Luke in the 3rd person.

The crowd quieted as they heard Paul speaking in a "Hebrew dialect" (Acts 21:40) known as Aramaic. This is the Semitic language which the Jews learned during their seventy-year Babylonian captivity and brought back with them when they returned to their Jewish homeland. It was probably around this time that the archaic Hebrew letters of the Bible were replaced with the block shaped letters so familiar to readers of the Hebrew Bible today. Like many modern Israelis, the first century Jews were multilingual. They spoke Aramaic, as well as Greek, the language of commerce and politics, and understood Hebrew when Scripture was being read in their synagogues.

Paul began his defense by rehearsing the facts of his birth, education and zeal for the law. The Apostle Paul was seeking to demonstrate that he was a true Jew, just as were his listeners (Acts 22:3). Recounting his education in Jerusalem under the renown rabbi Gamaliel must have added credibility to his testimony. Paul highlighted his fervor for the Jewish law and traditions by telling how he had persecuted followers of "the Way" (Jn. 14:6) to the death, arresting and imprisoning both men and women. His pursuit of such heretics was endorsed by the Sanhedrin who authorized Paul to arrest and extradite these wayward Jews to Jerusalem for trial (Acts 22:5).

Paul then explained that he was on his way to Damascus in fulfillment of his commission when he witnessed "a very bright light" suddenly flash from heaven. Falling to the ground, he heard a voice saying, "Saul, Saul, why are you persecuting Me" (Acts 22:7). The voice identified Himself saying to Saul, "I am Jesus the Nazarene whom you are persecuting." With a flash of insight through the illuminating ministry of the Holy Spirit, Paul suddenly realized that his attempts to serve God as a persecutor of Jesus' followers was accomplishing the very opposite of what he intended. Paul now realized that God had revealed Himself through Jesus, and to follow Jesus was to serve God. In new found faith, genuine repentance and sincere submission, Paul asked, "What shall I do, Lord?" (Acts 22:10).

Standing on the steps of the Antonia Fortress, Paul continued to recount his experience while his Jewish accusers listened quietly. They were probably wondering about the eventual outcome of this amazing story. Paul told of how he had been directed by Jesus to proceed on to Damascus where he would meet a Jewish follower of Jesus named Ananias. The Lord told Paul that Ananias would reveal "all that has been appointed for you to do" (Act 22:10).

Because he had been blinded by the bright light, Paul was led by hand to Damascus. There Ananias authenticated his authority as God's messenger by miraculously restoring Paul's sight. Then he said, "The God of our fathers has appointed you to know His will and to see the Righteous One and to hear an utterance from His mouth. For you will be a witness for Him to all men of what you have seen and heard" (Acts 22:14-15). After this, Paul reported that he underwent the ritual of immersion in water (*baptism*) to symbolize his spiritual cleansing and identify himself as a follower of Jesus, Israel's Savior and promised Messiah.

Paul continued his testimony, recounting his return to Jerusalem after his Damascus road encounter with Jesus. Praying in the temple, Jesus spoke to Paul saying, "Make haste, and get out of Jerusalem quickly, because they will not accept your testimony about Me" (Acts 22:18). In response to Paul's comments about his past life as a persecutor of believers and participant in the stoning of Stephen, Jesus said to him, "Go! For I will send you far away to the Gentiles" (Acts 22:21).

The mention of "the Gentiles" appears to have reminded the crowd of their accusation against Paul. They immediately stopped listening to his testimony and the riot that had led to Paul's arrest quickly resumed. The crowd began shouting, "Away with such a fellow from the earth, for he should not be allowed to live" (Acts 22:22). As his accusers continued shouting and throwing dust into the air, the commander gave the order to bring Paul into the Antonia

Fortress and have him scourged (Acts 22:24). A scourge was a leather whip imbedded with bits of sharp metal. Josephus tells of a man whose flesh was cut to ribbons and his bones laid bare by such punishment (*The Jewish War* VI. 303-04). While often done in preparation for execution, in Paul's case the purpose of this torture was to discover what he had done to cause such a riot in the temple.

As Paul was being "stretched out" with leather straps in readiness for the scourging, Paul must have decided that this was a good time to appeal to his Roman citizenship. Speaking to a centurion standing nearby, Paul said, "Is it lawful for you to scourge a man who is a Roman and uncondemned?" (Acts 22:25). Lysias, commander of the cohort, then asked Paul himself saying, "Tell me, are you a Roman?" While the commander had *purchased* his Roman citizenship, Paul explained that he was actually *born* a Roman (Acts 22:28). Upon hearing these words, Paul was immediately released by the soldiers who were preparing to scourge him. And the commander himself was fearful because he had violated Paul's rights as a Roman by putting him "in chains" (Acts 21:33; 22:29). As a Roman citizen, Paul was entitled to the rights of due process, including a public hearing before provincial authorities, prior to undergoing any punishment. Although we don't know any of the details, Paul's parents or ancestors had apparently received Roman citizenship. This meant that Paul had gained his Roman citizenship by birth rather than by some other means.

Paul had been saved from mob violence by the Roman soldiers and from scourging by his Roman citizenship. But his troubles in Jerusalem were far from over. On the next day after the riot in the temple, Paul was released by the Romans to stand trial before the highest religious court in the land, the Jewish Sanhedrin (Acts 22:30).

# Chapter 17
# Paul's Hearing before the Sanhedrin

After his arrest by the Roman commander in Jerusalem temple, Paul was taken into the Antonia Fortress, located on a rocky knoll overlooking the colonnaded outer court of the temple. There in the fortress honoring the memory of Marc Antony, Paul was kept in Roman custody overnight. On the day following his arrest, the commander ordered the chief priests and members of the Sanhedrin to assemble so they could examine Paul. Lysias was hoping to discover the charges against Paul which had led to the riot in the temple.

Luke, an eye witness of the proceedings, records that Lysias "brought Paul down" from the fortress and "set him before" the Sanhedrin, the Jewish religious court which met at the east end of the colonnaded Royal Porch of the temple (Acts 22:30). Although the Roman rulers were the highest authority in civil and governmental matters, the Sanhedrin was the highest *religious* authority and served as the final court of appeals on the interpretation and application of Jewish law.

Paul's hearing before the Sanhedrin was stormy. Standing before Ananias, the Jewish high priest (AD 47-66), Paul asserted his innocence by declaring that he had lived his life before God with a "perfectly clear conscience" (Acts 23:1). The high priest was so incensed by Paul's words that he ordered those standing nearby to strike him! Paul responded with anger saying, "God is going to strike you, you whitewashed wall!" (Acts 23:2-3). A whitewashed wall is an image of something that is unstable and crumbling, but has been covered with white paint to hide its defects. Paul withdrew his comment when he was informed that he was speaking to Israel's high priest, and quoted the words of the Torah, "You shall not speak evil of a ruler of your people" (Exod. 22:28).

You may be wondering why Paul didn't recognize the high priest by his distinctive robe, crown and breastplate. Some have suggested that Paul's eyesight was damaged and failing, perhaps due to his being blinded by his vision on the road to Damascus. Others interpret

Paul as simply commenting, "I didn't think Israel's high priest would command someone to strike an innocent man."

Paul must have realized that he was making no progress in his defense before the Sanhedrin, so he decided on a different tactic. Aware that the members of the council were made up of two competing factions—the Sadducees and the Pharisees--Paul was able to turn the focus away from himself and onto the theological differences between the two sects. Paul cried out saying, "Brethren, I am a Pharisee, a son of Pharisees; I am on trial for the hope and resurrection of the dead!" (Acts 23:6). You may recall that the Sadducees denied the concept of bodily resurrection since they didn't believe the doctrine was taught by Moses in the Torah (Josephus, *Jewish War* II.166-67; cf. Matt. 22:23-33). On the other hand, the Pharisees affirmed the biblical doctrine of the bodily resurrection (Dan. 12:2; Acts 23:8).

Paul's mention of the doctrine of the resurrection successfully derailed the attack against him. At this point, the Pharisees and Sadducees began a heated debate among themselves, with the Pharisees actually coming to Paul's defense! The leaders of the Pharisees declared, "We find nothing wrong with this man; suppose a spirit or an angel has spoken to him?" (Acts 23:9).

Seeing that the meeting with the Sanhedrin was getting nowhere in determining the cause of the previous day's riot, and fearing for the life of a prisoner who was under his protection, the Roman commander ordered his soldiers to return Paul to the Antonia Fortress (Acts 23:10).

That night, as Paul was kept as a prisoner in the fortress, the Lord appeared to him saying, "Take courage; for as you have solemnly witnessed to My cause at Jerusalem, so you must witness at Rome also" (Acts 23:11). This was the third appearance of the Lord to Paul since his first encounter on the Damascus road (Acts 18:9-10; 22:17-18). The mention of Paul's witness in Rome reflects God's future plans for Paul. He was going to Rome! But it would take two years for him to get there.

On the day after the volatile session before the Sanhedrin, more than forty Jews formed a conspiracy to murder Paul. They reported their plans to the Jewish chief priests and elders saying, "We have bound ourselves under a solemn oath to taste nothing until we have killed Paul" (Acts 23:14). To accomplish this, they asked the Jewish leaders to have Paul brought back to the Sanhedrin for further investigation. They would be waiting and ready to attack and kill him. Somehow the conspiracy became known to Paul's nephew, his sister's son, who was able to inform Paul and Lysias, the Roman commander (Acts 23:16-22). The commander instructed Paul's nephew to "tell no one" that the conspiracy had been discovered. He then took immediate steps to safeguard his prisoner.

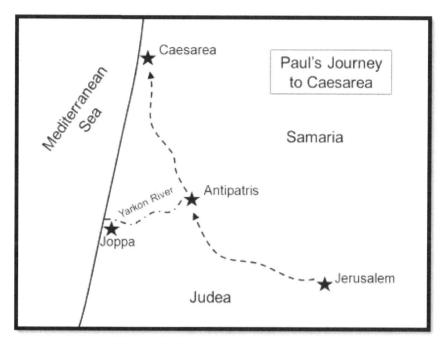

Figure 28  Paul's Journey to Caesarea

The Roman commander charged two centurions to make ready two hundred soldiers, seventy horsemen and two-hundred spearmen to transfer Paul under the cover of darkness to Caesarea, the Roman capital of the province of Judea. While Paul was used to walking, a horse was provided to expedite his exit from Jerusalem. The military escort also carried a letter written to Felix, the Roman procurator (AD 52-58), explaining Paul's arrest and the reason he was being transferred to Caesarea (Acts 23:25-30). In his letter, the commander reported that Paul had been accused over questions about Jewish law, but the charges provided no grounds for imprisonment or the death penalty.

In accordance with the commander's orders, Paul was taken by night to Antipatris, a fortified city named for Herod's father, Antipater.

The city was strategically located halfway between Jerusalem and Caesarea at the headwaters of the Yarkon River. The Yarkon flowed from abundant springs at Antipatris (ancient Aphek), crossed the coastal plain and emptied into the Mediterranean Sea just north of modern Tel Aviv. The day following Paul's arrival at Antipatris, the soldiers returned to their barracks in Jerusalem while the horsemen continued on to Caesarea where they presented their prisoner to governor Felix (Acts 23:32-33). Felix promised that Paul would have a hearing before his accusers when they arrived from Jerusalem. Until then, Paul was ordered to be kept in "Herod's *Praetorium*," the palace originally built by King Herod but later served as the official residence of the Roman governors of Judea. Herod's magnificent palace was prominently situated overlooking the sea with pleasing views of the Roman theater, hippodrome and Mediterranean sunsets.

Figure 29  This Roman aqueduct once carried water to Caesarea.

It was here in Caesarea that archaeologists later discovered an inscription bearing the name of the Roman official overseeing Jesus' civil trial, "Pontius Pilate, Prefect of Judea." Herod's former palace, the Roman *praetorium*, would be Paul's place of residence in

118

Caesarea where he would "shelter in place" for the next two years. For Paul, this would be a time of waiting, trusting and learning patience. But it would also be an opportunity for strategic witnesses before some of the most influential political and religious leaders in Roman Judea.

Figure 30  Audience Hall of Herod's Palace where Paul may have appeared before Felix, Festus and King Agrippa (Holylandphotos.com)

# Chapter 18
# Paul's Witness in Caesarea

Paul was imprisoned in Caesarea for two years, from early summer of AD 57 to late summer of AD 59. Caesarea, pleasingly situated on the Mediterranean Sea north of the ancient port of Joppa, served as the seat of the Roman government which ruled over Judea. The city had been built by King Herod and named for his patron, Caesar Augustus. Built to impress Herod's visitors from Rome, Caesarea boasted of a magnificent harbor, theater, hippodrome (for chariot races) and a temple dedicated to Rome's divine emperor, Augustus. Visitors arriving at the port of Caesarea could not help being impressed with the marble columned Temple of Augustus on a prominent bluff overlooking the harbor. They understood clearly from the appearance and appointments of the city that they were entering an outpost of Rome.

Figure 31 Caesarea *Maritima*. The field in the foreground was part of the original harbor.

Although Caesarea was primarily a Gentile city with a culture much like Rome, the discovery of a synagogue gives evidence that there was a community of Jews living there as well.

While awaiting his trial, Paul was held in Herod's palace, the *praetorium* (Acts 23:35), which was being used as the residence for the Roman administrators of Judea (Eckhard Schnabel, "Paul as a Prisoner in Judea and Rome," *LGCATR*, pp. 401-402). His confinement probably prevented him from moving about the city and preaching publicly, but Paul did have the opportunity to present the gospel to some of the civic leaders, including Felix, Festus and King Agrippa II.

## Imprisonment Under Felix

Paul was detained in Caesarea by the Roman governor, Antonius Felix (AD 52-58) for two long years (Acts 24:27). Felix had been the slave of Antonia, the mother of Emperor Claudius (AD 41-54), whose life was featured in the BBC series, "I Claudius." When Felix was set free, he rose to prominence and became a Roman procurator (or governor). Josephus reports that he was a harsh ruler who crucified bandits and put many to death with the sword (Josephus, *The Jewish War* II. 247; 252-53; 260; 271). The Roman historian Tacitus records that Felix was "a master of cruelty and lust who exercised the power of a king in the spirit of a slave" (*Historias* 5:9).

Five days after Paul's arrival in Caesarea, Ananias, the Jewish high priest, came with his attorney, Tertullus, to file charges against the apostle. After flattering the governor with words of thanks and praise for his administration of the province (Acts 24:2-4), Tertullus proceeded with his accusation against Paul. The essence of the charge was that Paul was a "real pest" who stirred up dissension and was the recognized "ringleader" of the Nazarenes (Acts 24:5). Tertullus then recounted Paul's so-called attempt "to desecrate the temple" and his subsequent arrest (Acts 24:6-9). Having presented his charges against Paul, the Jews who had accompanied Ananias and Tertullus to Caesarea joined in the attack, "asserting that these things were so" (Acts 24:9).

After hearing the charges, Felix nodded to Paul, granting him the right to speak in his own defense. After a brief courtesy, acknowledging the years of Felix's governorship over Judea, Paul explained that he had arrived in Jerusalem only twelve days before his arrest and had neither said nor done anything to incite a riot in Jerusalem (Acts 24:10-12). Next, Paul proceeded to explain that he was a follower of the "Way" and had been a faithful and law abiding Jew, believing all that was written in the Mosaic law and the Prophets. As a Pharisee, Paul asserted his belief in the doctrine of the resurrection and his blameless conscience before God and men (Acts 24:15-16). Paul went on to recount his visit to the Jerusalem temple for the purpose of presenting alms and offerings. He pointed to the "Jews from Asia" as those who had stirred up the crowd of worshipers and caused the disturbance. Paul concluded by declaring that there was no crime for which he should be charged and the "trial" was simply the result of his assertion of "the resurrection of the dead" (Acts 24:21).

Luke records that Felix was well acquainted with the Jewish sect, called "the Way," and knew that Paul was innocent of the charges against him. But he put off making a decision about Paul's case because of the presence of influential Jews from Jerusalem. He explained the delay, saying that he wanted to speak with Lysias, the Roman commander who had arrested Paul (Acts 24:22-23).

Sometime later, Felix and his Jewish wife, Drusilla (daughter of Herod Agrippa I), came to visit Paul and heard him speak about his faith in Jesus, Israel's Messiah (Acts 24:24). But the governor became fearful when Paul began talking about "righteousness, self-control and the judgment to come" (Acts 24:25). Felix quickly ended the discussion. But with the hopes of receiving a bribe from the apostle, he later sent for Paul for additional conversations. Felix was recalled by Emperor Nero in AD 58 and nothing further is known of him. When the next procurator, Festus, assumed office, Felix left Paul in custody as a "favor" to his Jewish accusers (Acts 24:27).

Imprisonment Under Festus

Governor Felix was succeeded by Porcius Festus who served in the office of procurator from AD 58 until his death in AD 61. His administration over Judea was not marked by the harsh rule and excesses which had characterized Felix. Josephus, in fact, commends him for restoring law and order, reporting that "he captured large numbers of bandits and put not a few to death" (*Jewish Wars* II. 271).

Three days after his arrival in Caesarea, Festus went up to Jerusalem to meet the chief priests and Jewish leaders (Acts 25:2). It didn't take long for them to bring up the subject of that trouble maker,

Paul. Once again, they brought their charges against Paul and asked that he be transferred to Jerusalem for trial. Luke reveals that their ulterior motive was to "ambush and kill him on the way" (Acts 25:3). In spite of the new governor's limited experience with the religious squabbles of the Jews, he didn't concede to their request. Instead, he invited the Jewish leaders to bring their charges against Paul in the Roman civil court *at Caesarea* (Acts 25:5).

Paul had been held by the Roman authorities for two full years when his case was reopened at Festus' tribunal. Standing before Festus and the Jewish leaders from Jerusalem, Paul persisted in asserting his innocence of all charges—violating Mosaic law, defiling the temple and dishonoring Caesar (Acts 25:8). Seeking to gain some goodwill from the Jewish leaders, Festus asked Paul if he was willing to return to Jerusalem and stand trial before the Sanhedrin. Paul replied, "I am standing before Caesar's tribunal, where I ought to be tried" (Acts 25:10). Fearing that a trial in Jerusalem couldn't be conducted with impartiality Paul continued. "If I am a wrongdoer and have committed anything worthy of death, I do not refuse to die; but if none of those things are true of which these men accuse me, no one can hand me over to them. I appeal to Caesar" (Acts 25:11).

The right of an appeal to Caesar was one of the cherished rights of a Roman citizen. It was customarily made to appeal the verdict of a lower court, but could be exercised at any stage in the court proceedings. The appeal to Caesar was recognized only in extraordinary cases which were not addressed by Roman statute laws. On the basis of the appeal, the case would be transferred to Rome for a final verdict to be made by the emperor, who at this time was the infamous Nero (AD 54-68).

Festus was in a difficult situation. He knew that Paul was innocent of any charges which would be of concern to a Roman court (Acts 25:25). But he also knew that his duties as procurator required him to report court proceedings relating to Paul's appeal to Caesar's tribunal. And Festus was uncertain as to what he would say in his report (Acts 25:26). This difficulty seems to have been resolved by a visit from a man well recognized by Rome, Herod Agrippa II (AD 50-100).

Agrippa was the son of Herod Agrippa I whose execution of James and imprisonment of Peter is recounted by Luke in Acts 12. His failure to give God glory, resulting in his subsequent death (Acts 12:23), is a sobering warning even for today. Agrippa, the great-grandson of Herod the Great, was reputed to be an authority on the Jewish religion. Perhaps by hearing from Paul, Agrippa could provide Festus some insights on what to report to Rome regarding Paul's case.

Anxious to provide a bit of background for the charges against Paul, Festus explained to Agrippa what he knew about the case (Acts 25:14-21). He reported that the charges against Paul were not of a criminal nature, but were over religious disagreements and reports "about a dead man, Jesus, whom Paul asserted to be alive" (Acts 25:19). Festus explained that Paul was unwilling to go to Jerusalem to stand trial before the Jewish leaders and had, instead, appealed to Caesar. Being a Jewish king, Agrippa apparently was interested in Paul's case. He told Festus, "I also would like to hear the man myself" (Acts 25:22). The governor was more than happy to comply and said, "Tomorrow you shall hear him."

## Paul Speaks Before King Agrippa II

Paul's hearing before King Agrippa took place in the late Summer of AD 59, shortly before his departure for Rome. The hearing before Agrippa didn't actually advance the trial, but was intended to provide Festus with additional information for his report. Beyond that, the hearing gave Paul another opportunity to tell the story of his spiritual transformation before "kings," as had been prophesied (Acts 9:15).

King Agrippa arrived at the hearing room "amid great pomp" accompanied by his sister and intimate companion, Bernice. She was of Herodian descent being the daughter of Herod Agrippa I and sister of King Agrippa II. After several failed marriages, she ended up in the court of her brother, with whom she was rumored to be living incestuously (Josephus *Antiquities* XX.7.3; Juvenal *Satires* VI). Later, during the Jewish war, she entered into a love affair with the Roman general and future emperor, Titus, but was dismissed when he became emperor in AD 79 (Tacitus. *Histories* II.2).

After King Agrippa II, the Roman commanders, and the prominent men of Caesarea had gathered, Paul was presented by Festus with a brief explanation of the background of the case. Then he added, "Since he himself appealed to the Emperor, I decided to send him. Yet I have nothing definite about him to write to my lord. Therefore, I brought him before you all and especially before you,

King Agrippa, so that after the investigation has taken place, I may have something to write" (Acts 25:25-26).

Paul began by expressing his appreciation for the opportunity to present his defense, appealing to Agrippa's expertise in Jewish customs and questions (Acts 26:2-3). He then rehearsed his own religious heritage as a strict Pharisee with faith in God's promise to "raise the dead" (Acts 26:4-8). Paul recounted his zealous persecution of the followers of Jesus, furiously pursuing them even to foreign cities to lock them up or put them to death. But his heavenly vision on the road to Damascus changed all that! Paul told of how he had met Jesus, Israel's resurrected Messiah, and received His commission to bear witness of the good news of "forgiveness of sins" through faith (Acts 26:9-18). His obedience to the heavenly vision, Paul explained, led to his being seized in the temple by Jews who were attempting to put him to death (Acts 26:19-21).

Not one to miss an opportunity to present the gospel, Paul began explaining how Moses and the Prophets had predicted that the Messiah would suffer and be raised from the dead to bring Jews and Gentiles into the spiritual light of God. But Festus interrupted the apostle, calling out loudly, "Paul, you are out of your mind! Your great learning is driving you mad" (Acts 26:24). Respectfully denying the charge, Paul declared that he was speaking "words of sober truth" (Acts 26:25).

Paul then addressed the guest of honor, King Agrippa. "Do you believe the Prophets? I know that you do" (Acts 26:27). If Agrippa responded by answering "No," his reputation as a "Jewish" king would be tarnished. But if he answered "Yes," then it would appear that he was supporting Paul over against his Jewish accusers. Playing it safe, King Agrippa brushed aside the question. His reply (Acts 26:28) can be interpreted in two possible ways depending on one's understanding of the word "short." Agrippa may have been saying, "In short, you are trying to persuade me to become a Christian." The other possibility is that the king was saying, "In a short time you will persuade me to become a Christian." Either way, it was indeed Paul's desire for not only Agrippa, but for *everyone* at the hearing to become as Paul, a follower of Jesus, *except for* his chains (Act 26:29).

With these words, King Agrippa rose to his feet, indicating an end to the hearing. Conferring among themselves, Agrippa and those with him agreed that Paul had done nothing worthy of imprisonment or death (Acts 26:31). Commenting to Governor Festus, King Agrippa said, "This man might have been set free if he had not appealed to Caesar" (Acts 26:32). But by making his appeal to Caesar, Paul had set in motion a legal procedure that had to be followed. The case was no longer under the jurisdiction of Festus, procurator of Judea. Paul must be sent to Rome.

Figure 32  Menora from a Jewish synagogue at Caesarea.
(Holylandphotos.com)

# Chapter 19
# Paul's Sea Voyage and Shipwreck

Paul began his voyage to Italy towards the end of the summer of AD 59, after two years and two months of incarceration at Caesarea. His arrest resulted from a riot that was sparked during his visit at the Jerusalem temple, but no formal charges had been made against him. Paul presented his defense before the Roman governors, Felix and Festus, but they had not granted his release. Finally, Paul exerted his right as a Roman citizen and appealed his case to Caesar. This appeal now required that Paul's case be transferred to Rome. Further details on his journey can be found in my article, "Paul's Journey to Rome" (*LGCATR*, pp. 411-429).

Paul's co-worker, Dr. Luke, accompanied Paul on this journey and provides a detailed account which is full of unique geographical and navigational terms. Luke's narrative has been called "one of the most instructive documents of ancient seamanship" (James Smith, *The Voyage & Shipwreck of St. Paul*). The Greeks had a great appreciation and respect of the Mediterranean Sea. Many of their accounts of Mediterranean voyages include a shipwreck. It is not too much to say that Luke's account ranks on a par with Homer's epic poem, *The Odessy*, in terms of excitement and travel adventure.

Paul was escorted to Rome by Julius, a centurion (commander of 80-100 soldiers), of a cohort (600 men) named for the emperor, Augustus. The ship's home port was Adramyttium, southeast of Troas. Julius knew that the ship would be stopping at various ports along the coast of Asia Minor and somewhere along the route he could transfer his prisoner to a ship going to Rome (Acts 27:2).

The first stop on the voyage was Sidon, located seventy miles north of Caesarea. Luke notes that Julius "treated Paul with consideration and allowed him to go to his friends and receive care" (Acts 27:3). From Sidon, the ship sailed north and east of Cyprus to get shelter from the prevailing winds which came out of the west during the summer months. The ship continued slowly against the wind, in a westerly direction along the coast of Asia Minor until arriving at the port of Myra. Egypt's Nile delta served as the chief source of grain for ancient Rome, and Myra was one of the main ports for the wheat fleet that carried grain to Rome. Ships in Rome's wheat fleet made one or more trips a year, bringing about 150,000 tons of grain to Rome annually (Lionel Casson, *Ships and Seamanship in the Ancient World*, JHU Press, 1985, p. 188). The city of Myra eventually became known for a generous bishop who gave gifts to the poor and is remembered today as "Saint Nicholas."

At Myra, Julius found a ship which was carrying a load of grain from Alexandria and would be continuing on to Italy (Acts 27:6). In addition to its cargo, the ship carried 276 passengers. Leaving Myra, the ship's progress became more difficult because of the strong winds blowing from the northwest. Reaching Fair Havens, on the island of Crete, the ship laid anchor to wait for more favorable weather conditions (Acts 27:8). It was fast approaching the end of the sailing season on the Mediterranean Sea. The period of "safe" sailing was during the spring and summer months. Because of life endangering winter storms, all travel on the open sea ceased by mid-November and didn't begin again until February. The transitional seasons during the late fall and early spring were considered discretionary, but risky. Luke notes that it was already October, for the Day of Atonement ("the fast") had already past (Acts 27:9).

Figure 33  Paul's Sea Voyage to Rome (*Baker's Concise Bible Atlas*, 1988. By permission of Baker Books, Baker Publishing Group)

Knowing that continuing on would be "dangerous," Paul advised that the ship winter over at Fair Havens to avoid the risk of being caught in an early winter storm. You might wonder what Paul knew about the dangers of sailing. According to his own testimony, he had already been shipwrecked three times (2 Cor. 11:25). But the ship's captain wasn't persuaded by Paul's words of warning (Acts 27:11). Since the harbor at Fair Havens was deemed unsuitable for wintering, it was decided to continue the voyage with the hopes of reaching the better protected harbor of Phoenix and spend the winter months there (Acts 27:12).

When the wind came up, the crew lifted the ship's anchor, raised the sails and began sailing along the south coast of Crete. But suddenly, as is often the case on the Mediterranean Sea, the weather dramatically changed. Luke records that "there rushed down from the land a violent wind, called *Euraquilo* ("northeaster") and the ship was caught in it (Acts 27:14-15). The gale pushed the ship away from the shore of Crete and it wasn't until they reached the shelter of a small island named Clauda that they were able to get the situation under control.

Luke records that the ship's crew took three precautionary measures in the face of the raging storm (Acts 27:16-17). First, they hauled the lifeboat, which was usually towed, onto the deck of the ship. Second, the crew undergirded the ship with cables to prevent the crashing waves from damaging the hull. Third, they lowered "the gear" (*skeuos*), referring to either (1) the sea anchor to prevent drifting into shallow water or (2) the tackle to prevent the sails being ripped to shreds by the storm wind.

The next day the storm did not let up, so the sailors began to jettison the cargo to lighten the ship (Acts 27:18). You may recall that the sailor's on Jonah's ship did the same thing in the midst of a storm (Jonah 1:5). On the third day, as what Luke calls "no small storm" continued and the hope of survival diminished, the crew took the more drastic measure of throwing the spare tackle overboard (Acts 27:19). These were desperate attempts by the storm weary sailors to survive the forces of nature that were battering them and their ship.

After days of being tossed about day and night by the storm, the Apostle Paul couldn't resist the temptation to say, "I told you so!" Standing among the passengers and crew, Paul said, "Men, you ought to have followed my advice and not to have set sail from Crete and incurred this damage and loss" (Acts 27:21). But he went on to offer words of comfort and hope. Paul reported that an angel had appeared to him saying, "Do not be afraid, Paul; you must stand before Caesar; and behold, God has granted you all those who are sailing with you" (Acts 27:24). The ship would be lost to the storm, but their lives would be spared through God's grace and protection. Paul then assured his fellow travelers, "Keep up your courage, men, for I believe God that it will turn out exactly as I have been told" (Acts 27:25).

If you have ever been seasick, you can imagine the misery of the sailors and passengers after fourteen days on a ship that's rocking and rolling about through a winter storm. The ship had been driven by the northeasterly winds to the Adriatic Sea, between Greece and the boot of Italy (Acts 27:27). During the night, the crew suspected that the drifting ship was approaching land (Acts 27:28-29). Perhaps they heard waves crashing the nearby rocky beach. Fearful of drifting onto the rocks, the sailors set out four anchors to secure the ship until the light of day. As the day began to dawn, Paul noticed that some of the crew members were attempting to abandon the ship and make it to shore in the lifeboat. But Paul alerted Julius and the soldiers, warning that they had to stay together to ensure that all would get safely ashore (Acts 27:30-31).

Since the sailors and passengers were in a weakened condition from not eating during the raging storm, Paul encouraged them to "take some food" and reminded them of God's promise that none of them would perish (Acts 27:24,33-34). Luke records that Paul then "gave thanks to God in the presence of all;" he broke bread and began to eat (Acts 27:35). Having been encouraged by Paul's words of assurance and prayer, the passengers and crew took food and ate. Strengthened by the food, they began to lighten the ship by throwing overboard the remaining cargo of wheat. They wanted the ship to draw as little water as possible so that it might run aground well up on the beach (27:38).

As the day dawned, the sailors didn't recognize the land before them, but they did see a bay with a beach where they could possibly land the ship. Cutting the anchors, they hoisted the rigging, intending to sail into the bay. Saint Paul's Bay, a small town located along the northern coastline of Malta, is the traditional location of where Paul and his companions arrived on the island. This was a major harbor in Paul's day. Remains of a Roman road and baths found in the area give evidence of first century occupation. But Carl Rasmussen has pointed out that Saint Paul's Bay "lacks sandy beaches, and thus would not qualify as 'a certain bay with a beach' and thus was probably not the place of the shipwreck (www.holylandphotos.org). He suggests that Paul's ship arrived on Malta at nearby Salina Bay, located just to the east of the traditional site. This understanding is based on Mark Gatt's book, *Paulus: The Shipwreck 60 AD* (2nd edition, Allied Publications, Valletta, Malta, 2017). Qawra Point is identified as the place where, according to Luke, "the two seas met," and was the location of the reef where Paul's ship went aground (Acts 27:41). In support of this identification is the discovery of four ancient anchors, as well as many other artifacts, under about 100 feet of water. This coincides with Luke's mention of "four anchors" which the sailors cast from the stern ship to secure it until daybreak (Acts 27:29). It is an exciting prospect to think that the anchors from Paul's ship have been discovered!

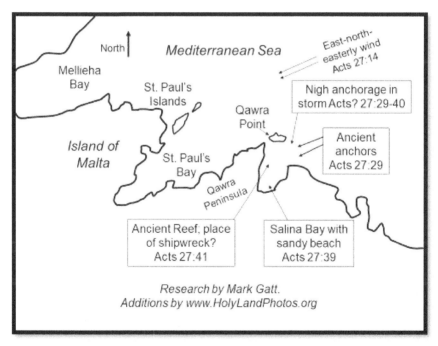

Figure 34 Paul's Shipwreck on Malta

What the sailors didn't realize as they approached an unknown island in the early morning light was that there was a reef "where the two seas [the Adriatic Sea and the bay] met" (Acts 27:41). The ship ran aground and the crashing waves began pounding against the stern of the ship. Under the force of the powerful waves, it didn't take long for the ship to begin breaking up. I recall witnessing this in Santa Cruz, California, when a sailboat went aground in Monterey Bay. Attempts to get the boat off the beach were unsuccessful and by the next morning the stern had been demolished by the pounding waves and surf was flowing in and out of the nearly submerged cabin.

The soldiers intended to kill the prisoners to prevent their escape; but Julius, desirous of delivering Paul safely to Caesar, intervened. He commanded that the prisoners swim or float ashore on debris from the ship (Acts 27:42-43). Luke concludes the account of Paul's fourth shipwreck by reporting, "And so it happened that they all were brought safely to land," just as God had promised (Acts 27:24).

It is worth noting the Jewish historian Josephus was shipwrecked in the same area on his voyage to Rome in behalf of some priests who had been unjustly accused. When the ship foundered in the "Sea of Adria," Josephus and other passengers swam all night before being rescued by another ship which carried them safely to Puteoli, the same port to which Paul would eventually arrive (Josephus, *Vita* 3).

# Chapter 20
## Paul's Journey on to Rome

As God had promised, all the passengers and crew survived the shipwreck and made it safely to shore. It was then that they discovered that the place they had landed was an island called Malta (Acts 28:1). Malta is the largest island in a group of small islands south of Sicily in the Mediterranean Sea. The island group is known today as the Republic of Malta. The place of Paul's arrival has been traditionally identified with "St. Paul's Bay" where remains of a Roman harbor and road have been discovered. Recent research suggests that Paul and his fellow passengers came ashore at Salina Bay, featuring a sandy beach (Acts 27:39), just east of the traditional site.

Luke reports that the native people of Malta showed "extraordinary kindness" to the survivors of the shipwreck, kindling a fire on the beach because of the cold and rain (Acts 28:2). Paul, who was not averse to working with his hands (Acts 20:34; 2 Thess. 3:8), was helping gather firewood when a poisonous viper in the bundle of wood bit into his hand (Acts 28:3)! When the islanders saw what had happened, they assumed that Paul would die, saying to each other, "Undoubtedly this man is a murderer, and though he has been saved from the sea, justice has not allowed him to live" (Acts 28:4). The word translated "justice" (*dike*) refers to Dike, the daughter of Zeus and goddess of justice and moral order in Greek mythology. The natives of Malta believed that the goddess of justice was not going to let this criminal escape. They had expected to see him "swell up" or "fall down dead," but nothing of that sort happened. When Paul shook off the viper into the fire and suffered no harm, they changed their minds about him. His miraculous survival led them to conclude that Paul was a god (Acts 28:6)! This wasn't the first time Paul had been mistaken as a god. It had happened before at Lystra where Paul and Barnabas were mistakenly identified as the visiting gods, Hermes and Zeus (Acts 14:11-12).

Luke reports that "the leading man of the island," by the name of Publius, welcomed Paul and his traveling companions and graciously "entertained" them for three days (Acts 28:7). The word translated "entertained" (*xenizo*) refers to hospitality and includes the idea of providing food and lodging (cf. Acts 21:16; Heb. 13:2). The kindness of Paul's host was returned when Paul prayed for and healed Publius' father of fever and dysentery (Acts 28:8). The mention of this and other healings (Acts 28:8) is a clue as to what Paul was doing during his time at Malta. Paul was not a medical missionary, but as in the case of Jesus, his miraculous healings served to authenticate the gospel message he was proclaiming (Matt. 4:23; 12:28). As he had done in so many places on his previous travels, Paul was preaching the gospel to the Gentile natives of Malta. Had there been a synagogue in the area, Luke would probably have mentioned Paul's ministry there as well.

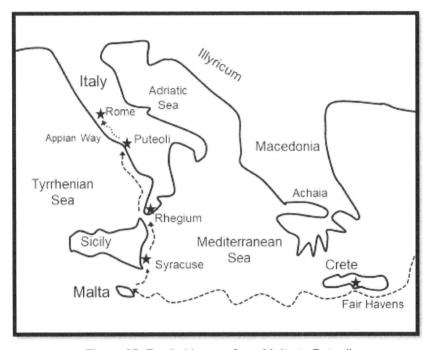

Figure 35  Paul's Voyage from Malta to Puteoli

The people of Malta treated Paul and his companions well. Luke notes that "they honored us with many marks of respect" (Acts 28:10a). And when the time arrived for Paul and his fellow travelers to depart, Luke comments that "they supplied us with all we needed" (Acts 28:10b). Although Paul had never intended to visit Malta, God had providentially provided that opportunity, and the apostle must have departed with pleasant memories of the winter he spent on the island.

About three months after the storm and shipwreck, the Mediterranean Sea was once again reasonably safe for travel. Julius was able to secure passage for Paul and his companions on a ship that had wintered on Malta and was also sailing for Rome. The home port of the ship was Alexandria, that intellectual center and Mediterranean port on the Nile delta. It was evidently one of the fleet of ships that transported wheat from the delta of Egypt to feed the populous of Rome. Luke notes that the figurehead on the bow of the ship featured the Gemini twins, Castor and Pollux. These were the sons of Leda, a Spartan queen, but conceived by different fathers. Castor was the mortal son of the king of Sparta, while Pollux was the divine son of Zeus. When Pollux asked Zeus to let his brother share his immortality, the twins were transformed into the Gemini constellation. The half-brothers were regarded as the patrons of navigation. It was believed that viewing their constellation at sea would bring good fortune, including a safe voyage.

Leaving Malta, the ship sailed for Syracuse, a port on the Ionian coast of Sicily, where it remained for three days before continuing the journey (Acts 28:12). The city Syracuse today features Greek and Roman ruins and is remembered as the birthplace of the famous mathematician, Archimedes (287-212 BC). Sailing from Syracuse, the next stop for Paul's ship was Rhegium, located on the tip of the toe of the boot of Italy, just across the water from Messina, Sicily. This is where the Allied forces invaded in 1943 to defeat the fascist regime in Italy. Two days later, with the help of a south wind, Paul and his traveling companions arrived at Puteoli in the Bay of Naples, the terminus for Rome's wheat fleet. Known as Puzzoli today, the port is located just across the bay from Pompeii, a city covered by the ash and volcanic debris which fell when Mount Vesuvius erupted on August 24th, AD 79.

Paul's sea voyage was over, but not his journey. Disembarking from the ship, Paul found some followers of Jesus at Puteoli who hosted him for a week before he set out walking about one hundred miles northeast on the *Via Campania* to Capua. There he turned northwest and continued his journey on the famous *Via Appia* (Appian Way) to Rome (Acts 28:14). The believers in Rome who had heard of Paul's arrival, came south to meet and welcome him. Some of the brothers met him at "the Market of Appius" (Appii Forum), about 43 miles south of Rome. Others met him at "Three Inns," about ten miles closer in. What an encouragement it was to be met and welcomed by those who shared his love for Jesus and who had, no doubt, read his letter, the epistle to the Romans. Luke concludes his account of Paul's long and hazardous sea voyage by commenting that Paul "thanked God" and "took courage" (Acts 28:15).

Figure 36  The Via Appia: Paul's Road to Rome (www.holylandphotos.org)

# Chapter 21
# Paul's Years in Rome

When Paul entered Rome, he had reached the heart of the ancient world. As a missionary strategist, he had longed to visit the eternal city on the Tiber River, the hub and focal point of the Roman Empire. Although still a prisoner, Paul now had the opportunity for witness and ministry that would radiate to all parts of the Roman world.

If you have had a chance to visit Rome, you know what an amazing city it is! The excavations at the Roman Forum and other public spaces reveal the achievements of its leaders and the worship of Rome's gods. The city has been universally recognized as the political and conceptual center of the Roman Empire (David A. DeSilva, "The Social and Geographical World of Rome, *The LGCATR*, pp. 430-449). DeSilva comments that the city of Rome was "the beating heart of the empire that encompassed the lands around the Mediterranean" (p. 433). The Apostle John may have had Rome in mind when he described "a great city that rules over the kings of the earth" (Rev. 17:18). It is little wonder that Paul wrote in his letter to the church at Rome that he "had for many years been longing to come you" (Rom. 16:23). The apostle recognized the strategic opportunities that the city of Rome provided to expand the outreach of the gospel.

What was Paul's situation like during his two years in Rome? Although he was still a prisoner (Acts 28:20) appealing to Caesar, Paul was granted a good deal of freedom. He was allowed to stay in his own rented quarters (Acts 28:30). Although his freedom was limited, Paul was able to receive and minister to visitors throughout his imprisonment.

During his confinement, Paul was under the care and protection of the praetorian guard (Acts 28:16, cf. Phil. 1:13), an elite military unit whose primary function was to guard the imperial palace and protect the emperor. They were also responsible for guarding political prisoners in the emperor's custody. The praetorian guard was a pampered, but powerful unit. The emperor Claudius (AD 41-54) was elevated to the throne by the praetorian guard after a group of praetorian guardsmen assassinated his predecessor, Caligula (AD 37-41). The praetorians received three times the ordinary legionary's pay and could retire after sixteen years of service. The soldiers guarding Paul were rotated so that, over the period of his incarceration, Paul was able to share the gospel with "the whole praetorian guard" (Phil. 1:13).

Paul didn't waste any time contacting the Jewish leaders after his arrival in Rome. Three days after entering Rome he called what might be termed a "press conference" to report the background and circumstances which accounted for his presence (Acts 28:17-19). Although he had been falsely accused and mistreated, Paul made no complaints or accusations against his Jewish kinsmen in Jerusalem. He simply reported the facts of his arrest, incarceration and appeal to Caesar. He concluded by stating, "I am wearing this chain for the sake of the hope of Israel" (Acts 28:20).

What was the "hope of Israel" to which Paul was referring? Was it the hope of the resurrection from the dead (Acts 23:6)? Or was Paul referring to the blessed hope of the Messiah's return and the establishment of His kingdom (Rom. 15:12-13; Tit. 2:13)? Whatever Paul had specifically in mind, the messianic promises of the Hebrew Scriptures were the basis for Paul's future hope (Rom. 15:4). This hope could be realized only through the Savior, Jesus.

The Jews that had gathered to hear from Paul had not yet learned of his case. They had received no letters nor had a messenger from Judea come to report anything negative about him (Acts 28:21). They were, however, interested in Paul's theological views, especially with regard to the disputed "sect" (*airesis*) of which he was a member and represented. It is evident from the term "sect" (or "party") that what has become known as "Christianity" was in Paul's day simply regarded as another stream of first century Judaism. A date was set for the Jewish leaders to come to Paul's lodging to hear more about his views.

On the appointed day, Luke records that "large numbers" of Jews came to hear the Apostle Paul. His presentation focused on the biblical theme of "the kingdom of God" and how God's plan for the ages had been predicted by Moses and the Prophets, culminating in the redemptive work of Jesus (Acts 28:23). Moses wrote of Him (Deut. 18:15). The Prophets spoke of Him (Isa. 53). Paul was explaining, in essence, that Jesus was the Messiah of biblical prophecy. Some of the Jews were persuaded by his arguments, but others clung to their own traditions and simply "would not believe" (Acts 28:24).

As the Jews began to leave, the apostle had one closing word for them. Paul pointed out that the prophet Isaiah, through the ministry of the Holy Spirit, had predicted their response to his message. The Lord had revealed to Isaiah that because of Israel's unbelief, his prophetic message would not be received. Isaiah had announced to the people of Israel, "You will keep on hearing, but will not understand; and you will keep on seeing, but will not perceive; for the heart of this people has become dull, and with their ears they scarcely hear, and they have closed their eyes" (Acts 28:26-27; Isa. 6:9-10). What was true in Isaiah's day, was also true in the time of Jesus (Matt. 13:14-15). And now Isaiah's prophecy of Israel's unbelief was, sadly, being realized again in Paul's day.

But we need not despair over Israel's future. According to biblical prophecy, Israel's unbelief won't last forever. When Messiah Jesus returns someday in the future, a remnant of Israel will witness His coming, repent, and embrace their Messiah (Zech. 12:10-13:1; Rom. 11:26). Paul's pattern of ministry was always to present the good news of the coming of Israel's Messiah to the Jews first. But now that they had rejected Paul's message, he would turn his attention elsewhere, announcing the message of God's provision of salvation to the Gentiles (Acts 28:28). Paul's listeners departed, arguing with each other over the meaning and significance of his words.

Luke concludes his account of Paul's stay in Rome reporting that during the next two years, Paul was living in his own rented quarters, welcoming visitors, "preaching the kingdom of God and teaching concerning the Lord Jesus Christ" with all openness and without hindrance (Acts 28:30-31).

Although Luke did not record it, Paul also engaged in a writing ministry during his two years of house arrest in Rome. Four of Paul's epistles (Ephesians, Philippians, Colossians and Philemon) can be traced to this period of his life. Paul's letter to the Ephesians was probably written first, around AD 60. Paul refers to himself as a "prisoner" (Eph. 3:1; 4:1) and used the armor of the Roman soldier, who was guarding him, as a metaphor for the believer's defenses in spiritual warfare. Paul encouraged the Ephesians to recognize their position as believers "seated in the heavenlies" (Eph. 2:6) with Jesus and to live their lives in keeping with their new identity as "saints" (holy people) in Christ.

Paul's letter to the Philippians was probably written in the spring of AD 62, not long before his release. In this letter Paul wrote of his imprisonment for the cause of Christ (Phil. 1:13) and his defense and confirmation of the gospel (Phil. 1:7). He referred to the praetorian guard, that elite group of Roman soldiers to whom he witnessed as they were guarding him (Phil. 1:13). In spite of his imprisonment, God was at work and Paul was rejoicing! He wrote to encourage the Philippians to "rejoice in the Lord" whatever the circumstances.

Paul's letters addressed to the Colossians and to Philemon were evidently written and sent at the same time, late in the spring of AD 62. Both letters mention Paul's imprisonment (Col. 4:3, Philm. 10,13) and his letter to Philemon alludes to the apostle's anticipated release (Philm. 22). Paul's letter to the church at Colossae focused on the preeminence of Jesus and the believer's completeness in Him. The accompanying letter to Philemon, the master of the runaway slave, Onesimus, was intended to encourage reconciliation between the two who were now united in Christ. Paul appears to have been suggesting that Philemon take the additional step of emancipating Onesimus, welcoming him back "no longer as a slave, but more than a slave, as a beloved brother" (Philm. 1:16)

The perplexing question we are left with as we come to the end of Luke's account in Acts is, "What happened next?" Was Paul executed? Was he released? Did the statute of limitations expire during which the prosecutors were allowed to present their case? We will explore these intriguing questions in the next chapter.

# Chapter 22
# Paul's Life After Acts

Luke concluded the book of Acts reporting that Paul stayed two full years in Rome in his own rented quarters, apparently under some form of house arrest (Acts 28:30). But what happened next?

Some scholars believe that Paul was tried and executed. But since Luke does not record Paul's death, others have suggested that he was exiled for several years and then brought back to Rome to be executed by orders from Nero. But against these views is the fact that Paul anticipated his own release when he wrote to the Philippians (Phil. 1:25; 2:24). In his letter to Philemon, written near the end of his imprisonment, Paul asked Philemon, "Prepare me a lodging, for I hope that through your prayers I will be given to you" (Philm. 22). In addition, there is no place in the chronology of the book of Acts where Paul's epistles to Timothy and Titus fit into the historical narrative. If Paul wrote these letters, they must fit somewhere else in the life of the apostle.

I believe the evidence points to the probability that Paul was released after two years of house arrest and engaged in further ministry before his death. Perhaps the statute of limitations expired and Paul was released for lack of any formal complaint by his accusers. It appears that Paul was later charged with more serious crimes and experienced a second imprisonment, as described in 2 Timothy (1:8; 2:9; 4:6-8), which ended in his death. While Paul's life after Acts 28 remains a historical puzzle, there are sufficient clues in his letters--especially in his epistles to Timothy and Titus--to offer a likely itinerary. For additional resources on this intriguing study, consider my article, "Paul's Travels After Acts" *LGCART*, pp. 455-463).

Since Paul had written to Philemon requesting that he prepare him a lodging (Philm. 22), he probably set out for Asia Minor soon after being released by the Roman authorities. The most reasonable route to Philemon's home in Colossae would be to sail from Rome's port at Puteoli to Ephesus where he had spent three years on his third journey (Acts 19). After visiting the believers at Ephesus, Paul would have followed the Meander River to the Lycus Valley, the location of Colossae and the home of Philemon to whom Paul had written in anticipation of his forthcoming visit. He was probably interested in making sure that Philemon and his runaway slave, Onesimus, who had come to faith through Paul's ministry in Rome, had been reconciled (Philm. 17-20).

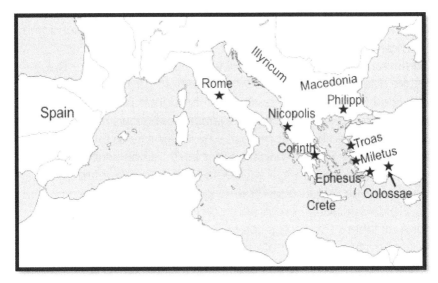

Figure 37  Paul's Travels After Acts

The next clue in reconstructing Paul's travel itinerary after Acts 28 is found in 1 Timothy 1:3, "I urged you upon my departure for Macedonia, remain on at Ephesus." After his scheduled visit in Colossae, Paul appears to have returned to Ephesus where he left his young protégé, Timothy, to give leadership to the church there. Anxious to visit believers in other churches he had established, Paul left Ephesus, crossed the Aegean Sea and arrived in Macedonia (1 Tim. 1:3). Why Macedonia? Paul provided a clue in his letter to the Philippians that he wished to visit the believers there, and wrote that he would be "coming shortly" (Phil. 2:24). Reaching Macedonia by ship, Paul would have disembarked at Neapolis, as he had done on his second journey (Acts 16:11), and continued a short distance north to greet the church and enjoy fellowship with his friends at Philippi.

In his letter to Timothy, Paul had expressed his hope of returning to Ephesus. He explained in his letter, "I am writing these things to you, hoping to come to you before long; but in case I am delayed, I write so that you will know how one ought to conduct himself in the household of God, which is the church of the living God, the pillar and support of the truth" (1 Tim. 3:14). If Paul's "hope" was realized, then he would have returned to Ephesus after spending time with the believers in Macedonia.

Paul's travel itinerary becomes more speculative at this point. In his letter to the believers at Rome, Paul had written of his plans to travel to Spain (Rom. 15:24), and the early Christians believed he had done so. Clement, an early church leader in Alexandria, wrote that Paul "traveled to the extreme limit of the west" (1 Clement 5:7), understood to be a reference to Spain. The Muratorian Canon, the oldest known list of New Testament books (AD 170), makes reference to "the journey of St. Paul to Spain." There appears to be a well-established early church tradition that Paul had a ministry in Spain, and this likely took place after his release from his first Roman imprisonment. According to local tradition, Paul preached the gospel at Terraco (modern Tarragona), located on the northeast coast of Spain and regarded as the most important city in Spain during the first century AD. The Cathedral of Tarragona, built over a site previously occupied by a first century Roman temple, preserves the tradition of St. Paul's visit (Eckhard Schnabel, "Paul in Spain and Crete, *LGCATR*, pp. 450-454).

Where might Paul have traveled after visiting Spain? A clue is found in his letter to Titus, where Paul wrote, "For this reason I left you in Crete, that you would set in order what remains and appoint elders in every city as I directed you" (Titus 1:5). Recall that Paul had wanted to winter at Fair Havens on the island of Crete during his voyage to Rome (Acts 27:9-12), but the captain's decision to continue on led to their being caught in the storm and shipwrecked on Malta. Paul's return Mediterranean Sea voyage from Spain would have provided him with the perfect opportunity to minister the gospel on Crete. Two ancient writers, Philo and Tacitus, mention Crete among the Greek islands that had significant Jewish communities (Philo, *On the Embassy to Gaius*, 282; Tacitus, *Histories* 5:11; Schnabel, p. 453). Paul was no doubt anxious for the opportunity to bring the good news of Israel's resurrected Messiah to these Jewish communities. Titus must have been traveling with the apostle and was left on the island to do follow-up and give leadership to the church after Paul's departure.

Several additional clues about Paul's travels after Acts 28 can be found in the Pastoral Epistles. A verse in Titus indicates that Paul once again traveled to Greece as evidenced by his instructions for Titus to meet him in Nicopolis for the winter (Titus 3:12). Nicopolis was founded by Caesar Augustus to commemorate his victory in 31 BC over Antony and Cleopatra and became the capital of the Roman province of Epirus Vetus. The fact that Nicopolis was a major port and transportation center reflects, once again, Paul's mission strategy to focus his evangelistic efforts on major population centers and regional hubs. Another visit to Corinth, where he had spent a year and a half on his second journey (Acts 18:1-18) is evidenced by Paul's comment to Timothy, "Erastus remained at Corinth" (2 Tim. 4:20).

Paul's return to Asia Minor is also reflected in his second letter to Timothy. He apparently revisited Miletus where he had convened a conference with the Ephesian elders on his way back to Jerusalem. Unable to stay there longer, Paul wrote Timothy that he left Trophimus sick at Miletus (2 Tim. 4:20).

Persecution against Christians was intensifying at this time in the Roman empire, and Paul was a well-recognized leader in this messianic movement. The fact that Paul appears to have been on the run, fleeing from arresting authorities, is evidenced by another comment he made at the end of his last letter to Timothy. "When you come bring the cloak which I left at Troas with Carpus, and the books, especially the parchments" (2 Tim. 4:13). Paul may have been in such a hurry to escape from his pursuers that he left town without his books and coat!

In this chapter, I have sought to reconstruct Paul's itinerary after Acts 28. But what happened next? Where does the evidence take us from here? The biblical record, as well as early church tradition, indicates that the Apostle Paul spent the last days of his life in the city of Rome.

# Chapter 23
# Paul's Final Imprisonment and Death

Having traveled and ministered for about four-and-a-half years (spring of AD 62 to fall of AD 67) after being released from his first imprisonment, Paul was arrested again and brought to Rome (2 Tim. 1:8,16-17). We don't know the details or reason for his arrest, but Paul reports being treated more harshly than his first Roman imprisonment which was more like a situation of house arrest (Acts 28:30). Now the conditions were different. In his final letter to Timothy, Paul explains that he was suffering "imprisonment as a criminal" (2 Tim. 2:9).

Anticipating his impending death, Paul wrote his last words to Timothy from the Mamertine Prison, located adjacent to the Roman Forum.

Figure 38  Rome's Marmertine Prison

From this damp, dark prison cell, Paul exhorted Timothy, "Be sober in all things, endure hardship, do the work of an evangelist,

147

fulfill your ministry" (2 Tim. 4:5). Then he added, "I am already being poured out as a drink offering, and the time of my departure has come. I have fought the good fight, I have finished the course, I have kept the faith" (2 Tim. 4:6-7).

According to the early church historian, Eusebius, the martyrdom of Paul took place in the thirteenth year of Nero. This commenced in October, A.D. 67, although Saint Jerome (A.D. 347-420), translator of the Bible into Latin, places it in A.D. 68. Since Paul had asked Timothy to join him in Rome before winter (1 Tim. 4:21), it is likely that Paul died in the spring of A.D. 68. According to early tradition, Paul was beheaded outside the city of Rome on the *Via Ostiense* (Ostian Way) and buried in the catacombs south of the city. There is evidence that his body was later moved and was placed in a tomb under Rome's Basilica of St. Paul Outside the Walls, the church depicted on the cover of this book.

Figure 39  The Gate of Paul on the Ostian Way

Some years ago I traveled with one of my professors, Dr. Ralph Alexander, on a study tour of Turkey, Greece and Rome, visiting the sites and cities where the Apostle Paul ministered. On the last day of the tour, I arose early to take my morning run along the Tiber River to the Ostian Gate, known today as *Porto san Paolo*, "Paul's Gate." As I stood there by "Paul's Gate," I reflected on the fact that this location

148

is our last point of contact with the apostle whose encounter with Jesus on the Damascus road was the catalyst which changed him from being a persecutor of Christians to a proclaimer of the gospel.

Paul continued his life as a believer in the God of Abraham, Isaac and Jacob. But he had become a follower of Jesus. From his Damascus road experience on, he lived his life as the *Jewish* Apostle Paul. As I stood by Paul's Gate, near the place where he was executed, I reflected on his transformed life and thanked God for his amazing calling and faithful ministry.

The death of the Apostle Paul was not the end of his ministry and influence. His thirteen letters are a major contribution to the literature of the New Testament. Paul's gospel message of salvation by grace, through faith apart from works (Eph. 2:8-9) is foundational to the Christian faith. His life continues to be an example to all believers as he said, "Be imitators of me just as I also am of Christ (1 Cor. 11:1). Because of Paul's ministry, the faith would live on. The end of Paul's life was but a beginning.

Figure 40 Basilica of St. Paul Outside the Walls

# Part 2  The Teachings of Paul

The "story of Paul" is not limited to a chronology of his life, travels and ministry activities. The Apostle Paul was a traveling evangelist who was called to proclaim the gospel. But he was also a gifted teacher. Through his letters, the Apostle Paul has provided us with a great treasury of divine revelation and life changing truth. In this section of Paul's story, we will focus on what the apostle believed and taught. Here we will consider what can be regarded as the major topics of Paul's theology.

I fully recognize that I don't have the final word on all that Paul believed and taught. My goal in this section of the book is to encourage further study. I hope you can use these brief essays as a foundation from which you can take the next step in your own studies. If your understanding of some of Paul's teachings is different than mine, let's recognize areas of agreement and commit ourselves to further study of the points where we differ. For many years I have quoted to my students the wise counsel of William Sanford LaSor (1911-1991), Professor of Old Testament at Fuller Theological Seminary. In the introduction to his book dealing with the controversy regarding the Dead Sea scrolls, he wrote, "We have nothing to fear from the truth; only ignorance can hurt us. New truths always challenge old opinions. But new truths never destroy old truths; they merely separate truth from falsehood" (*The Dead Sea Scrolls*, 1972, p. 27).

Saul of Tarsus sat at the feet of Rabbi Gamaliel to study and learn the Torah. I invite you to sit at the feet of Rabbi Paul to study, learn and *apply* the teachings of the New Testament Scriptures. What did Paul teach?

## About Abraham

As a "Hebrew of Hebrews" (Phil. 3:5), the Apostle Paul had high regard for the patriarch Abraham, the first person in the Bible to be called a "Hebrew" (Gen. 14:13). That Abraham was an important figure in Paul's theology is evidenced by the fact that he is mentioned seventeen times in his letters to the Galatians, Romans and Corinthians. Paul wanted his readers to know that the doctrine of "salvation by faith" was not something newly invented by Jesus, His apostles or by Paul himself, but that this truth can be traced all the way back to Abraham. Paul quoted Genesis 15:6, "Abraham believed God, and it was reckoned to him as righteousness" (Gal. 3:6; Rom. 4:3), to show that Abraham was saved by faith. The fact that Abraham was declared righteous (Gen. 15:6) *before* being circumcised (Gen. 17:24-27), makes it clear that his salvation was not the result of rituals, works or ceremonial traditions.

Paul is not only interested in the fact that Abraham was saved by faith, but that God's promise to Abraham, to bless the world, has application for all humanity. In Galatians 3:8, Paul explained that God preached the gospel ("good news") to Abraham when He promised, "All the nations will be blessed in you." Paul explained to the Galatians that God's great promise to Abraham (Gen. 12:2-3), is not just for Abraham, but "his seed" (Gal. 2:16). And while Abraham had many descendants ("seed" in the plural sense), his ultimate "seed" or descendant through whom the world would be blessed is the Messiah, Jesus. What Paul is saying is that through Jesus, Israel's promised Messiah, *all* the nations would experience spiritual blessing. This means that what holds true for Abraham, is equally true for both Jews and Gentiles. Abraham was saved by faith. His descendants are saved by faith. And the non-Jewish people of the nations can also be saved and blessed by faith. There is no other means by which a person can be righteous in the sight of God except *by faith.*

In discussing the fact that both Jews and non-Jews are saved the same way Abraham was saved, Paul pointed out that *all* believers become "sons of God" and members of God's spiritual family "through faith" (Gal. 3:26). In a life-redefining declaration Paul writes, "There is neither Jew nor Greek, there is neither slave nor free man, there is neither male nor female; for you are all one in Christ Jesus" (Gal. 3:28). The barrier that distinguished and separated Jews from Gentiles has been broken down in Christ "who made both groups into one" (Eph. 2:14). But there is even more good news for Gentile believers. Paul declared that Gentiles who belong to Christ are not merely second class citizens in God's great kingdom. Rather, by placing their trust in Israel's Messiah, they have become

"Abraham's descendants, heirs according to promise" (Gal. 3:29). Paul was a physical descendant of Abraham. But non-Jewish believers in Jesus become Abraham's *spiritual* descendants and heirs of God's promised blessings through faith. Although the Laney family is of Irish descent, I am a spiritual "son of Abraham" on the basis of faith in Israel's promised Messiah.

## About Adam

According to Scripture, Adam was the first human being God created. But that view has recently come into question. In his book, *Evolutionary Creation* (2008), Denis Lamoureux wrote "Adam never existed, and this fact has no impact whatsoever on the foundational beliefs of Christianity." Tremper Longman, formerly professor at Westmont College, wrote, "There is nothing that insists on a literal understanding of Adam." And Dan Harlow, formerly of Calvin College, declared, "Whether or not Adam was historical is not central to biblical theology."

The Apostle Paul took a different view. If Paul were here today, I think he would ask these contemporary theologians, "How can the Bible's theology be true if the historical events on which theology is based *never happened*?" It is quite clear from his letters that Paul believed in a literal, historical Adam.

Paul wrote Timothy, "For it was Adam who was first created, and then Eve" (1 Tim. 2:13). Then he commented about what happened in the garden of Eden that while Eve was deceived by the tempter, Adam was *not* deceived. Adam sinned with the full knowledge that he was disobeying God (1 Tim. 2:14). In 1 Corinthians 15:21-22, Paul compares the God-man, Jesus, with the first man, Adam. Through the first man, Adam, came sin and death. But through Christ, comes resurrection and eternal life. In Adam, "all die," but in Christ, all believers "will be made alive." If Adam was not a historical figure, then Paul's analogy breaks down. You can't have a historical Jesus without a historical Adam.

In Romans 5, Paul elaborates on the historical actions of Adam and the significance for the human race. Paul wrote, "Just as through one man, sin entered into the world, and death through sin, and so death spread to all men, because all sinned" (Rom. 5:12). Theologians debate exactly how the human race is related to Adam's sin. Some believe that Adam represented the human race, and that when he sinned by eating the forbidden fruit, Adam "voted for humanity's rebellion." Consequently, we all were condemned as sinners because of Adam's vote. Others believe that in some real or genetic way, all humanity was "in Adam," and when Adam sinned, all humanity *participated* in his sin. In whatever way our connection with Adam is understood, Paul makes it clear that *all* have sinned (Rom. 3:23, 5:12). As a result, "death reigned from Adam until Moses" (Rom. 5:14), not because of violating the Mosaic law, but because all humanity became sinners through the actions of the first man, Adam.

Paul makes it clear in Romans 5:18-21 that all humanity falls into one of two families. There is the family of Adam, which is characterized by disobedience, sin and death. And by contrast, there is the spiritual family of Jesus, characterized by obedience, righteousness and eternal life. The question each person must ask is, "In which spiritual family do I belong?" Am I still in the family of Adam, leading from disobedience to sin and death? Or have I been adopted by faith into the family of Jesus, resulting in righteousness and eternal life?

# About Adoption

Paul was familiar with the Roman law concerning adoption and he refers to this cultural background three times in his letter to the Romans and once each in Galatians and Ephesians (Rom. 8:15,23; 9:4; Gal. 4:5; Eph. 1:5). The Greek word for adoption (*huiothesia*) means "son placing." The concept of "son placing" or adoption was very familiar to people living in first century Roman society. Sometimes a son would be adopted to provide a family with a male heir. This was the case with Augustus Caesar and the emperor Tiberius, both of whom were adopted by imperial families needing an heir.

There were four things that characterized adoption in Roman law (Francis Lyall, *Roman Law in the Writings of Paul*, p. 83). *First*, the adoptee's debts were cancelled. *Second*, the adoptee received a new name. *Third*, the adoptee started a new life as part of a new family. *Fourth*, the adoptee would gain inheritance rights. Paul drew on this cultural background to explain what happens when a person enters into God's spiritual family. This has great application for believers. Paul explained to the Romans that as believers in Jesus, they have received a spirit of "adoption as sons" by which they are privileged to call God "Abba! Father" (Rom. 8:23). The Aramaic word, "Abba," is a term of affection and endearment. It could be rendered "Dad," and reflects the personal and intimate relationship that God's children enjoy with their heavenly Father.

Adoption into God's family means that believers are God's sons and daughters whose debts (sins) have been forgiven (1 Cor. 6:9-11). Their former life as unbelievers is over, and they have begun a new life in Christ (2 Cor. 5:17). No longer does God regard them as "sinners," but now they are greeted as "holy ones" or "saints" (1 Cor. 1:2; 2 Cor. 1:2). As God's adopted children, believers receive the glorious inheritance of personal salvation and eternal life (Rom. 6:22-23).

One of my colleagues at Western Seminary had three children of his own. Then he and his wife added three more children to their family through adoption. The fathers of the three had abandoned their children, and their mother was physically and emotionally unable to care for them. The three boys were neglected, desperate and headed for a life of misery and trouble. But when they were adopted into a strong Christian family, *everything* changed. They have a new name, a new mom and dad and a new family. Their future, once dismal, is now bright and hopeful. What a beautiful picture of what God has done for us! How blessed we are as believers to have been adopted into *God's* family!

## About Baptism

The practice of baptism was not something invented by John the Baptizer, Jesus or the Apostle Paul. The ritual of immersion in water was a well-established Jewish tradition in the time of the first century. Cleansing from ritual impurity by pouring or dipping in water appears throughout the Hebrew Bible (Lev. 15:4-5, 16-18). In the time of Jesus, before entering the Jerusalem temple to offer a sacrifice, Jewish worshipers would remove their clothes, enter a pool (*miqveh*) where they would immerse themselves completely in water as a means of ritual purification. Approximately forty of these pools or ritual baths have been discovered by archaeologists near the southern entrances to the Jerusalem temple.

In addition to symbolizing purification from ritual impurity, immersion in a *miqveh* served as a ritual of identification. If a Gentile (non-Jewish) man wanted to convert to Judaism, in addition to being circumcised and offering the required sacrifice, he would undergo an immersion in water, thus identifying himself with the Jewish people. Women would follow the same procedure except for circumcision. The ritual of immersion in water served as an initiation into the Jewish community.

John practiced this water ritual when he *baptized* people in the Jordan River, inviting them to repent of their sins and join his messianic movement (Matt. 3:6). Jesus' disciples also practiced *baptism* as an initiation into the community of Jesus followers (Jn. 3:22; 4:1-2).

The Greek word *baptizo*, from which we get the word "baptize" simply means "to dip or immerse." The word is used to describe ships that sink, people who drown and garments that are immersed into a vat of dye. The Greek word for immersion in water (*baptize*) is not actually translated in the New Testament, but is simply transliterated into English, leaving the meaning of the word to be variously interpreted by church leaders and ecclesiastical authorities. But from the original meaning of the word ("to immerse") comes the concept of a change in identity. When a woolen garment was dipped into purple dye, it took on a new identity. And so *baptism* in the Christian context illustrates and symbolizes how a believer takes on a new identity through faith in Jesus.

Paul recognized baptism as a ritual of identification for someone leaving paganism to believe in and follow Jesus. To be "baptized in the name of Jesus" was to become *identified* as a follower of Jesus. Paul himself was baptized after his Damascus road experience (Acts 9:18). And he baptized others (Acts 16:33, 1 Cor. 1:16). But Paul recognized that salvation comes by faith in Jesus, not through the water ritual of immersion. He told the Corinthians, "Christ did not send me to baptize, but to preach the gospel" (1 Cor. 1:17). In his clear statements about the gospel, baptism is never included in the formula for salvation (Eph. 2:8-9; Rom. 10:9-10). Yet, Paul did not regard baptism as unimportant.

In his letter to the Romans, Paul points to the importance of baptism as symbol of what happens in the life of a new believer in Jesus (Rom. 6:3-4). He uses the image of baptism as a picture of the believer's change in identity, being separated from the old life and united with Christ. The key to understanding Paul's words here is to remember that immersion into water is a symbol of identification. Paul wanted his readers to understand that when they came to faith in Jesus, it was like a dying and rising again. The ritual of immersion is like a burial. And coming up out of the water is like resurrection to new life. Paul was saying that those who believe in Jesus have been identified (*baptized*) into His death (Rom. 6:3). Having been identified with Christ in His death, believers are identified with Him in His resurrection (Rom. 6:5). Just as Jesus rose from the dead, so His followers are raised to "walk in newness of life" (Rom. 6:4). The ritual of immersion in water (*baptism*) is a beautiful picture of what happens when we become followers of Jesus.

While baptism remains an important symbol of our new identity and spiritual life, this water ritual is not necessary for salvation. Forgiveness and cleansing from sin is a gift of grace received by those who trust in Jesus, not the result of baptism or any righteous deeds (Titus 3:5-7). The thief on the cross died without being baptized. Yet because of his faith, Jesus told him, "Today you will be with me in paradise" (Lk. 23:43).

# About Children

Although Paul used the words "my true child" and "my beloved son" metaphorically when referring to his spiritual relationship with Timothy (1 Tim. 1:2; 2 Tim. 1:2), there is nothing in the Bible to suggest that the apostle had any physical children of his own. But he was interested in the spiritual lives of children and gave them two direct commands. Paul instructed children to "obey your parents in the Lord, for this is right" (Eph. 6:1). The command is a present imperative which is best translated, "keep on obeying." He issued the same command in his letter to the children at Colossae, but added the explanation, "for this is well-pleasing to the Lord" (Col. 3:20). Children are in the care of and under the authority of their parents until they assume adult responsibilities, such as leaving home and becoming financially independent.

Paul's second command to children comes directly from the Ten Commandments. Paul wrote, "Honor your father and mother (which is the first commandment with a promise), so that it may be well with you, and that you may live long on the earth" (Eph. 6:2; Exod. 20:12).

The word translated "honor" means to "regard with value" or "appreciate." Like the command "obey," this is a present imperative which means, "keep on honoring." I believe this command has application to adult children as well as those still at home under the authority of parents. Paul is suggesting that valuing, appreciating and caring for one's parents is a lifelong responsibility. This may include such things as phone calls, Mother's Day and Father's Day cards, and personal assistance that may be necessary when parents enter their senior years.

Paul notes that the commandment to honor one's parents comes with a promise, "that it may be well with you, and that you may live long on the earth" (Eph. 6:3). Under Mosaic law, a child who dishonored his parents through stubborn rebellion and disobedience was to be executed by stoning (Deut. 21:18-21). According to this instruction, obedient children in the Old Testament period actually *did* live longer than a stubborn or rebellious one! But what Paul was emphasizing for followers of Jesus is that it is in our own best interest to recognize, value and honor the heritage that we receive from our parents. This is not always easy, for parents are not perfect people. Some parents have abused and hurt their children. This was true in Paul's day as well as in the twenty-first century. But one way to "honor" an abusive parent is by forgiving them and seeking reconciliation.

Although Paul may not have had children of his own, he was familiar with the responsibilities that come with parenting. He admonished fathers not to "provoke" their children to anger (Eph. 6:4) or "exasperate" them with unreasonable rules that would make them "lose heart" and give up trying to obey (Col. 3:21). In a more positive context, Paul reminded the Thessalonians how he was gentle among them, "as a nursing mother tenderly cares for her own children" (1 Thess. 2:7). There is no image so sweet as a mother tenderly cradling a nursing baby in her arms. A hungry, crying baby will become quiet and content as the child enjoys a mother's touch and nourishment.

A few verses later, Paul switched the metaphor to that of the father and recalls that during his visit at Thessalonica he was "exhorting and encouraging and imploring each one as a father would his own children" (1 Thess. 2:11). The images of a loving father and nurturing mother were used by Paul to highlight the gentle and responsible manner by which he ministered to the Thessalonian believers.

# About Christ

Jesus Christ was *central* in the life and teaching of the Apostle Paul. It would be impossible to summarize in a short essay everything Paul wrote about Jesus. But let's consider some of his key teachings.

1. *Jesus is the divine Son of God.* The first thing Paul said about Jesus in the synagogues after his Damascus road experience was, "He is the Son of God" (Acts 9:20). Paul wrote that Jesus was "declared the Son of God with power by the resurrection from the dead" (Rom. 1:4). He is the "visible image of the invisible God" (Col. 1:15), "For in Him all the fullness of deity dwells in bodily form" (Col. 2:9).

2. *Jesus is the Creator of all things.* Paul informed the Colossians, "For by Him all things were created, both in the heavens and on earth, visible and invisible, whether thrones or dominions or rulers or authorities—all things have been created through Him and for Him" (Col. 1:15).

3. *Jesus is the descendent of Abraham.* Jesus is the one in whom the covenant promises of God to Abraham (Gen. 12:2-3) are ultimately fulfilled (Gal. 3:16).

4. *Jesus is the Messiah of Israel.* In the synagogues of Damascus, Paul was proving by the prophetic Scriptures that "Jesus is the Christ" (Acts 9:22). The Greek word "Christ" (*Christos*) means "anointed one" and translates the Hebrew *Mashiach*. Whenever Paul refers to Jesus as "Christ," he is affirming that Jesus is Israel's promised Messiah (Rom. 6:3-4).

5. *Jesus died for sinners.* Paul wrote, "God demonstrates His own love toward us, in that while we were yet sinners, Christ died for us" (Rom. 5:8). A "sinner" is anyone who falls short or "misses the mark" of God's standard of righteousness. That includes all of us (Rom. 3:23). Jesus' death provided the ultimate and final sacrifice for our sins (1 Cor. 15:13, Eph. 5:2).

6. *Jesus was raised from the grave.* The death, burial and resurrection of Jesus is central to the proclamation of Paul's gospel (Acts 13:28-33; 1 Cor. 15:4).
7. *Jesus provides forgiveness of sins.* Through Jesus' sacrifice on the cross, believers enjoy something they could have never earned, the "forgiveness of sins" (Acts 13:38). Paul told the Ephesians that the forgiveness of our trespasses is "according to the riches of His grace" (Eph. 1:7).
8. *Jesus satisfied God's wrath.* Because of God's holiness, He must respond to sin with an expression of His wrath. But Jesus is the "propitiation" who quenches or satisfies God's wrath. Paul wrote that we are "saved from the wrath of God through Him" (Rom. 5:9). Through His sacrifice, Jesus satisfied God's wrath on sin (Rom. 3:25).
9. *Jesus is our redeemer.* The word "redeem" means to "buy back." Jesus did this when He paid the price of our transgressions with His own precious blood (Rom. 3:24, Eph. 1:7) and bought us out of slavery to sin.
10. *Through faith in Jesus, believers are justified.* The central core of Paul's teaching about Jesus is that through faith in Him and His sacrifice, believers receive something they could never achieve by keeping the Mosaic law. Paul wrote, "Through Him everyone who believes is freed (*justified*) from all things, from which you could not be freed (*justified*) through the law of Moses" (Acts 13:39). Paul traced his teaching on justification by faith to the experience of Abraham (Rom. 4:1-3) and the words of Habakkuk (Rom. 1:17, Gal. 3:6). Believers are justified or "declared righteous" not by the works of the law but "through faith in Jesus Christ" (Gal. 2:16).
11. *Jesus death terminates the Old Covenant law.* Because of Jesus' sacrifice, the Old Covenant contract has been terminated (Rom. 10:4) and replaced by the New Covenant (Jer. 31:31-34) which Jesus enacted by His death.
12. *Jesus leads the way to resurrection life.* Paul taught that because Jesus is the "first fruits" of the resurrection (1 Cor. 15:20), believers in Jesus will also be raised. The "first fruits" means that there will be more to come. Paul writes of the order of resurrection, "Christ the first fruits, after that those who are Christ's at His coming" (1 Cor. 15:23, 1 Thess. 4:16).

13. *Jesus is seated at God's right hand.* Paul informed the Colossians that, having ascended to heaven, Jesus is seated at the right hand of God (Col. 3:1) where He rules over God's present kingdom (Col. 1:13).
14. *Jesus leads and rules His church.* Although Jesus is in heaven, He serves as the authoritative head of His church (Eph. 5:23) to whom believers are called to submit and obey.
15. *Jesus is coming again.* Paul taught that Jesus is coming again (1 Thess. 2:19) to resurrect the dead in Christ and gather His followers to be with Him forever (1 Thess. 4:15-17).
16. *Jesus will judge Satan at His return.* While believers will be gathered to Christ at His return, Satan and his deluded captives will be judged "because they did not receive the love of the truth so as to be saved" (2 Thess. 2:8-10).

While most of these teaching points may appear more theological than practical, Paul's relationship with Jesus was both truly practical and deeply personal. This is particularly reflected in his letter to the Philippians. There Paul confessed to the Philippians, "For me to live is Christ" (Phil. 1:21). For Paul, Jesus was the sum total of what his life was all about. Jesus also provided Paul an example for how to live humbly, serving others (Phil. 2:5-8). Paul's relationship with Jesus gave purpose and direction to his life. He likened himself as a runner, striding toward Jesus, his ultimate goal in running the race of life (Phil. 3:13-14). Finally, for Paul, Jesus was the all-sufficient One who met his needs, both physical and spiritual (Phil. 4:19). For Paul, Jesus was *everything*. Little wonder, then, that Paul proclaimed Jesus, with the goal of helping others find *their* completeness in Christ (Col. 1:28).

## About the Church

Paul was a church planter. Throughout his missionary travels, Paul was busy preaching the gospel and establishing churches. Although Jesus mentioned the church just twice (Matt. 16:18; 18:17), Paul had quite a bit to say about the church (*ekklesia*) and constantly referred to it in his letters. In the Greek speaking world of Paul, the term *ekklesia* was used to describe any duly convened assembly of citizens. The word was used in the ancient Greek translation of the Hebrew Bible (the Septuagint) to refer to the assembly or congregation of the people of Israel. The Greek word *ekklesia* simply refers to an assembly of people who have been called together. In the New Testament, the word refers to an assembly of people who have been summoned or called together by God.

The word "church" (*ekklesia*) is used by Paul in three different ways. First, Paul used the word to refer to the body of Christ, the universal church of all who believe in Jesus as God's Son and Savior of the world (1 Cor. 10:32; 12:28; Phil. 3:6). Second, Paul used *ekklesia* to refer to any assembly of Jesus followers gathered together for worship (1 Cor. 11:18, 14:9,23). Finally, Paul used the word to identify a particular local church, such as the "church of the Thessalonians" (1 Thess. 1:1) or the "church of God which is at Corinth" (1 Cor. 1:1).

It is significant that Paul never used the word "church" to refer to a building. The church is not a place or a structure, but a community of believers who have gathered under the leadership of Christ to worship, serve and proclaim the good news of God's provision of salvation through Jesus. The first century congregations didn't have a designated building for their gatherings, but met in homes for worship, prayer and teaching (Rom. 16:5; 1 Cor. 16:19; Col. 4:5).

While Christ is present wherever "two or three" believers are gathered (Matt. 18:20), not every gathering of believers constitutes a meeting of the church. The meeting of the church has spiritual leadership. Paul wrote that Christ "is the head of the church" (Eph. 5:23), but he also appointed elders and deacons to lead and serve local congregations (1 Tim. 3:1-13). Paul instructed the Corinthians that when they gathered as a meeting of the church, they were to remember Christ by partaking in the Lord's supper (1 Cor. 11:17-26). In Paul's letter to young Timothy, he provided instructions on "how one is to conduct himself in the household of God" (1 Tim. 3:15). In that context, Paul instructed Timothy "to give attention to the public reading of Scripture, to exhortation and teaching" (1 Tim. 4:13). In a later letter, Paul told Timothy, "Preach the word; be ready in season and out of season; reprove, rebuke, exhort with great patience and instruction" (2 Tim. 4:2). Similarly, he wrote Titus to "keep on speaking things which are fitting for sound doctrine" (Tit. 2:1).

Paul's instructions about the church led us to understand that the church is a congregation of believers who are gathered together in the name of Jesus to worship, pray, observe the Lord's supper and receive instruction from the Word of God. While local congregations are under the leadership and authority of pastors and elders, the CEO of the church is Jesus Christ (Eph. 5:23-24).

## About Church Discipline

Some years ago I wrote a book, "Your Guide to Church Discipline" (Bethany House Publishers). If I were to retitle the book today, I would call it "Your Guide to Spiritual Accountability." The words "Church Discipline" sound like Christians are chasing down sinners and beating up on them to make them stop sinning. That's not what it is about! Church discipline, or *spiritual accountability*, is simply the act of loving and caring for someone who is on the way to a spiritual disaster. God calls believers to care enough about each other to intervene and help one another get back on track spiritually. I recall a situation in my own church were church discipline was being applied. Someone spoke up and said, "This is the most unloving thing a church can do to one of its members." According to Scripture, the most unloving thing a church can do is to *ignore* someone on the path to self-destruction. The most loving thing we can do is to reach out, confronting the situation and offering the struggling believer a helping hand.

This is exactly what Paul asked the Corinthians to do with regard to the man who was sleeping with his father's wife (1 Cor. 5). Jesus outlined four basic steps for spiritual accountability in the body of Christ: Private reproof, private conference, public announcement, and public exclusion (Matt. 18:15-18). Paul was applying those steps in dealing with the immorality he was confronting at Corinth. But the instructions, written in his previous letter (1 Cor. 5:9-11; 2 Cor. 2:4), had been ignored. The Corinthian believers were having a difficult time applying the guidelines given by Jesus and had failed to follow through with the last of the four steps--removal of the offender from fellowship with the congregation. So the Apostle Paul commanded that they finish the job, "Remove the wicked man from among yourselves" (1 Cor. 5:13).

The good news is that the Corinthian church finally obeyed Paul and the offender was disciplined, not as a judgment, but as an encouragement to repent. The purpose of church discipline is always to encourage repentance and restoration to fellowship with Christ and the church.

When the church at Corinth carried out the required discipline, the offender's conscience was pricked by the Holy Spirit and he repented. But now there was a need for follow-up and restoration. Since this important step had been neglected, Paul wrote a follow-up letter. In 2 Corinthians 2:5, Paul reminded the Corinthians of the situation that had caused much sorrow and grief. Church discipline had been applied and the man had repented. But now they needed to take the next step. Paul wrote that the Corinthians should forgive, comfort and "reaffirm their love" for the repentant offender (2 Cor. 2:6-7). To neglect this important step can create a situation which Satan can use to create bitterness, discord and dissention in the church (2 Cor. 2:11).

Church discipline, or spiritual accountability in the community of believers, is always designed to lead to restoration of fellowship with Christ and His people. When believers repent and turn back to Jesus, they are to be welcomed back into the congregation. If they refuse to repent, after being given sufficient time and opportunity for the Spirit to do His work, they must be excluded and regarded as unbelievers (1 Cor. 5:11), not to be humiliated or shunned, but as with all unbelievers, lovingly evangelized.

# About Circumcision

In keeping with God's instructions to Abraham (Gen. 17:10-12) and the law given by God at Mount Sinai (Lev. 12:3), the Apostle Paul was circumcised (Phil. 3:5). The English word is derived from the Latin, meaning, "to cut around." Circumcision refers to the removal of the foreskin of a male's penis. Circumcision was practiced before the time of Abraham, as evidenced by Egyptian tomb art, but the custom was given special significance in God's covenant with Abraham. God told Abraham that circumcision on the eighth day was a sign of His "everlasting" covenant with Israel (Gen. 17:13). Even non-Israelite males wishing to share in community and worship with the people of Israel were required to be circumcised (Exod. 12:48).

You might be wondering why God gave His people such a strange rite as the sign of His covenant. The Bible doesn't answer that question, but I have a suggestion. Making their home in Canaan, the Israelites were surrounded by people who worshiped pagan deities, like Baal and Asherah, through sexual acts. The sign of circumcision would serve as a visible reminder that the Israelites were dedicated to the worship of Yahweh, not false deities!

Circumcision was intended to be an outward and visible sign of an inward and invisible relationship with the God of Israel. Unfortunately, it was practiced as an external rite without recognizing its spiritual significance. Therefore, Moses and Jeremiah spoke of "circumcision of the heart" (Deut. 10:16; Jer. 4:4). By the time of the Apostle Paul, circumcision had become a tradition that simply distinguished Jews from Gentiles. Along with other rituals which were detailed in the Mosaic law, circumcision had become for many Jews a means of gaining right standing before God. They believed that circumcision was a requirement for being saved (Acts 15:1,5). This understanding was in sharp conflict with the gospel which had been revealed by Jesus to the Apostle Paul.

Paul preached that circumcision was never intended as a means of achieving right standing or righteous before God, for Abraham was declared righteous on the basis of his faith *before* he was circumcised (Gen. 15:6; 17:24). Paul taught that a person "is not justified by the works of the Law, but through faith in Christ Jesus" (Gal. 2:16). Paul viewed the requirement that Gentile believers be circumcised as a form of spiritual slavery that removed the blessing and benefit of all sufficient grace (Gal. 5:1-2). He insisted that "in Christ Jesus neither circumcision nor uncircumcision means anything, but faith working through love" (Gal. 5:6).

For Paul, circumcision had theological significance as the sign of God's covenant with Israel and served as a mark of Jewish identity. It was right and appropriate for Jewish boys to be circumcised. But Paul insisted that circumcision was not a means of gaining righteousness and should *not* be required for non-Jewish men who have come to faith in Jesus. Paul urged believers to accept the circumstances in which they come to faith, whether circumcised or uncircumcised, and not seek to change their situation (1 Cor. 7:18-20). At the end of his letter to the Galatians where Paul hammered out his teaching on this subject, he wrote, "For neither is circumcision anything, nor uncircumcision, but a new creation. And those who will walk by this rule, peace and mercy be upon them, and upon the Israel of God" (Gal. 6:15-16).

# About Circumstances

A circumstance is the situation in which you find yourself apart from your own personal plans. Often, unplanned circumstances are significant factors in the major turning points of our lives. The unplanned circumstances of a college conference led me to meet a young lady who introduced me to her younger sister…who later became my wife! Unplanned circumstances led to my forty-year career as a professor at Western Seminary. Unplanned circumstances led me to spend a summer in Israel, a life-defining experience which eventuated in my post-graduate studies and career emphasis on the historical geography of the Holy Land. So many of the twists and turns in our lives are the result of unplanned circumstances.

The Apostle Paul believed that God, through His sovereignty, rules over the circumstances of our lives. Concerning God's work in the spiritual lives of believers, Paul wrote, "And we know that God causes all things to work together for good to those who love God, to those who are called according to His purpose" (Rom. 8:28). He went on to explain that circumstances which may appear on the surface to be merely "chance," are divinely determined by God to guide the steps of our spiritual journey (Rom. 8:29-30). Paul further declared to the Ephesians that our salvation was not something we have chosen and determined for ourselves, but that the boundaries of our lives have been marked out beforehand ("predestined") by God who "works all things after the council of His will" (Eph. 1:11).

Paul's belief in God's sovereignty over life's circumstances was not just armchair theology. During his first Roman imprisonment, Paul wrote to the Philippians reporting that, "my circumstances have turned out for the greater progress of the gospel" (Phil. 1:12). Paul was under house arrest, awaiting trial. He was not sure of the outcome, but was determined to exalt Christ "whether by life or by death" (Phil. 1:20). Yet in the midst of these dire circumstances, Paul was content (Phil. 4:11) because he knew that God was in control. Paul revealed in his letter to the Philippians that he was able to experience peace and joy knowing that God was working through the circumstances in his life for the advancement of the gospel.

An important lesson we can learn from Paul is that our personal peace is not determined by our circumstances, but by resting in the confidence that the Prince of Peace is in control. Philippians 4:13, "I can do all things through Him who strengthens me," is often quoted in various contexts. But the original context in Paul's letter to the Philippians is that because of God's benevolent sovereignty over believers' lives, we can find contentment "in any and every circumstance" (Phil. 4:12).

# About Clothing

You may be surprised to see "clothing" on the list of Paul's teachings. But clothing is a topic addressed as early as Genesis 3:15 where God clothed Adam and Eve with animal skins to replace the fig leaves that they had fashioned to cover their nakedness. One of my classmates at Dallas Seminary wrote a whole master's thesis on the biblical theology of clothing! In Paul's day clothing was so important that a person was considered "naked" (*gumnos*) whether totally without clothing or clad in a light undergarment, as was the case with Peter when he was fishing (Jn. 21:7). Most of us take clothing for granted and think about it mostly when it is missing. If you have ever left your coat behind after visiting somewhere, you can identify with Paul who asked Timothy, "When you come, bring the cloak which I left at Troas with Carpus (2 Tim. 4:13).

In his instructions concerning women in the assembly, Paul instructed Timothy that they should "adorn themselves with proper clothing, modestly and discreetly, not with braided hair and gold or pearls or costly garments" (1 Tim. 2:9). Regardless of contemporary fashion, Paul insists that modest and discreet apparel is the standard for followers of Jesus. While this is true of both men and women, Paul's particular concern here is in the context of men and women gathered together for worship. Since men are wired to respond to visual stimulation, Christian women are encouraged to help men keep their spiritual focus by dressing modestly. Three areas are specifically mentioned: hair, jewelry, and expensive clothing. Paul's mention of "braided hair and gold" may be a reference to the custom of dancing girls braiding their hair with gold bangles which shimmered and clattered as they moved. Expensive jewelry and clothing which sets one apart from other worshipers, attracting undue attention, is not conducive to an atmosphere of worship. On the positive side, Paul added that "good works" may adorn the lives of women "making a claim to godliness" (1 Tim. 2:10). The words, "making a claim" (*epaggello*), can be better translated, "proclaiming." Paul is saying that women can make a "proclamation" of godliness by their modest, God-honoring dress.

In his letter to the Corinthians, Paul used the concept of clothing as a metaphor to contrast our present, temporal existence with our future immortality. He likens our present, earthly experience to being "naked" or "unclothed" as we await our future "dwelling from heaven" (2 Cor. 5:2-3). Paul wrote, "For indeed while we are in this tent, we groan, being burdened, because we do not want to be unclothed but to be clothed, so that what is mortal will be swallowed up by life" (2 Cor. 5:4). For Paul, this mortal life was like being "naked" in contrast with the imperishable, spiritual body we will enjoy in heaven when God will "transform the body of our humble state into conformity with the body of His glory" (Phil. 3:21). What a glorious hope for the future!

## About the Conscience

Paul believed that all people, including unbelievers, have a conscience which commends what is right and condemns what is wrong. The Greek word translated "conscience" (*suneidesis*) means "to know with," and suggests the idea of self-knowledge or self-judgment. A person's conscience enables them to distinguish moral good from moral evil. In his letter to the Romans, Paul explained that when unbelieving Gentiles responded in obedience to the commands of God's law, they were responding to their God-given conscience, "the work of the law written in their hearts…alternately accusing or else defending them" (Rom. 2:15). While one's conscience can serve to guide one's behavior, Paul recognized that it was possible for a person to reject that leading and "become seared in their own conscience as with a branding iron" (1 Tim. 4:2). A seared conscience may be similar to a "defiled" conscience which is no longer sensitive to the sinfulness of sin (Titus 1:15).

Paul often appealed to his conscience as a guiding factor in his own decisions and actions (Rom. 9:1; 13:5). He lived in such a way so as to maintain a "good," "blameless," or "clear" conscience (Acts 23:1, 24:16; 2 Tim. 1:3). He recognized that his own teaching must be the outflowing of a "pure heart" and a "good conscience" (1 Tim. 1:5). Along with keeping the faith, Paul commanded his disciple, Timothy, to keep "a good conscience" (1 Tim. 1:9). A "clear conscience" is listed as a requirement for those aspiring to serve as deacons (1 Tim. 3:9).

While a person's conscience can serve as an indicator of moral right and wrong, it is possible to have a conscience that is overly sensitive due to influence from one's culture or background. Paul refers to believers who have a "weak" conscience and feel it is wrong for them to eat certain foods (1 Cor. 8:7-12). Although there is nothing morally wrong with eating foods which God has provided, their weak conscience condemns them for it. Encouraging them to go ahead and eat the food can "wound" their conscience and damage a person's spiritual life (1 Cor. 8:12). Paul believed that while "all things are lawful," not all things are helpful or spiritually edifying (1 Cor. 10:23). And while "nothing is unclean in itself" (Rom. 14:14), Paul has determined to avoid questionable things to avoid causing someone with a weak conscience to stumble spiritually (1 Cor. 8:13). He wants all believers to do the same. Paul wrote, "We who are strong ought to bear the weakness of those without strength and not just please ourselves" (Rom. 15:1).

## About the Day of the Lord

The "Day of the Lord" is an important theme throughout the Bible. Thirteen out of sixteen Prophets contribute to our understanding of this topic. While "the Day of the Lord" can refer to historical events of military defeat and other forms of divine judgment (Lam. 1-2, Ezek. 13:1-9, Jer. 46:2-12, and Isa. 22:1-14), most references speak of a future or eschatological day of coming judgment on disobedient Israel and unbelieving nations. The prophet Joel declared, "Alas for the day! For the day of the Lord is near; and it will come as destruction from the Almighty (Joel 1:15; also Zeph. 1:14-18). But the Day of the Lord is not just a day of wrath and judgment on the disobedient. In eschatological contexts, it also includes deliverance, blessing and restoration for the righteous. The prophet Amos announced the blessings which would follow Israel's repentance, "I will restore the captivity of My people Israel, and they will rebuild the ruined cities and live in them; they will also plant vineyards and drink their wine, and make gardens and eat their fruit" (Amos 9:14-15; also Isa. 4:2-6, Hosea 2:18-23, Joel 3:18-21, Micah 4:6-8). Based on a study of the Prophets, we can define the Day of the Lord as that period of time during which God will deal with Israel and the nations through judgment and deliverance.

The Apostle Paul, of course, was familiar with this biblical theme and further develops it in his letters to the Thessalonians. Paul had spoken about end time events during his ministry at Thessalonica, but wrote two follow-up letters to correct some misunderstandings and assure his readers that the Day of the Lord had not yet arrived. While Jesus taught that His return would be preceded by warning signs (Matt. 24:29-30), Paul explained that the Day of the Lord would commence unexpectedly. He wrote, "For you yourselves know full well that the Day of the Lord will come just like a thief in the night. While they are saying 'peace and safety!' then destruction will come upon them suddenly like labor pains upon a woman with child, and they will not escape" (1 Thess. 5:2-3). Note the repeated contrasts between "you" (believers) and "them" (unbelievers) in 1 Thess. 5:1-11. Paul made it clear that the wrathful judgments of the Day of the Lord are not intended for Jesus' followers, but for unbelievers. He emphasized this with the words, "For God has not destined us for wrath, but for obtaining salvation [*deliverance*] through our Lord Jesus Christ" (1 Thess. 5:9).

In Paul's second letter to the Thessalonians, he offered evidence to correct those who believed that the Day of the Lord had already arrived (2 Thess. 2:2). According to Paul, two events will precede the beginning of this day of wrath and judgment. "Let no one in any way deceive you, for it [*the Day of the Lord, v. 2*] will not come unless the apostasy comes first, and the man of lawlessness is revealed, the son of destruction" (2 Thess. 2:3). The "man of lawlessness" is a reference to the "little horn" of Daniel 7:8, the anti-Christ of the end time (cf. Dan. 9:27). His appearance marks the beginning of the Day of the Lord.

The Greek word translated "apostasy" (*apostasia*) is derived from a verb meaning "depart from" (*aphistemi*). The basic root meaning of *apostasia* is "departure." The context clarifies the meaning of this word. Since Paul was writing about "the coming of our Lord Jesus" and particularly that aspect of the event which

170

relates to "our gathering together with Him" (2 Thess. 2:1; also 1 Thess. 4:17), the word translated "apostasy" clearly refers to the gathering and *departure* of believers to be with Jesus (ie. the rapture). Two events, then, must precede the Day of the Lord--the rapture and the revelation of the anti-Christ. According to Paul, the Day of the Lord constitutes a time of future chastening on unbelievers which is designed to bring them to repentance so they can enjoy all the blessings God has prepared for His people in eternity.

# About Deacons

The word translated "deacon" (*diakonos*) in the Bible literally means "servant." A deacon is someone who serves. The best example of this is in Acts 6 where the apostles selected seven men to "serve" (*diakoneo*) the church by caring for the needs of some widows who were being neglected (Acts 6:1-6). By taking charge of this task, they freed the apostles to focus their attention on prayer and the ministry of the Word. Although they were not called "deacons," the church office of deacon is probably derived from this historical situation.

While the word "deacon" can be used in a general sense to refer to anyone who serves (1 Cor. 3:5; 2 Cor. 3:6; Eph. 3:7). It is also used by Paul to designate a church office, the office of deacon. This is how Paul uses the word in his letter to Timothy where he sets forth the qualifications for the church offices of elder (3:1-7) and deacon (3:8-13). Some have regarded the office of deacon as lesser than that of elder and requiring fewer spiritual qualifications. But that doesn't seem to be Paul's view. The spiritual qualifications for the two offices are nearly identical. Deacons have a different role in the body of Christ than elders, but they are equally important for the spiritual health of the church and one is not superior to the other in qualifications or importance.

There is some debate as to whether Paul intended for there to be a church office of female deacons. In presenting the qualifications for the office of deacon, Paul writes, "Women must likewise be dignified, not malicious gossips, but temperate, faithful in all things" (1 Tim. 3:11). Paul may have been suggesting that the office of deacon can be filled by qualified men and women, as perhaps evidenced by the example of Phoebe (Rom. 16:1). On the other hand, Paul could be emphasizing that since deacons often serve together with their wives, the spouses of deacons must be exemplary. Whatever you conclude about the *office* of deaconess, both women and men are encouraged to use their gifts in serving the church. Phoebe stands as a prominent example of a woman whose service to the church Paul noted and appreciated.

## About Death

The Bible tells us that there have been just two people who left planet earth without undergoing the experience of physical death—Enoch (Gen. 5:24) and Elijah (2 Kings 2:11). Everyone else since the time of Adam has died. Paul explained to the Romans that physical death came about as the result of sin. He said, "Just as through one man sin entered into the world, and death through sin, so death spread to all people, because all sinned" (Rom. 5:12). Paul emphasized that death wasn't just the natural consequence of sickness or old age, but that death is something we earn as the "wages of sin" (Rom. 3:23). While death rules and reigns over fallen humanity, Jesus' sacrifice for sin and resurrection from the grave have broken the bonds of death. While the followers of Jesus still die, death doesn't have the final say regarding their future.

While the "sting of death" is still present in our sin-damaged world, Paul thanks God for the victory over the grave which was achieved through the death and *resurrection* of Jesus Christ (1 Cor. 15:55-57). Paul believed that when God's reign over His creation is fully realized in His future kingdom, "the last enemy [death] will be abolished" (1 Cor. 15:26). But in the meantime, death is still an enemy, and people will still die.

The death of a friend or loved one leaves us with a feeling of physical loss and emotional sadness. I have repeatedly experienced this in my own family with the passing of my mom, dad and brother. But Paul wants us to know that we can find comfort in the fact that believers will be reunited with their loved ones in some future day. Paul explained to the Thessalonians that when Jesus returns for His people, "the dead in Christ will rise first" (1 Thess. 4:16). That's good news. But it gets even better! Paul added in the next verse, "Then we who are alive and remain will be caught up together with them in the clouds to meet the Lord in the air, and so we shall always be with the

Lord" (1 Thess. 4:17). Notice the words, "together with them." Paul is referring to the ultimate reunion of believers with those who have gone before them in death. Confidence in the resurrection of believers means that there is a biblical basis for consolation and comfort in death of a loved one in Christ (1 Thess. 4:18).

There is a lot of speculation about what happens to a believer when they breathed their last breath and die. Paul answers that question with clarity in his words to the Corinthians where he explained that while we are "at home" in our earthly bodies, we are "absent from the Lord" (2 Cor. 5:6). Then he added, "I prefer rather to be "absent from the body and to be at home with the Lord" (2 Cor. 5:8). Our bodies remain in the grave until they are raised and glorified at the return of Jesus. But the immaterial part of our bodies (soul or spirit) is eternally present with Jesus from the moment of death. And with Paul we say, "Thanks be to God, who gives us the victory through our Lord Jesus Christ" (1 Cor. 15:57).

## About Divorce

Divorce is a difficult and painful subject for many believers. It is rare today for a family to be untouched by the experience of loved ones, friends, or church members who have been through the trauma of a marital breakup. Of course, there is a great deal of controversy about whether or not divorce is permitted under certain circumstances. But we need to put the painful experiences and controversy aside for a moment and consider what Paul said about this subject. We should also pray for God's guidance in discovering and applying the truth of His Word.

Paul regarded marriage as a lifelong relationship. According to Paul, death and death alone ends a marriage. This is evident by his words, "A wife is bound as long as her husband lives; but if her husband is dead, she is free to be married to whom she wishes, only in the Lord" (1 Cor. 7:39). Also, "For the married woman is bound by law to her husband while he is living; but if her husband dies, she is released from the law concerning the husband" (Rom. 7:2). Concerning the permanence of marriage, Paul wrote, "I give instructions, not I, but the Lord, that the wife should not leave her husband" (1 Cor. 7:10). Yet Paul recognized that in a fallen world, marriages sometimes fail. In such a case, Paul offered two alternatives to those who have been divorced: (1) be reconciled with your spouse or (2) live your life as a single person (1 Cor. 7:11). According to Paul, a person who has been divorced should seek reconciliation or actively pursue the single life. A new marriage is simply not an option which Paul presents to his readers.

But what about Paul's words, "Yet if the unbelieving one leaves, let him leave; the brother or the sister is not under bondage in such cases, but God has called us to peace" (1 Cor. 7:15). While these words have been interpreted as allowing for remarriage in the case of desertion, Paul doesn't mention remarriage in this verse at all. He knows of the concept of remarriage, and presented this as an option for widows (1 Cor. 7:39). It is unlikely that Paul would prohibit divorce and remarriage in 1 Corinthians 7:10-11 and then allow it in 7:15. The phrase "not under bondage" literally means "not enslaved." Paul taught that a deserted believer is not so bound to preserve the marriage union that he or she must follow the deserter around like a slave. Being enslaved is contrasted with being at peace. Rather than living as slave to an unwilling spouse, believers can be at peace with the abandonment while recognizing the two options relevant to their situation (1 Cor. 7:11).

But what about Paul's words in 1 Cor. 7:28, "but if you marry, you have not sinned"? The key to any verse is its context. In 1 Cor. 7:25-28 Paul was giving instructions to unmarried people ("virgins"). He had been pointing out the advantages of living as a single person. But some young people in Corinth who had made plans to marry were wondering if it was sinful for them to go ahead with their wedding. Paul responded by writing that people in a state of marital freedom (1 Cor. 7:27), such as engaged virgins (*parthenoi*), commit no sin should they go ahead and marry. Yet, Paul preferred the single life for himself (1 Cor. 7:7) and was convinced that, at least for widows, this results in a "happier" life (1 Cor. 7:40).

Like all other sin, divorce is something which God hates (Mal. 2:16). But in saying that, I want to emphasize that God is *always* willing to forgive and restore the repentant. For further study of the biblical teaching on marriage and divorce, consult my book, *The Divorce Myth* (Bethany House Publishers) and *Divorce and Remarriage: Four Christian Views* (InterVarsity Press, 1990).

# About Elders/Overseers

The term "elder" (*presbuteros*), referring to a person in their senior years, has a rich history in the biblical world. Moses selected seventy elders to assist him in leading the people of Israel (Num. 11:16). In the time of Jesus, elders provided leadership in Israel's Sanhedrin and Jewish synagogues (Matt. 16:21, Acts 4:5). The Apostle Paul adopted and adapted the office of elder to give leadership in the messianic congregations he and Barnabas had established. When they were returning from their first missionary journey, Paul and Barnabas revisited the cities of Lystra, Iconium and Antioch where they "appointed elders" in every church (Acts 14:23).

When Paul was returning to Jerusalem toward the end of his third journey, he stopped at Miletus for a meeting with the elders of the church at Ephesus. Paul exhorted the Ephesian elders to guard themselves and the people among whom "the Holy Spirit has made you overseers, to shepherd the church of God" (Acts 20:28). Here we discover that another term for "elders" is "overseers." The term "elder" speaks of the spiritual maturity required for the office, while the term "overseer" focuses on the responsibility of spiritual oversight. But notice also the words, "to shepherd the church of God." The verb "to shepherd" speaks of the *function* of the elder/overseers. As a shepherd leads, feeds and cares for the flock in his charge, so the elders are responsible to shepherd (or pastor) the church family. The Apostle Peter emphasized this role when he exhorted the elders to "shepherd the flock of God among you" (1 Pet. 5:1-2).

In his letter to Timothy, who had been charged with providing spiritual leadership to the church at Ephesus, Paul explained that the office of elder may be rightfully desired, but certain requirements must be met. The first and last qualifications highlight the kind of man who can rightfully fill the office. The elder/overseer, first of all, must be a man who is "above reproach" (1 Tim. 3:2). The word suggests personal character that is not open to criticism or question. The last qualification is that the elder must have a "good reputation" with those outside the church (1 Tim. 3:7). What Paul is referring to in these qualifications is integrity. The elder/overseer must be a person of integrity. There is no such thing as a "minor lapse" in integrity. Who would want to fly in an airplane which had a "minor lapse" in its structural integrity?

Paul listed additional qualifications for the office of elder. These include the areas of his marriage ("husband of one wife"), gifting ("able to teach"), social relationships ("hospitable," "not pugnacious"), family life ("managing his household," "children under control") and experience ("not a new convert"). Paul set a high bar for those aspiring to church leadership. Not all will meet the qualifications to fill the office of elder. But by the continued workings of God's grace, some will be able to serve and lead the church as elders.

# About Election

In keeping with the clear teaching of the Hebrew Scriptures, Paul believed in the biblical doctrine of election (Deut. 7:6-8, Amos 3:2). The Apostle Paul believed that as a function of His sovereignty, God has the right and authority to choose. He believed that God chose Jacob instead of Esau to be the heir of the covenant He made with Abraham (Rom. 9:10-13). Paul believed that Jacob's descendants, the people of Israel, were chosen to receive the covenants, the law and the promises of God (Rom. 9:4). And Paul believed that God chose angels as instruments for doing His will (1 Tim. 5:21).

In addition to God's sovereign choice of Jacob, Israel, and certain angels, Paul taught that individuals are chosen by God to respond with faith and believe the gospel (Rom. 8:33; Titus 1:1). In his letter to the Ephesians, Paul wrote, "Blessed be the God and Father of our Lord Jesus Christ, who has blessed us with every spiritual blessing in the heavenly places in Christ, just as He chose us in Him before the foundation of the world (Eph. 1:3-4). He assured the Thessalonian believers, "God has chosen you from the beginning for salvation through sanctification by the Spirit and faith in the truth" (2 Thess. 2:13).

Paul's teaching on the doctrine of election is difficult for us to understand, accept, and appreciate. For many, it seems unfair that God would choose some and not others. It seems that God is playing favorites. Paul responded to the objection that election is unfair in his letter to the Romans. Paul wrote, "What shall we say then? There is no injustice with God, is there? May it never be! For He says to Moses, 'I will have mercy on whom I have mercy, and I will have compassion on whom I have compassion.' So then it does not depend on man who wills or runs, but on God who has mercy" (Rom. 9:14-16). In other words, Paul was saying that since God is the sovereign Creator and Ruler over the universe, He has the right to choose. Since no one is deserving of God's mercy, His choosing is simply a reflection of His sovereign grace. Election is not a doctrine for unbelievers, focusing on their exclusion; but a doctrine for believers, focusing on the blessing of being included in God's family. It is not just about us. Paul emphasized that the sovereignty of God in election is "to the praise of the glory of His grace" (Eph. 1:6).

When I was in grade school and joined my friends for a game of baseball, the two team captains selected the players they wanted on their team. The best players were always chosen first. Not being a talented ball player, I was among the *last* to be chosen. But the encouragement I have found in Paul's teaching on election is that I was chosen by God at the very *beginning*, "before the foundation of the world" (Eph. 1:4). The encouragement and blessing of election for believers is knowing that even though we weren't the best players, God has chosen us to be on His team.

## About Faith

What is faith? Faith is the attitude of someone who believes that something is true and reliable. The writer of Hebrews declares that "Faith is the assurance of things hoped for, the conviction of things not seen" (Heb. 11:1). When we are persuaded that something is true and rely on that truth, we are demonstrating our faith. Although we can't see God, believing that He exists is an expression of personal faith. During my son's career in the Navy, he made about a dozen parachute jumps. His faith in the parachute gave him the confidence to jump out of an airplane, trusting that the parachute would open and gently carry him back to earth.

Paul taught that while salvation is a free gift from God, the gift of salvation must be appropriated by faith. In his letter to the Romans, Paul quoted from Genesis 15:6 to show that righteousness was credited to Abraham by faith. "For what does the Scripture say? 'Abraham believed God, and it was credited to him as righteousness'" (Rom. 4:3,9). The fact that Abraham was declared righteous before he was circumcised, was highlighted by Paul as evidence that righteousness is not achieved by the works of the law but by faith (Rom. 4:13).

Paul insisted that what was true for Abraham is true for everyone. Salvation is always by faith in accordance with God's amazing grace. Paul made this crystal clear in his letter to the Ephesians, "For by grace you have been saved through faith; and that not of yourselves, it is a gift of God; not as a result of works so that no one may boast" (Eph. 2:8-9). Not only is salvation a gift, but the very faith that is necessary to receive it comes to us as God's gift! In other words, there is no salvation without faith, and the faith necessary for salvation comes to us as a grace gift. Grace is the basis of salvation and faith is the channel by which it is received. If I were to offer you the gift of a hundred-dollar bill, you would need faith in my character to make good on the offer in order to come by my house and collect what was promised.

If salvation is a gift that is received by faith, where do works come into the picture? Paul has made it clear that works are not the basis of our salvation (Gal. 2:16; Eph. 2:9); but they do have a part to play in our spiritual lives. In his discussion of the process of salvation, Paul added these important words, "For we are His workmanship, created in Christ Jesus for good works, which God prepared beforehand so that we would walk in them" (Eph. 2:10). For those who are saved by faith, God has prepared opportunities for them to express their faith by how they live. Good works are the expression of a genuine faith, not the means of achieving salvation or earning a right standing before God.

I have never had sufficient faith in a parachute to strap one on and jump out of an airplane. But I have taken an even greater leap of faith by placing my eternal future in the care of my Savior, Jesus. He is the best and most trustworthy "parachute" available to get us safely from this sin-cursed earth to our eternal home in heaven.

## About the Flesh

According to Paul, people have a spirit, soul and body (1 Thess. 5:23). The distinction between "spirit" and "soul" is debated, but it is clear that our personhood includes both spiritual and physical parts. The physical part of our being is our "flesh" (sarx). Paul acknowledges that despite the differences in their physiology, both

178

human beings and animals are made of "flesh" (1 Cor. 15:39). This is also true of Jesus who was "revealed in the flesh" (1 Tim. 3:16). Paul uses this word to describe how his "flesh," his physical body, "had no rest" because of the affliction he experienced in Macedonia (2 Cor. 7:5).

In addition to describing the physical body as "flesh," the word *sarx* is sometimes used by Paul as a metaphor for his spiritual life before coming to faith in Jesus. "For while we were in the flesh, the sinful passions, which were aroused by the Law, were at work in the members of our body to bear fruit for death" (Rom. 7:5). Paul used the terms "flesh" and "Spirit" to make a clear contrast between believers and unbelievers. He wrote, "while those who are in the flesh cannot please God," but added that the readers of his letter were "not in the flesh but in the Spirit" (Rom. 8:8-9).

A major question is raised by Paul's words in Romans 7:14 where he writes, "I am of flesh (*sarx*), sold into bondage to sin." Is Paul referring to his life before coming to faith in Jesus, or is he describing his struggle with sin as a believer? Is Paul indicating that believers in Christ have a sinful (fleshly) nature that encourages sin? I suggest that in Romans 7:14-25, Paul is dealing with the problem of his fleshly, physical body which is in conflict with his new, regenerate person—his deepest and truest self. Paul has been set free from the dominion of sin (Rom. 6:14), but he still is living life on earth with a physical body, his "flesh". Paul's deep desire, based on his new identity in Christ, is to please God. Yet his "flesh" wages war against his mind and heart, tempting him to do things contrary to God's will (Rom. 7:21-24). Relying on his own resources means defeat. But through the New Covenant provision of the indwelling ministry of the Holy Spirit, there is victory (Rom. 8:1-4).

Paul described the same conflict of "flesh" and "Spirit" in his letter to the Galatians. He wrote, "For the flesh sets its desire against the Spirit, and the Spirit against the flesh; for these are in opposition to one another, so that you may not do the things that you please" (Gal. 5:16). While our physical bodies are not intrinsically bad, our flesh can be used for evil purposes. Believers are called to present their bodies "as instruments of righteousness to God" (Rom. 6:13). This decision is an act of the will based on the recognition of our new identity as adopted sons and daughters of the Creator and King of the universe. Believers who forget their identity as saints destined for glory (Eph. 1:1-14), may respond to the physical longings and memories of the flesh (*sarx*). But Paul provides the key to spiritual victory. He implored believers to live by the power and enablement of the Holy Spirit, adding the encouraging assurance, "and you will not carry out the desire of the flesh" (Gal. 5:16).

## About Gentiles

Incredible as it may seem, Abraham, the revered patriarch of Israel, wasn't Jewish (a descendant of Judah). He wasn't even an Israelite (a descendent of Jacob). Abraham was a non-Jew, a non-Israelite with whom God entered into an eternal covenant (Gen. 12:2-3). The big surprise to many Jews is that Abraham was a Gentile. A "Gentile" is simply someone who is not Jewish. The Greek word (*ethnos*) refers to a group of people of the same nation or identity. While it can be used of the Jewish people (Lk. 7:5), the predominate use in the New Testament is to non-Jewish people or nations. Since Gentiles in the first century spoke Greek rather than Hebrew or Aramaic, the terms "Greek" (*hellen*) and Gentile (*ethnos*) became rather interchangeable.

Shortly after the apostle's life-changing encounter with Jesus on the Damascus road, God revealed to Ananias that Paul would proclaim the gospel "before the Gentiles and kings and the sons of Israel" (Acts 9:15). Paul understood and embraced this mission. He wrote to the Ephesians, "To me, the very least of all saints, this grace was given, to preach to the Gentiles the unfathomable riches of Christ" (Eph. 3:8). Out of a deep love for his own Jewish people, Paul always went to the Jews first to tell them about the coming of Israel's Messiah. But when they rejected his message, Paul turned his attention to the Gentiles (Acts 13:46).

Some believers who had come to faith in Jesus from a Jewish background insisted that Gentile followers of Jesus needed to be circumcised and follow the laws given by God to Israel at Mt. Sinai. Paul insisted that this was not only unnecessary, but undermined the principle of salvation by grace (Gal. 2:16; 5:1-5). Gentile salvation by grace through faith, apart from the works of the law, was a theme that Paul repeatedly emphasized in his preaching of the gospel. Since Abraham came to faith and was declared righteous as an "uncircumcised Gentile" (Rom. 4:1-22), non-Jewish people could enter into God's spiritual family the same way. Paul declared that circumcision "which is of the heart" distinguished a Gentile believer apart from the physical procedure (Rom. 2:29).

In his letter to the Ephesians, Paul made it crystal clear that believing Gentiles were not second class citizens in God's family. Paul reminded them that as unbelievers they were once "separate from Christ, excluded from the commonwealth of Israel, and strangers to the covenants of promise, having no home and without God in the world" (Eph. 2:12). Then he triumphantly added that as believers in Christ, they were "no longer strangers and aliens, but fellow citizens with the saints, and are of God's household" (Eph. 2:19). This is very good news indeed for Gentile believers!

## About Giving

Paul was a giver as well as being the recipient of giving. When the believers in Antioch learned of the famine and economic struggles in Jerusalem, they sent a money gift to the church in the care of Barnabas and Saul (Acts 11:27-30). While Paul often worked his trade to avoid being a burden to newly established congregations (2 Thess. 3:7-8), he welcomed financial assistance during his imprisonment (Phil. 4:18).

Paul taught the principle of giving by his example and his words. In his letter to the Corinthians, the apostle provided four important guidelines for giving. First, giving should be regular and systematic. Paul instructed the Corinthians that on the first day of the week they should "put aside and save" some of their income as a collection for the needs of the church (1 Cor. 16:2a). Second, giving should be proportionate. Paul instructed that a believer should give "as he may prosper" (1 Cor. 16:2b). Paul wasn't concerned about the amount of the gift, but the attitude of the donor, "for God loves a cheerful giver" (2 Cor. 9:7). Third, Paul insisted that giving should be done without pressure or compulsion. He wanted the collection by the Corinthian church to be completed before he arrived so that his presence would not be taken as pressure to give (1 Cor. 16:2). Finally, Paul taught that giving should be carefully administered. He asked the Corinthian church leaders to appoint trustworthy men from their congregation to carry the gift to Jerusalem (1 Cor. 16:3). Paul was careful to protect his own reputation and personal integrity. He wanted the collection to be handled in such a way that there would be no questions raised about his handling of the money.

It is significant that in his teaching on giving, Paul said nothing about tithing. Tithing under the Old Covenant law was more than just ten percent. According to the law, there were *three* tithes (Deut. 14:22-29) amounting to 23% annually. Tithing often focuses attention on fulfilling an obligation rather than responding to needs from the heart. And tithing can hinder us from doing what we could do by making us think that we have done enough. There is nothing wrong with tithing. But neither is there anything wrong with giving 5%, 15% or 30% of one's income. Some believers may be capable of giving less and others have the resources to give more. God can be equally pleased with a gift of five dollars from a poor widow and a gift of a million dollars from a wealthy business owner. The ultimate spiritual value of the gift depends on the attitude of the donor's heart (Mk. 12:41-44).

In Acts 20:35, Paul quoted Jesus as saying "It is better to give than to receive." Interestingly, this quote is nowhere found in the gospels. Paul may have received this proverb from the oral tradition passed on by other apostles or from Jesus Himself. Why is it better to give than to receive? First, giving enables us to share in the lives and ministries of other believers. Second, through giving, God uses us to bless others. Third, giving reminds us of how God demonstrated His love by sending the gift of His Son. God doesn't need our giving to accomplish His eternal purposes for the church and the world (Psa. 51:10). But through open handed generosity, believers have the privilege of partnering with God in accomplishing His kingdom work.

# About Good Works

While Paul makes it very clear that good works are not the basis for our salvation (Ephesians 2:8-9), they have an important place in the lives of Jesus' followers. Paul explained to the Ephesians that believers are "created in Christ Jesus for good works, which God prepared beforehand that we should walk in them" (Eph. 2:10). Good deeds are the fruit of a living and vital faith. God provides opportunities for us to help and serve others. Through His leading and the empowerment of the Holy Spirit, we respond and become the hands and feet through which Jesus ministers to people's physical and spiritual needs.

Good works are such an important part of Paul's teaching that they are mentioned five times in his short letter to Titus. Titus was instructed to be an "example of good deeds" (Titus 2:7), to "be ready for every good deed" (Titus 3:1) and to "engage in good deeds" (Tit. 3:8). Part of his duties as Paul's representative on the island of Crete was to instruct the believers "to meet pressing needs, that they may not be unfruitful" (Titus 3:14). Peter records that during His earthly ministry, Jesus "went about doing good" (Acts 10:38). Believers are called to follow His example.

# About Government

Paul recognized four spheres of authority in which believers are called to submit: church, home, work and government. In each of these areas, believers are instructed to recognize and obey the leaders that God has placed over them. In his letter to the Romans, Paul instructed his readers "to be in subjection to the governing authorities" (Rom. 13:1). The Greek word translated "subjection" (*hupotasso*) means "to arrange under" and was used in a military context of soldiers forming up for battle. Under the authority of their commander, soldiers would go to their assigned positions in preparation for warfare. As soldiers were "under orders" given by their commander, so believers are under the orders of governing authorities.

Submission to governing authorities is not always easy, especially in Paul's day when the tyrant Nero ruled the Roman empire. So Paul explained the reason for a believer's subjection to government. He wrote, "For there is no authority except from God, and those which exist are established by God. Therefore, he who resists authority has opposed the ordinance of God" (Rom. 13:2). Paul was saying that God raises up authority figures and replaces them at His pleasure. Since this is true, our obedience to God is to be demonstrated by our submission and obedience to divinely ordained authorities. Reinforcing this point, Paul calls government "a minister of God" for good (Rom. 13:4).

Paul went on in Romans 13 to explain the purpose of government. Civil authorities are divinely intended to promote good and deter evil. Those who submit to the authorities have nothing to fear from "the sword" that government is authorized to use. Those who refuse to submit and disobey the laws established by the governing authorities will bring "wrath" upon themselves. Paul was reminding believers that breaking the law leads to painful and sometimes life threatening consequences.

Submission to civil authority is not just about obeying the law. Submission includes the concept of support, such as paying taxes (Rom. 13:6). Paul further commanded, "Render to all what is due them: tax to whom tax is due; custom to whom custom is due; fear to whom fear is due; honor to whom honor is due" (Rom. 13:7). Supporting governing authorities includes praying for those in leadership. Paul wrote Timothy, "I urge that entreaties, prayers, petitions and thanksgivings be made on behalf of all people, for kings and all who are in authority…. This is good and acceptable in the sight of God our Savior" (1 Tim. 2:1-3).

Submitting to and supporting the divinely ordained governing authorities is not always easy! It wasn't easy for Paul. It may not be easy for you. We may disagree with their political agendas and their executive enactments, but we can still honor and pray for our leaders, including our president, representatives, governors, mayors, and policemen. Are these national and community leaders on your prayer list?

## About the Gospel

We all can agree that Paul preached "the gospel." But what exactly does this mean? What is the *content* of the gospel Paul preached? The Greek word translated "gospel" (*euangellion*) means "good news." Paul told the Ephesian elders that the calling he had received from the Lord Jesus was "to testify solemnly of the gospel ("good news") of the grace of God" (Acts 20:24). Paul believed that he was personally set apart by God as an apostle to proclaim "the gospel of God" (Rom. 1:1). This "good news" centers on the coming of Jesus as Israel's Messiah, Savior and King.

Paul summarized the basic elements of this "good news" in his letter to the Corinthians. Paul wrote, "I make known to you brethren, the gospel which I also preached to you, which you also received, in which you also stand" (1 Cor. 15:1). He proceeded to outline four essential elements of the gospel: (1) Messiah's death for our sins, according to Scripture; (2) His burial, authenticating his death; (3) His resurrection on the third day, according to Scripture; and (4) Jesus' resurrection appearances, authenticating His resurrection (1 Cor. 15:3-8).

Paul insisted that the gospel he preached should never be modified or distorted, as was happening in the churches of Galatia where some were preaching a "different (*heteros*) gospel" (Gal. 1:6). Since there is only one true gospel, Paul took what seems like an extreme step in calling down God's judgment on anyone preaching a gospel contrary to the message they had received (Gal. 1:8-9). Saying it twice for emphasis, Paul declared, "let him be accursed!"

Why must Paul's gospel be kept free from alteration or modification in light of further needs or changes in culture? Paul answered that question, writing "For I neither receive it from man, nor was I taught it, but I received it through a revelation of Jesus Christ" (Gal. 1:12). Paul's gospel was not a message passed down to him from the other apostles or church tradition. Paul's gospel was totally accurate and trustworthy because it was revealed to him directly from Jesus! For this reason, the followers of Jesus must guard the purity of the good news, not adding to, subtracting from or compromising the gospel in any way.

Theologians have debated whether "the gospel" includes more than the death, burial and resurrection of Jesus. While 1 Cor. 15:3-4 captures the essence of the gospel, the Bible presents us with a larger picture of this good news. When Paul began proclaiming the gospel in the synagogues of Damascus, he was declaring that "Jesus is the Son of God" and proving by the Scripture that Jesus is Israel's Messiah (Acts 9:20,22). In his message delivered in the synagogue at Antioch, Paul was announcing that "God has brought to Israel a Savior, Jesus" (Acts 13:23). In addition to his review of Israel's history culminating in the coming of Jesus, Paul declared that "forgiveness of sins" is granted to those who believe in Him (Acts 13:38-39). The good news that Paul preached also included instruction about the "kingdom of God" (Acts 20:25; 28:31) which was announced by Jesus (Matt. 4:23). Paul believed that the kingdom of God was a present, spiritual reality into which believers enter by faith (Col. 1:13; Rom. 14:17) and will be culminated by the Messiah's return to redeem Israel (Rom. 11:26) and reign over His creation (1 Cor. 15:24-26). The gospel is more than the death, burial and resurrection of Jesus. The gospel includes all the "good news" that Paul preached about God's provision of salvation through Jesus and His promised blessings for Israel and the nations.

## About Grace

The word "grace" captures the distinguishing message of the Bible in both the Old and New Testaments. The Greek word translated "grace" (*charis*) refers to something that is freely given as a favor, not paid for or earned by the recipient. God in His inestimable grace planned and provided salvation for sinners who deserved His wrath. Paul declared to the Ephesians, "For by grace you have been saved through faith; and that not of yourselves, it is a gift of God" (Eph. 2:8). To the Romans he wrote, "But if it is by grace, it is no longer on the basis of works; otherwise grace would no longer be grace" (Rom. 11:6).

It was in appreciation of this "unmerited favor" that John Newton, former slave trafficker, penned the words, "Through many dangers toils and snares, I have already come; 'Tis grace that brought me safe thus far, and grace shall lead me home" (*Amazing Grace*). Author and Bible teacher, Jerry Bridges remarked, "Your worst days are never so bad that they are beyond the *reach* of God's grace. And your best days are never so good that they are beyond the *need* of God's grace." Well known author and speaker, Philip Yancy, said, "Grace does not depend on what we have done for God, but rather what God has done for us."

Ask people what they must do to get to heaven and most reply, "Be good." The teaching of Paul corrects this. He taught that all we must do is acknowledge our desperate need and cry, "Help!" Paul explained to the Philippians that in spite of his Jewish heritage and obedience to the Mosaic law, his righteousness as a follower of Jesus was not derived from the law but "through faith in Christ" (Phil. 3:9).

Highlighting God's grace in his own life, Paul told Timothy, "I was formerly a blasphemer and a persecutor and a violent aggressor, and yet I was shown mercy" (1 Tim. 1:13). Then Paul added, "Jesus Christ came into the world to save sinners, among whom I am foremost of all" (1 Tim. 1:15). In other words, if God can forgive and redeem Paul, God can save anybody! God's grace is truly amazing. *Amazing* grace!

# About Head Coverings

In spite of the controversial nature of this topic, I decided to include it since Paul devotes a half of a chapter of First Corinthians to the subject. What Paul wanted the Corinthians to do is pretty clear. How this applies to believers in the 21st century is a subject of considerable debate.

A little cultural background will help us understand the issue. According to Jewish custom a bride went bare-headed until her marriage, as a symbol of her freedom. When she married, she wore a veil as a sign that she was under the authority of her husband. It is quite probable that both Jewish women and respectable Greek women wore such a head covering in public (Conzelmann, *First Corinthians*, p. 185). The problem was that there were Christian women in the church at Corinth who were not wearing the traditional covering (1 Cor. 11:5-6). The idea of a "veil" is suggested, but not actually mentioned in the Greek text. Paul simply refers to those who are "covered" or "uncovered."

Paul began by pointing out that God has established an order of authority both in the spiritual and the natural realm. He wrote, "I want you to understand that Christ is the head of every man, and that man is the head of a woman, and that God is the head of Christ" (1 Cor. 11:3). The word "head" (*kephale*) was used by Paul as a metaphor referring to a position of hierarchy in God's order of authority. God the Father is in a position of authority over His Son. Jesus is in a position of authority over a man (*aner*). And the man (husband) is in a position of authority over a woman (ie. his wife). It is crucial to understand that rank or hierarchy doesn't necessarily involve inequality since Jesus is subordinate to His Heavenly Father, yet the two are spiritually equal (Jn. 10:30; 14:9).

Paul continued in his letter to the Corinthians by explaining that both the man and the woman have the potential to bring shame upon themselves (1 Cor. 11:4-5). The man does this by ministering with a covered head. The woman disgraces herself by ministering with an uncovered head. Since an adulterous wife would have her hair shorn,

Paul regards an uncovered woman as behaving like an immoral person.

But what is the context in which the woman is asked to wear the head covering? Paul wrote that Christian women are obligated (1 Cor. 11:10) to cover their heads when "praying and prophesying" (1 Cor. 11:5). Some commentators have suggested that Paul is referring to women using their speaking gifts in the meeting of the church. But Paul's regulations for using speaking gifts in meeting of the church appears to contradict this (1 Cor. 14:34-35). It is not until 1 Cor. 11:17-18 that Paul begins writing about an assembled congregation. It is very likely, then, that Paul's instructions about the head covering apply in situations where women are using their gifts in meetings apart from the regular meeting of the church where elders are appointed to lead and preach.

Paul provides several reasons why this regulation should be followed by women when praying and prophesying. First, it reflects creation order. The first woman, Eve, was created from man and for him (1 Cor. 11:8-9). The head covering symbolizes and reflects God's design for man and woman in terms of leadership and authority. Second, the head covering should be worn "because of the angels" (1 Cor. 11:10). Refusing to wear a head covering would offend the holy angels who are present when the church is gathered for worship. Third, Paul pointed out that God's created order in nature (*phusis*) reflects a distinction between men and women by the length of their hair (1 Cor. 11:14-15). While there are notable exceptions, men generally wear shorter hair than women. Fourth, while some might object to Paul's regulation, he concluded his instruction saying, "We have no other practice, nor have the churches of God" (1 Cor. 11:16).

It seems clear to me that Paul wanted the women at Corinth to wear the traditional head covering while praying and prophesying when they gather for such purposes outside the regular and official meeting of the church. But does this regulation have application for believers today in 21st century churches? Should Christian women *today* wear a head covering when praying or prophesying publicly? Would contemporary believers understand the spiritual significance of this practice today? It has been suggested, based on 1 Cor. 11:15, that a woman's long hair may take the place of the head covering. Others have suggested that the head covering is a symbol that might be updated to something more suitable, like a wedding ring. Some Christian leaders have chosen to teach their congregations about the significance of the biblical symbol and have encouraged women to follow Paul's recommended practice. Whatever believers decide on this intriguing and troublesome issue, they must strive to maintain harmony with each other and respect the diversity of opinion. Out of love for Christ and one another, we must focus on what we as believers share in common (Phil. 2:1-2) rather than on the issues where we differ.

## About Heaven

Paul did not have a lot to say about the eternal home of believers in Jesus. He taught that Jesus had ascended "far above all the heavens" (Eph. 4:10) and was seated there at the right hand of God (Rom. 8:34) "in the heavenly places" (Eph. 1:20). Paul told the Thessalonian believers that they were awaiting God's "Son from heaven" (1 Thess. 1:10) who would one day descend from heaven, raise the dead in Christ, and gather the living believers to Himself so they could remain with Him forever (1 Thess. 4:16-17).

Although the followers of Jesus were living on earth, Paul told the Philippians that their "citizenship was in heaven" (Phil. 3:20). In his first letter to the Corinthians, Paul contrasted our earthly and heavenly bodies. Since our mortal bodies of flesh and blood are not suited for our eternal existence, our "earthly" bodies will one day be replaced with "heavenly" bodies (1 Cor. 15:40). Paul explains that "as we have borne the image of the earthy, we shall also bear the image of the heavenly (1 Cor. 15:49). Paul used the image of a "tent" versus a "building" to contrast our earthly and heavenly existence. "For we know that if the earthly tent which is our house is torn down, we have a building from God, a house not made with hands, eternal in the heavens" (2 Cor. 5:1). It is in our heavenly body that we will experience God's promise of eternal life (Rom. 6:23).

Although Paul didn't describe what heaven will be like, he assured the Corinthians that to be "absent from the body" is to be "at home with the Lord" (2 Cor. 5:8). And living forever with Jesus is really what heaven is all about.

# About the Holy Kiss

I know this isn't the most significant of Paul's teachings, but he does repeatedly instruct the believers to "greet one another with a holy kiss" (Rom. 16:16; 1 Cor. 16:20; 2 Cor. 13:12; 1 Thess. 5:26). What is going on here? What kind of greeting did Paul have in mind?

Greeting people with a kiss was an ancient custom in the Middle East and is still practiced in many cultures today. The kiss is usually delivered to the cheek, but in some cultures it lands on the lips! This kind of greeting would make many contemporary believers uncomfortable, especially in our post-COVID 19 culture. This Christian greeting is designated as "holy," setting it apart from romantic or intimate kissing. The holy kiss is like the kiss I have given my mother, my sister and my daughters. It is a kiss on the cheek that communicates my love more personally than a verbal greeting, a handshake or a hug.

While greeting one another with a holy kiss is a biblical imperative, there is a danger involved. Clement of Alexandria, a 2nd century theologian who taught in Alexandria, Egypt, offered this warning:

"And if we are called to the kingdom of God, let us walk worthy of the kingdom, loving God and our neighbor. But love is not proved by a kiss, but by kindly feeling. But there are those that do nothing but make the churches resound with a kiss, not having love itself within. For this very thing, the shameless use of a kiss, which ought to be mystic, occasions foul suspicions and evil reports. The apostle calls the kiss holy. When the kingdom is worthily tested, we dispense the affection of the soul by a chaste and closed mouth, by which chiefly gentle manners are expressed" (*Ante-Nicene Fathers*, Vol. II, Chapter 12, p. 291).

A kiss on the cheek can be a warm, Christian greeting. But Clement warned that it should never be used to take advantage or fuel personal pleasure.

How should 21st century followers of Jesus respond to this biblical command? For the most part, Christians in the West simply ignore it, relegating this instruction to the culture of the Ancient Near East. Others have modified it into a "holy handshake." But how does a common hand shake become "holy?" How can the handshake become a distinctively Christian greeting? Perhaps with the accompanying words, "He is risen!"

With care and caution, I have on occasion used the "holy kiss" as a Christian greeting. I recall giving a kiss to a dear professor and mentor when he retired from Western Seminary. I planned to kiss him on the cheek, but he suddenly turned and the kiss landed on his lips! Neither he nor I was embarrassed by this expression of *agape* love. Years later I shared this story at his memorial service, adding that he was the only man I had ever kissed on the lips!

# About the Holy Spirit

Shortly after Paul's encounter with Jesus on the road to Damascus, he met the Holy Spirit. Ananias was sent by Jesus to tell Paul, "be filled with the Holy Spirit" (Acts 9:17). Luke records that when Paul and Barnabas left Antioch on their first missionary journey, they were "sent out by the Holy Spirit" (Acts 13:4). Luke reports that when Paul was ministering for the Lord, he was "filled (or empowered) by the Holy Spirit" (Acts 13:9). On his second missionary journey, Paul was directed "by the Holy Spirit" not to proceed to Asia (Acts 16:6), but to continue on to Troas. Toward the end of his third missionary journey, the Holy Spirit revealed to Paul that afflictions awaited him in Jerusalem (Acts 20:23). When quoting Isaiah 6:9-10 to the Jews at Rome, Paul said that "the Holy Spirit spoke through Isaiah the prophet to your fathers." These references to the work of the third Person of the Tri-unity (Trinity) demonstrate the important place the Holy Spirit had in the life and ministry of the Apostle Paul.

Paul believed that the Holy Spirit was one of the three, co-equal members of the Godhead (2 Cor. 13:14) and that He indwells believers along with the Father and Son (Rom. 8:9-11). Paul taught that the Holy Spirit has an active ministry in the life of Jesus' followers. The Holy Spirit regenerates people, giving them new life in Christ (Titus 3:5). In fulfillment of God's promise of a New Covenant (Ezek. 36:27), the Holy Spirit personally indwells believers (Rom. 8:9). The Holy Spirit initiates believers, baptizing them into the body of Christ (1 Cor. 12:13). The Holy Spirit puts God's seal on believers, verifying their identity as His people (Eph. 1:13; 4:30). Paul wrote of the Holy Spirit sovereignly dispensing "spiritual gifts" to believers "just

191

as He wills" (1 Cor. 12:4,11). And to enable believers to live a life that is pleasing to God, the Holy Spirit fills and empowers believers (Eph. 5:18; Gal. 5:16). Paul told the Corinthians that no one could say "Jesus is Lord," except by the supernatural and powerful workings of the Holy Spirit.

# About Hope

There are times of difficulty in our lives when we struggle to be confident about the future. The loss of a job, the break-up of a relationship or a worldwide pandemic often cause people to lose hope. But according to the Apostle Paul, the followers of Jesus have every reason to be the most hopeful people in town! Along with faith and love, "hope" is one of the three great pillars of the Christian faith (1 Cor. 13:13).

For many people, the word "hope" is a synonym for "wish," as in, "I wish I had a million dollars!" But the Greek word for hope (*elpis*) has a much stronger nuance. Both the noun and verb forms of the word express a "confident expectation" about something future. When Paul told members of the Sanhedrin that he was on trial for "the hope and resurrection of the dead" (Acts 13:6), this wasn't something he merely wished for. Paul was absolutely confident in God's promise of the resurrection of believers (1 Cor. 15:20-22). It is best that we remove the thought of uncertainty from our biblical theology of hope. Greek scholar, William Barkley wrote, "The Christian hope is not simply a trembling, hesitant hope that perhaps the promises of God may be true. It is the confident expectation that they cannot be anything else than true" (*New Testament Words*, p. 76).

Why could Paul have such a hopeful attitude in the face of the inevitable trials and troubles of life? First, Paul's attitude of hope was well grounded in Scripture. Paul told the Romans, "For whatever was written in earlier times was written for our instruction, that through the perseverance and the encouragement of the Scriptures, we might have hope" (Rom. 15:4). Paul was saying that the message found in Scripture provides a basis for hope. Second, God's covenant promise to Abraham and his descendants is a basis for hope. Paul told King Agrippa that he was on trial "for the hope of the promise made by God to our fathers" (Acts 26:6). Third, the person and work of Jesus

192

provided Paul with hope. Paul began his letter to Timothy referring to "Christ Jesus who is our hope" (1 Tim. 1:1). Fourth, the truths of the gospel gave Paul hope. He exhorted the Colossians not to drift from "the hope of the gospel" which they had received (Col. 1:23). Fifth, Paul was convinced that God is the basis for hope, not only for the Jews, but also for the Gentile nations. Quoting from the prophet Isaiah, Paul wrote, "There shall come the root of Jesse and He who arises to rule over the Gentiles; in Him shall the Gentiles hope" (Rom. 15:12, cf. Isa. 11:10). Finally, the Lord is characterized by Paul as "the God of hope." He prayed for the Romans, "Now, may the God of hope fill you with all joy and peace in believing that you may abound in hope by the power of the Holy Spirit" (Rom. 15:13).

Paul was convinced that the promises of God, fulfilled by the coming of Jesus, provided him with abounding hope, energized by the powerful workings of the Holy Spirit! And the hope that we have through Christ continues into the future as we anticipate "the blessed hope" of His return (Titus 2:13). Believers may be confident that in whatever difficult circumstances they may encounter, God has not left them without hope (1 Thess. 4:13). Our hope is not in better circumstances. Our hope is not in our health, wealth, family or career. Our hope is in God—and in Him alone!

## About Immortality

It was the German philosopher, Friedrich Nietzsche, who introduced the concept that "God is dead." Advocates of the Enlightenment or "Age of Reason," spreading through Europe in the 17th through 19th centuries, believed advances in science and philosophy had removed the need for God and the necessity of His existence. The Apostle Paul had a different view. He used the word "immortal" to describe God's nature. The Greek word (*athanasia*) means "without death" or "deathless." Paul blessed God as the "only Sovereign, the King of Kings and Lord of lords, who alone possesses immortality" (1 Tim. 6:15-16). This means that God exists eternally. He has not died. He does not change. Paul used a different word, also translated "immortal," in his letter to Timothy. Paul wrote, "Now to the King eternal, immortal, invisible, the only God, be honor and glory forever and ever" (1 Tim. 1:17). This Greek word (*aphthartos*) means "without corruption" or "incorruptible." This reveals that God's holiness, sovereignty, love and faithfulness will never be diluted or diminished. All that God is, He will always be. God's divine attributes won't be 100% today and 98% next week. Speaking through the prophet Malachi, God declared, "I the Lord, do not change" (Mal. 3:6). James, the Lord's brother, wrote that with God, "there is no variation or shifting shadow" (James 1:17).

This quality of immortality, which is always true of God, becomes true for Jesus' followers when they receive their glorified bodies. Paul explained to the Corinthians that "flesh and blood cannot inherit the kingdom of God; nor does the perishable inherit the imperishable" (1 Cor. 15:50). Paul explained further that when Jesus returns to raise the dead, "We shall be changed. For this perishable must put on the imperishable, and this mortal must put on immortality" (1 Cor. 15:52-53). Paul is referring to the "deathless" existence believers will enjoy for eternity. While our mortal bodies must die, this experience is only temporary. While the "sting of death" remains with us, death itself has been defeated through Christ's resurrection. In preparation for the eternal state, death itself will be judged and cast into the lake of fire (Rev. 20:14).

Paul taught that immortality for believers will be more than an on-going, "deathless" existence in glorified bodies. He explained to the Corinthians that what is now "mortal," will one day "be swallowed up by life" (2 Cor. 5:4). Immortality includes the *quality* of life that believers will enjoy as they live in God's presence forever. This may be what Jesus had in mind when He prayed, "This is eternal life, that they may know You, the only true God, and Jesus Christ whom You have sent" (Jn. 17:3).

## About Israel

Paul was an Israelite (Phil. 3:5). He had much to say about his people, the nation of Israel. After his encounter with Jesus on the Damascus road, God revealed to Ananias that this former persecutor of the church was "a chosen instrument of Mine, to bear My name before the Gentiles and kings and the sons of Israel" (Acts 9:15). While Paul was the "apostle to the Gentiles," he never passed up an opportunity to present the gospel to his own Israelite people (Acts 9:20, 13:5,14). Paul had no doubt that the nation of Israel was chosen by God (Acts 13:17) as the people through whom He would bless the world with the Messiah and Savior, Jesus (Acts 13:23; Rom. 9:5). The problem, as Paul detailed it in Romans, is that the nation of Israel rejected the promised Messiah instead of welcoming and receiving him. What was God to do? Would He reject the nation of Israel because of the people's unbelief and disobedience to the message Jesus proclaimed?

Paul spent three chapters of his letter to the Romans to answer these questions and explain how the nation of Israel fits into God's plan. Paul began this discourse reminding the Roman believers that the nation of Israel has received great blessings and promises. God gave to Israel "the glory and the covenants and the giving of the law and the temple service and the promises" (Rom. 9:4). But in spite of these many gracious blessings, the people of Israel sought to pursue their relationship with God through works instead of by faith. Paul wrote that Israel "stumbled over the stumbling stone" (Rom. 9:32), their Messiah. Instead of accepting by faith the righteousness provided through Jesus and the New Covenant, the people of Israel persisted in unbelief, refusing to "heed the glad tidings" which the Prophets had announced (Rom. 9:16). But did God give up on Israel? No! God continued reaching out to His people. Paul quoted Isaiah who spoke for God saying, "All the day long I have stretched out my hands to a disobedient and obstinate people" (Rom. 10:21).

Paul continued in Romans 11 to emphasize that while the nation of Israel rejected God's Messiah, God didn't reject Israel. Paul pointed out that there has always been a remnant of faithful Israelites among the descendants of Jacob. Paul himself is a primary example (Rom. 11:1). Even in the time of Elijah when Ahab ruled Israel with wicked Jezebel, there were "seven thousand" who had not bowed the knee to Baal (Rom. 11:4). Paul explained that in the sovereignty of God, something good has come through Israel's unbelief—the grafting in of believing Gentiles into the family of God (Rom. 11:11-17). And while the nation of Israel has experienced a "partial hardening," when God has completed His work among the non-Jewish people, "all Israel will be saved" (Rom. 11:26). From a divine perspective, Israel continues to be a people chosen and beloved of God whose gifts and calling are irrevocable (Rom. 11:28-29).

Paul is very clear about the future for the ethnic people of Israel as the recipients of unconditional promises and future blessings. But there are those who say that since Israel rejected their Messiah, God has replaced the nation of Israel with the company of believers known as "the church." This perspective is known as "replacement theology." According to this teaching, the nation of Israel becomes morphed into the church and the promises to Israel are spiritually applied to Christians. The covenant promises about the land and a nation (Gen. 12:1-3, 2 Sam. 7:12-16) are interpreted spiritually as describing heaven. An appeal is made to Romans 9:6, "They are not all Israel who are descended from Israel." But Paul wasn't eliminating ethnic Israel from God's program. Rather, he was saying in Romans 9:6 that physical descent from Abraham does not necessarily make someone a child of God and a recipient of His promises. God's covenant promises to the nation of Israel will be literally fulfilled by a believing remnant of the descendants of Abraham.

Instead of removing Israel as the recipient of God's unconditional covenant promises, I believe that the physical promises to Israel, concerning the land and nation, will be fulfilled by the physical descendants of Abraham *when* they repent and accept their Messiah. Zechariah anticipates that day when God "will pour out a Spirit of grace" on the house of David and inhabitants of Jerusalem, and the people of Israel "will look upon Me [Messiah] whom they have pierced" and believe (Zech. 12:10). This is already beginning to take place as increasing numbers of Jewish people are recognizing *Yeshua* (Jesus) as their Messiah and finding their Jewish faith completed in Him.

## About Jesus

It is truly amazing how someone so antagonistic against Jesus and His followers could become such a committed follower and proclaimer of the gospel. For many years, the Holy Spirit had been prodding Saul's heart and convicting his conscience. Then he met Jesus on the road to Damascus and everything changed. After several days in Damascus, Saul "began to proclaim Jesus in the synagogues, saying, 'He is the Son of God'" (Acts 9:20). What Paul believed about Jesus is illustrated by his Sabbath sermon at the synagogue in Pisidian Antioch (Acts 13:16-41). Paul believed that in keeping with God's promises to their ancestors, Jesus came as Israel's Messiah and Savior. He died to provide forgiveness of sins and was raised from the dead in fulfillment of prophecy.

The essence of what Paul believed about Jesus is recorded by Luke in Acts 13:39, "Through Him everyone who believes is freed [*justified*] from all things, from which you could not be freed [*justified*] through the Law of Moses." Paul developed this great theme more thoroughly in his letters to the Galatians and the Romans where he emphasized that believing in Jesus as Israel's Messiah and Savior results in being justified or "declared righteous" by faith (Gal. 2:26; Rom. 5:1). Paul believed and taught that Jesus was fully God and fully man (Col. 2:9; 1 Tim. 2:5), a sinless Savior (Acts 13:23; 2 Cor. 5:21), Israel's Messiah (Acts 17:3), the sovereign Lord of all (Phil. 2:9; 2 Cor. 4:5) and reigning King over all creation (1 Cor. 15:25; 1 Tim. 1:17; 6:15). For more on what Paul believed about Jesus, see the topic, "About Christ."

## About Jews

When the kingdom of Israel divided in 931 BC after the death of Solomon, Jereboam was made king over the ten northern tribes which became known as the kingdom of Israel. The southern tribes (Judah and Simeon), under the leadership of Rehoboam, became known as the Kingdom of Judah. The Israelites in the north were taken captive by Assyria in 722 BC and never returned to their homeland. With a few exceptions, they disappeared from Israel's history. The southern tribes were taken captive by Babylon in 586 BC, but returned in 537 BC to reoccupy their native homeland. Since the group that returned was from the tribe of Judah, they were known as "Judeans," the designation from which the term "Jew" (*'Ioudaios*) is derived. In its original sense, a "Jew" was someone from the tribe of Judah. In this sense, Paul, being of the tribe of Benjamin, was an Israelite, but not a Judean (a "Jew"). By the time of the New Testament, the word "Jew" became the general designation of those who lived in the land of Israel, worshiped God at the Jerusalem temple and obeyed the teachings of the Mosaic law. Jews (or Judeans) were distinct from non-Jews (Gentiles) who worshiped many gods or no god. This background helps us understand the term "Jew" as it appears in the New Testament. While it has religious connotations, the word "Jew" was primarily a geographical and ethnic designator, as in "Judean."

Paul used the word "Jew" to refer to those of the tribe of Judah who adhered to the beliefs, traditions, and worship of the people of Israel. Paul understood that he was commissioned to preach "to Gentiles and kings and the sons of Israel" (Acts 9:15). In keeping with his love for his own people, Paul's custom was to preach "to the Jew first" (Rom. 1:16). Even after his Damascus road encounter with Jesus, Paul identified himself as a "Jew" (Acts 21:39, 22:3), a Jew who believed in Jesus. He recognized that being a "Jew" was more than just a matter of circumcision and involved an attitude of the heart, not just the removal of a bit of flesh (Rom. 2:28-29). In his letter to the Galatians, Paul taught that in Christ, the distinctions between "Jew" and "Greek" (non-Jews) are removed so that "all are one in Christ Jesus" (Gal. 3:28). Believers entering into the New Covenant by faith experience such a spiritual renewal that there is no longer a distinction "between Jew and Greek, circumcised and uncircumcised, barbarian, Scythian, slave and freeman, but Christ is all and in all" (Col. 3:11). A Christian's true identity is based on being a new person in Christ, not their ethnic background or socio-economic status.

## About Justification

As a faithful monk in the Roman Catholic tradition, Martin Luther struggled with how he could be righteous enough to have a relationship with an infinitely righteous God. In spite of his fasting, Bible reading and prayer, Luther realized that his best attempts at being holy fell short of God's righteous standard. Finally, as he studied God's Word, his eyes were opened to a wonderful truth. While he could never earn enough righteousness through his personal piety or good works to satisfy God, he could be "declared righteous" or "justified" through faith in his Savior Jesus. While all have sinned and fallen short of God's righteous standards (Rom. 3:23), believers in Jesus are "justified as a gift by His grace through the redemption which is in Christ Jesus" (Rom. 3:24). Justification by faith, apart from meritorious works, became the great theme of the Protestant Reformation and remains an essential teaching of biblical Christianity.

Paul developed the theme of justification by faith in his letters to the Galatians and the Romans. Paul used the Greek word *dikaioo* to describe what happens when someone believes in Jesus. God looks at their lives and says, "You have missed the mark. You have fallen short of My righteousness standards. But Jesus has taken your sin upon Himself and died in your place. On the basis of your faith in His saving work, I will place your sin on Him and put His righteousness on you."

Justification means that God has declared us righteous based on the gift we have received through faith in Jesus. Paul wanted his readers to know that justification by faith is nothing recently revealed or newly invented. Abraham was declared righteous by faith (Gen. 15:6; Rom. 4:1-5). Likewise, David was justified by faith apart from works (Rom. 4:6-8). The prophet Habakkuk presented the principle of justification by faith in the Hebrew Bible when he wrote, "The just shall live by faith" (Hab. 2:4).

Paul wanted his readers to know that God wasn't cheating or simply playing with words when He declared believers "righteous." Since God is a just and holy judge, He couldn't just ignore our sin or "sweep it under the rug." Our sin had to be judged. The penalty for sin must be paid. But since Jesus paid for our sins by the sacrifice of His life, God can "be just and the justifier of the one who has faith in Jesus" (Rom. 3:26). As a result of being justified by faith, those who were formerly the subjects of God's holy wrath "have peace with God through our Lord Jesus Christ" (Rom. 5:1). The good news of justification by faith is captured for us in Romans 8:1 where Paul wrote, "Therefore, there is now no condemnation for those who are in Christ Jesus." Ponder those words, "No condemnation." Instead of being condemned for our sins, the gift of complete acquittal is available to each of us through faith in the saving work of Jesus.

## About Justice

The other day on my morning run, I saw a popular sign reflecting the protests over the tragic shooting deaths of black Americans by the police. The sign read, "No justice; no peace." People today are calling for justice—justice for black Americans; justice for women; justice for the unborn; justice for the "Dreamers" (DACA). When will there be "justice for all" which is promised by the U.S. Constitution and highlighted in our Pledge of Allegiance? Americans have looked to lawmakers, the courts and judges with the hope of getting justice. But they have often been disappointed.

The Apostle Paul believed in a God of justice. The Greek word for "justice" (*dike*) denotes "what is right." The Greeks believed in *Dike* (counterpart to the Roman *Justitia*), a goddess of justice, who would inflict a just punishment on the guilty. When the poisonous viper attached itself to Paul's hand, the observer assumed that Paul was a murderer and "Justice (*Dike*) has not allowed him to live" (Acts 28:4). The word is used by Paul to refer to the just "penalty" (*dike*) for rejecting God and His provision of salvation through Jesus (2 Thess. 1:8-9). Paul used a related word (*dikaios*) to refer to what God has declared to be right. He told the Thessalonian believers that it was "just (*dikaios*) for God to repay with affliction those who afflict you" (2 Thess. 1:6). On the other hand, God was "right" or "just" in acquitting believers of their guilt and consequent punishment on the basis of their faith in Jesus (Rom. 3:26).

When most people ask for justice, they are appealing for the rights, freedoms and opportunities they believe they deserve. But when Paul writes about justice, he is referring to God being "right" in executing judgment on those who have rejected Him and His ordinances (Rom. 1:32). Many people are demanding justice *now*. But Paul assures us that justice is coming and it is not going to be nice. God's justice means that we get what we deserve (2 Thess. 1:9). I am thankful that the justice I deserved fell upon Jesus. As a result, I can enjoy "peace with God" (Rom. 5:1). Believers receive both *peace* and *justice* through the person and work of Christ.

## About the Kingdom of God

John the Baptizer preached about the kingdom of God, as did Jesus and the Apostle Paul. The kingdom of God is one of the great themes that ties together the various facets of God's message in the Bible. Yet while Jesus' parables tell us what the kingdom of God is like (Matt. 13), the Bible doesn't actually provide a definition. I think we can correctly assume that a "kingdom" requires a king, a domain and a people who occupy the domain, living under the authority of the king. With this in mind, I believe the "kingdom of God" can be described as "God's people, in God's place, under God's rule."

The kingdom of God existed when David represented and ruled for God over His people in the land of Israel. That was a literal kingdom. But the Bible reveals that there is more to the kingdom of God than physical realities. Paul explained to the Colossians that God "rescued us from the domain of darkness, and transferred us into the kingdom of His beloved Son" (Col. 1:13). This verse (along with Lk. 17:20-21,18:16; Jn. 3:3,5) indicates that the kingdom of God exists today as a *spiritual* reality. The miracles of Jesus demonstrate that the kingdom order has been inaugurated. When Jesus gave sight to the blind, healed the sick, caused the lame to walk, cleansed lepers, and liberated those with demons, he was providing a picture of what God's kingdom is all about. His resurrection marked the beginning of the fulfillment of one of the great kingdom promises (Dan. 12:2). Jesus, the resurrected Messiah and King is seated *today* at God's right hand, ruling over God's people who live under His authority in the body of Christ. We could rightly say that the kingdom of God is a present, spiritual reality which will be culminated when Jesus returns to rule over His people, in His land, during His promised messianic kingdom (Lk. 1:32-33; Acts 1:6; Rev. 19:11-16, 20:1-6).

Throughout his ministry, Paul preached and taught about the kingdom of God. He regarded those who assisted him as "fellow workers for the kingdom of God" (Col. 4:11). Paul encouraged the new believers at the recently established churches that the pathway into God's kingdom would not be easy. He said, "Through many tribulations we must enter the kingdom of God" (Acts 14:22). Paul emphasized that the kingdom of God was not focused on physical experiences, like "eating and drinking," but on the spiritual realities of "righteousness and peace and joy in the Holy Spirit" (Rom. 14:17). He rebuked the arrogant at Corinth, saying that the kingdom of God does not consist in people's boastful words, but in God's power (1 Cor. 4:20). In Rome, Paul spoke to representatives of the Jewish community, "solemnly testifying about the kingdom of God and trying to persuade them concerning Jesus, both from the law of Moses and from the Prophets" (Acts 28:23). Luke records that "the kingdom of God" was the central theme of Paul's preaching and teaching during his two years of house arrest in Rome (Acts 28:30-31). Throughout his preaching, Paul made it clear that self-made righteous was insufficient grounds for entering the kingdom of God. Yet the worst of sinners could experience forgiveness and enter freely into God's kingdom, enjoying all its blessings through faith in Jesus Christ (Eph. 5:5).

## About the Law

What did Paul have to say about the law? While whole dissertations have been written on this topic, this brief summary will help you begin thinking about this important topic. What comes to your mind when you hear or read the word "law"? Most Christians think of rules, limits and legalism. But Paul, being fluent in the Hebrew language, would have known that the Hebrew word for "law" (*torah*) simply means "instruction." The "law" is God's instruction. God gave Israel the law, His instruction, to teach His people how to live in covenant relationship with their Creator.

Paul used the New Testament word for "law" (*nomos*) in several different ways. The word *law* can refer to civil law, the law of the land (Rom. 7:1). It can also refer to a "principle" or "norm" that influences a person's conduct (Rom. 7:21-23). Frequently, the term "law" refers to the Mosaic law which was given by God to the people of Israel at Mt. Sinai (Rom. 2:25; 1 Cor. 9:9; Gal. 3:12; 1 Tim. 1:8-9). Finally, Paul used the word *nomos* to refer to the "law of Christ" (Gal. 6:2), the teachings of Jesus embraced by faith (Rom. 3:27) and applied in our lives by the ministry of Holy Spirit (Rom. 8:2).

God had given the law to instruct His people and guide them in covenant relationship with Him. But during the years before the coming of Jesus, the law came to be understood more as a legal code of conduct. Obeying the law was thought to secure a person's standing before God. Strict observance of the letter of the Mosaic law became the basis for God's acceptance of the individual. Paul totally rejected this. Paul taught that it is impossible to attain righteousness by keeping the law (Gal. 2:16, 3:2l). Due to the weakness of the human flesh (Rom. 8:3) and the sinfulness of the human nature (Rom. 7:23), people cannot consistently keep the law. Paul taught that keeping the Mosaic law cannot be the basis for justification

(Rom. 3:28) or sanctification (Gal. 3:2-3). According to Paul, the purpose of the law was to reveal humanity's sin (Rom. 3:20, 7:7) and point people to Jesus (Gal. 3:24).

Paul avoided throwing out the law along with legalistic traditions of Judaism. Paul explained to the Roman believers that God's law is "holy, righteous and good" (Rom. 7:12). The law expresses the will of God and was designed to lead His people to blessing and prosperity (Rom. 7:10, Lev. 18:5). Paul never rejected the Mosaic law. What he objected to was the idea that Gentile believers must embrace Jewish law and traditions as a basis for their complete salvation. Must believing Gentiles become law-keeping Jews in order to be saved? Paul answered with a resounding "No!" (Gal. 2:16).

Paul insisted that "Christ is the end [*telos*] of the law for righteousness to everyone who believes" (Rom. 10:4). Jesus is the end of the law in two ways: *First,* Christ fulfilled the law in His Person. He came under the law to redeem those under the law (Gal. 4:4-5). He became a curse for us (Gal. 3:13), canceling the debt against us (Col. 2:14). His work not only wipes out the curse of the law, but fulfills the demands of the Old Covenant for us (Matt. 5:17), presenting before the Father a positive righteousness for all those who are in Him. *Second*, the law is abrogated as a contractual obligation. Jesus' death inaugurated the New Covenant which abolishes the commandments and ordinances and ends the ethnic distinction between Israel and the Gentiles in Christ (Eph. 2:11- 18). All believers, whether Jew or Gentile, share a New Covenant identity in Christ.

Paul regarded the law as the expression of God's will for believers. But he taught that the righteousness of the law would be fulfilled not by human resources and ability, but by the power of the Spirit (Rom. 8:3-4). Paul upheld the law of God as an essential element of the New Covenant (Jer. 31:33). By the power of the Holy Spirit, believers under the New Covenant will "walk in God's statutes" and "observe His ordinances" (Ezek. 36:27). The relevant application of the Mosaic law is evidenced by Paul's appeal to specific Old Testament commands as normative for Christian conduct (Rom. 13:8- 10). The Mosiac law, as a contractual obligation with the nation of Israel, ended when the New Covenant was inaugurated by the sacrifice of Jesus (Heb. 8:6). This means that certain requirements concerning circumcision, foods, feasts, and Sabbath keeping are terminated (Col. 2:16). Although followers of Jesus are not under the Old Covenant legislation, the moral principles of the law, which reflects God's holiness, are abiding and relevant for followers of Jesus today. God's will that His people live holy lives has not changed (Lev. 19:2, 1 Thess. 4:7). This is why it is important for believers to study the *Torah*, God's "instruction," to discover the principles and applications that can guide our lives and conduct today.

## About Lawsuits

Have you ever been involved in a lawsuit? When a pastor friend of mine sold his house, it was thoroughly inspected and approved before the deal was closed. Then a year later, the sewer system failed. My friend offered to pay half the cost of the repair, but the new owner filed a lawsuit, insisting that he pay the full amount. Lawsuits happen today as they did in antiquity. Is it ever appropriate to take a fellow believer to court? Paul addressed this practical issue in his letter to the Corinthians.

The Apostle Paul recognized that disagreements and disputes between Christians will occur. But raising a rhetorical question, he pointed out that such disagreements should be adjudicated before believers and not in the civil courts. He wrote, "Does any one of you, when he has a case against his neighbor, dare to go to law before the unrighteous and not before the saints?" (1 Cor. 6:1). The word "unrighteous" refers to the unbelieving judges. Paul called for believers to settle their differences through mediation before believers rather than through the courts. Paul questioned the wisdom of trusting in unbelieving judges, who embrace the world's standards, rather than submitting to the judicial wisdom of a fellow believer in Christ (1 Cor. 6:4-6).

The alternative to having a believer mediate the case is not easy to accept. Paul wrote that it would be better to be "wronged" and accept the loss than to bring a dispute between believers before unbelieving judges in civil court (1 Cor. 6:7). Appealing to broader principles, Paul pointed out that since unbelievers will not inherit the kingdom of God, they are not qualified to judge disputes between church members (1 Cor. 6:9-11).

Based on Paul's instructions, disputes between believers must be settled by believers. Since Paul's concern was to maintain harmony in the body of Christ as a witness to the world, he didn't address the question of bringing a case against a non-believer before judges in a civil court. Nor did he comment on the appropriateness of self-defense in court. Yet Paul appears to have recognized the legitimacy of defending oneself before unbelieving judges, as he did on several occasions (Acts 16:37; 24:1-21; 25:9-11; 2 Tim. 4:16). Many people look to the courts to secure justice for themselves and others. But since the courts are human institutions ruled by human judges, they often disappoint us. Our confidence as believers is not in the courts, but in the Lord, our Lawgiver and Judge (Isa. 33:22).

# About Liberty

In 1964, Richard Longenecker published a book titled, *Paul, Apostle of Liberty* (Eerdmans). Some years later, British scholar, F. F. Bruce, published a book titled, *Paul, Apostle of the Heart Set Free*, (Eerdmans, 1977). Both of these distinguished New Testament scholars acknowledged in the title of their books that *liberty* or freedom in Christ was a major emphasis in Paul's writings. Paul used the Greek word *exousia* to refer to the "right" or "authority" that believers have to make certain decisions based on their conscience. But one's conscience must always be guided by loving concern for others. Paul wrote, "Take care that this liberty [*exousia*] does not somehow become a stumbling block for the weak" (1 Cor. 8:9). Paul devoted three chapters in his letter to the Corinthians (1 Cor. 8-10) to developing this theme of "love limited liberty." He concludes, "All things are lawful, but not all things are profitable. All things are lawful, but not all things edify. Let no one seek his own good, but that of his neighbor" (1 Cor. 10:23-24).

Paul used the word "freedom" (*eleutheros*) to describe how believers have been liberated from the ceremonial obligations of the Mosaic law. Just as physical death ends one's obligation to civil law

(Rom. 7:1-3), so believers "were made to die to the law through the body of Christ" (Rom. 7:4). Through faith in Jesus and His saving work, believers have been "released from the law" (Rom. 7:6). Paul was saying that the followers of Jesus have been set free from the limitations of the Old Covenant (Mosaic law) and can now enjoy the blessings and benefits of the New Covenant. Contrasting the Old Covenant with the New, Paul exclaimed, "Now the Lord is the Spirit, and where the Spirit of the Lord is, there is liberty" (2 Cor. 3:17).

In his warning to the Galatians who were being encouraged to retreat to the Old Covenant ceremonies and regulations, Paul wrote, "It was for *freedom* that Christ *set us free*; therefore, keep standing firm and do not be subject again to the yoke of slavery" (Gal. 5:1). Commenting on Paul's words "freedom" and "set us free," Vine writes, "the combination of the noun with the verb stresses the completeness of the act...indicating both its momentary and comprehensive character; it was done once for all" (*Vine's Expository Dictionary of New Testament Words*). Followers of Jesus have been "called to freedom" (Gal. 5:13). Under the guidance of the Holy Spirit and loving sensitivity toward our fellow believers, we enjoy a life of liberty in Christ.

## About the Lord's Supper

On the night before his crucifixion, Jesus celebrated Passover with His disciples in the upper room of the house of John Mark's mother, Mary, in Jerusalem. Jesus took two of the traditional elements from the Passover Seder (service) and gave them additional significance (Lk. 22:14-20). Jesus took some of the unleavened bread from the Passover table, broke it and gave it to his disciples saying, "This is My body which is given for you; do this in remembrance of Me" (Lk. 22:19). Then, taking a cup of the Passover wine, Jesus said, "Drink from it all of you, for this is My blood of the [new] covenant, which is poured out for many for forgiveness of sins" (Matt. 26:27-27; Lk. 22:20).

Following Jesus' instructions, the Corinthians were observing the Lord's Supper at a meal which became known as an "*agape* [love] feast" (Jude 12). This observance was intended to be a special time

206

of fellowship where believers enjoyed a good meal together and used some of their food to remember and celebrate what Jesus had done in their behalf. The problem was that they were participating in the Lord's Supper in a manner that dishonored Jesus and undermined the spiritual unity of the body of Christ. There were divisions, inequity, and a neglect of proper preparation (1 Cor. 121:18, 21, 28). These problems may have been due in part to the different economic backgrounds of the believers. In a stinging rebuke, Paul wrote, "When you meet together, it is not to eat the Lord's Supper, for in your eating each one takes his own supper first; and one is hungry and another is drunk" (1 Cor. 11:20-21). Then he questioned, "Do you despise the church of God and shame those who have nothing? What shall I say to you? Shall I praise you? In this I shall not praise you" (1 Cor. 11:22).

Paul then reviewed the true meaning and significance of the Lord's Supper. He traced this teaching to Jesus Himself, as indicated by the words, "I received from the Lord..." (1 Cor. 11:23). Quoting Jesus, Paul reminded the believers that they were to eat the bread and drink from the cup "in remembrance" of Him (1 Cor. 11:24-25). Then he added that the observance of the Lord's Supper constitutes a proclamation of the Lord's death (1 Cor. 11:26). In other words, everyone who participates in the Lord's supper is preaching a mini-sermon ("proclaiming") about the person and work of Jesus! Since Passover was a joyous celebration of God's redemptive work for Israel, the Lord's Supper should be a joyful proclamation and celebration of the believers' redemption through Jesus.

Paul concluded his teaching on the Lord's Supper with an admonition and warning. He admonished the believers at Corinth to examine their own spiritual condition before joining in the celebration (1 Cor. 11:28), for to participate in the Lord's Supper in an irreverent or unworthy manner dishonors our Savior.

Paul's warning highlights the serious nature of participating in the Lord's Supper. To eat the bread and drink from the cup in an unworthy manner invites God's discipline (1 Cor. 11:29-32). Paul didn't want to discourage believers from participating in a communion service. He simply wanted to make sure that Jesus was the focus in this special time of remembrance, worship and celebration.

# About Love

It was my privilege to give the commencement address at Western Seminary's graduation celebration the year I retired as a full time professor. The text which I selected for my message was 1 Timothy 1:5, "The goal of our instruction is love, from a pure heart, a good conscience and a sincere faith." I emphasized in my message that if our graduates learned the biblical languages (Hebrew and Greek), systematic theology, as well as pastoral and counseling skills, but didn't learn to love God and others, we have failed in the task of training Christian leaders. Agape love is one of the central teachings of the New Testament and is repeatedly highlighted in the writings of Paul. The love which characterized the life and ministry of Jesus is set forth as the pattern for His followers. Paul said, "Walk in love, just as Christ also loved you..." (Eph. 5:2).

Jesus told His disciples that *agape* love would be the identifying mark of those who follow Him. He said, "By this all people will know that you are My disciples, if you have love (*agape*) for one another" (Jn. 13:35). But what is true love like? What does it do? What is the nature of the "love" which identifies someone as a follower of Jesus?

Paul helped the Corinthians answer these questions in the classic and best known text on "love" in the Bible. In 1 Corinthians 13, Paul described *agape* love as the most preeminent, most permanent and most noble virtue. He began by emphasizing the absolute necessity of love. Whatever gifts one has and sacrifices one endures, it all adds up to a big "zero" if love is lacking (1 Cor. 13:1-3). Nothing can make up for the absence of love. Paul went on to describe what he means by "love" (Cor. 13:4-7). The Apostle Paul made it clear to the Corinthians that he was not referring to an emotion or feeling, but a sacrificial commitment to the ultimate good of another person. Love is patient, kind, not jealous, not boastful or arrogant, not unbecoming, not self-seeking, not easily provoked, does not keep account of wrongs done, does not rejoice in unrighteousness, but in truth; bears, believes, hopes and endures all things. I could spend the rest of my life just trying to live out and apply the implications of this teaching! Paul concluded his exposition on *agape* love by reminding his readers that it is the greatest of virtues because it will never fail nor fade away (1 Cor. 13:13). Tongues will cease. Prophecy will come to an end. But *agape* love alone will mark the followers of Jesus throughout eternity. I wonder if people can see evidence of *agape* love in me?

## About Marriage

June 5, 1971, was a major milestone in my life journey. It was on that day that I entered into a marriage relationship with my college sweetheart, Nancy Lilly. I thought I knew something about marriage from books, teachers, and counselors. But during that first year of marriage, I discovered that I had a lot more to learn. And I am still learning about this very special relationship that God instituted to create the human family.

In Paul's teaching on marriage, he directed the Ephesians back to Genesis where God established marriage for Adam and Eve. "For this reason, a man shall leave his father and mother and be joined to his wife, and the two shall become one flesh" (Gen. 2:24; Eph. 5:31). Based on this verse, Paul believed that marriage was designed by God to be a "one flesh" relationship between a man and a woman. The expression "one flesh" refers to the sexual union of the husband and wife as they share their bodies in marital intimacy. The children that may result from this union are a beautiful illustration of the "one flesh" relationship, sharing in the physical features and character traits of both their mother and father.

Paul explained that the marriage relationship was divinely designed to illustrate the love, sacrifice and intimacy that characterizes the relationship between Christ and His church. Referring to marriage, Paul explained, "This mystery is great, but I am speaking with reference to Christ and the church" (Eph. 5:32). So in the marriage relationship, the husband is called to love his wife "as Christ loved the church" and the wife is called to "respect" or "honor" her husband (Eph. 5:25,33).

Husbands sometimes wonder how to get the respect and honor they think they deserve. The answer is simple. Love your wife as Christ loved the church *by* sacrificing, serving and lifting her up. Behind every happy wife is a husband who washes dishes, changes diapers, vacuums the rug, takes out the garbage, washes the car, picks up his clothes, helps with the laundry, takes his family to church, reads the Bible, leads his family in prayer and is sensitive to his wife's emotional and physical needs. Behind every happy husband is a wife who loves, honors, appreciates and respects her husband. *And* shares herself with him in sexual intimacy.

Paul taught that marriage was designed by God to be a lifelong relationship. At the end of a lengthy chapter on divorce and remarriage, Paul explained that a wife is "bound" to her husband as long as he lives, "but if her husband is dead, she is free to be married to whom she wishes, only in the Lord" (1 Cor. 7:39). Paul made an almost identical statement in his letter to the Romans when he wrote, "For the married woman is bound by law to her husband while he is living; but if her husband dies, she is released from the law concerning her husband" (Rom. 7:2). Paul believed and taught that death, and death alone, ends the marriage relationship and provides freedom to remarry (Rom. 7:3; 1 Cor. 7:10-11). For further study on this subject, refer to the section "About Divorce" in this book or read my book, *The Divorce Myth* (Bethany House Publishers, 1981).

Some people hope that getting married will make them happy and fulfilled people. But Paul wrote that the *single* life provides greater opportunities for a fulfilling life of ministry and regards it a "happier" state (1 Cor. 7:32-35,40). A believer's joy and fulfillment is to be found in Christ, not dependent upon a marriage relationship (Phil. 4:11-13). Dr. Helene Dallaire, a single woman, professor of Hebrew, and friend, wrote on her FaceBook page, "Contentment does not come from marital status. It comes from the Lord. Following God and serving Him wholeheartedly is what the Christian life is about, whether single or married."

## About Money

Before someone invented money (an estimated seven thousand years ago), people simply exchanged something they had for something they needed. "I'll give you this stone hammer for a chunk of that goat meat." These days, most people use money to buy things they need. For many of us, our money is in the bank and we use a credit card ("plastic money") to make our purchases. Whatever your preference, we all need money (and lots of it) to live in our 21st century world.

Paul had some important things to teach us about money. In his letter to young Timothy, to whom he had entrusted leadership at the church of Ephesus, Paul wrote that "Godliness is a means of great gain when accompanied by contentment…. If we have food and covering, with these we shall be content" (1 Tim. 6:6-8). Paul warned that the desire to "get rich" leads to temptation which can result in making choices which lead to "ruin and destruction." Does that mean that money is bad? We often hear the warning, "money is the root of all evil." But that is a distortion of what Paul said. He explained to Timothy, "For the love of money is a root of all sorts of evil, and some by longing for it have wandered away from the faith and pierced themselves with many griefs" (1 Tim. 6:10). It is not money, but the *love* of money that leads to evil. Paul was warning Timothy, and the church at Ephesus, of the folly of devoting one's life to the accumulation of wealth.

In concluding his letter to Timothy, Paul wrote, "Instruct those who are rich in this present world not to be conceited or to fix their hope on the uncertainty of riches, but on God, who richly supplies us with all things to enjoy" (1 Tim. 6:17). You might think this just applies to millionaires. But I think it applies to all of us. Not all, but most of us have a roof over our heads, clothes on our backs and food in the frig. By Third World standards, we are rich! Paul is saying, "Trust in God, not your savings, investments or retirement plan." All that the world regards as "riches" is ultimately very "uncertain," as the rise and fall of the stock market clearly demonstrates.

So how can those who are "rich" steer clear of "the love of money"? Paul answered that question for Timothy, and for us. He said, "be rich in good works, be generous and ready to share" (1 Tim. 6:18). The best way to keep yourself from the love of money is to practice the discipline of giving it away. Use your riches to help others. Be generous in giving to your church, your missionaries, worthy ministries and charities. Instead of selling something you no longer need, find someone who has a need and give the item away.

By giving money and possessions away, you will discover the joy of open-handed generosity and store up treasure in heaven.

## About the New Covenant

The Bible is divided into two major sections. There is the Hebrew Bible, called the "Old Testament," and the Greek Bible, called the "New Testament," or more correctly, "The New Covenant." The "Old" Covenant was established at Mt. Sinai when Moses sprinkled the blood of a sacrifice on the people and said, "Behold the blood of the covenant, which the LORD has made with you in accordance with all these words" (Exod. 24:8). While this is usually referred to as the "old" covenant, the writer of Hebrews prefers the term, "first covenant" (Heb. 8:7, 9:1), avoiding implications often associated with something considered "old." The "new" covenant was established when Jesus offered Himself as a sacrifice for the sins of the world saying, "This cup which is poured out for you is the New Covenant in My blood" (Lk. 22:20). The second half of our Bible is named for the "New Covenant" which Jesus inaugurated by His death (Heb. 8:6).

The provisions of the New Covenant were revealed by the Prophets in the Hebrew Bible. Jeremiah and Ezekiel prophesied that although the people of Israel had broken the covenant and would go into exile, God would renew His special relationship under the provisions of a "new" covenant. These provisions are elaborated in Ezekiel 36:25-28 (see also Jer. 31:31-34, Isa. 55:3, 61:8-9) and are ultimately secured for God's people through the person and work of Jesus, Israel's Messiah. The New Covenant provides the following:

1. Spiritual cleansing and forgiveness of sin. "I will sprinkle clean water on you" (Ezek. 36:25, Jer. 31:34, 1 Jn. 1:9).
2. Spiritual rebirth regenerating the soul. "I will give you a new heart and put a new spirit within you" (Ezek. 36:26, Titus 3:5).
3. The indwelling ministry of the Holy Spirit. "I will put My Spirit within you" (Ezek. 36:27, Jn. 14:17).
4. Empowerment for godly living. "I will...cause you to walk in My statutes, and you will be careful to observe My ordinances" (Ezek. 36:27, Jer. 31:33, Rom. 8:4-5).
5. A vital relationship with the living God. "So you will be My people,

and I will be your God" (Ezek. 36:28, Jer. 31:33-34, Jn. 1:12).

While the New Covenant is said to be made with "the house of Israel and with the house of Judah" (Jer. 31:31), Paul taught that believing Gentiles are heirs to the promises of God on the basis of their faith in Jesus (Gal. 3:14,29; Rom. 4:16). Participation in the New Covenant by faith enables believing Gentiles to share in the rich spiritual heritage of the people of Israel. Those who were once "separate from Christ, excluded from the commonwealth of Israel, and strangers to the covenants of promise, having no hope and without God in the world" have been "brought near" by the blood of Christ (Eph. 2:12-13). As a result, believing Gentiles "are no longer strangers and aliens," but "fellow-citizens with the saints, and are of God's household" (Eph. 2:19). Together, believing Jews and believing Gentiles are one people of God.

So significant is the New Covenant in relationship to Christian life and ministry that the Apostle Paul by the Spirit of God is pleased to call the followers of Jesus "ministers of a New Covenant" (2 Cor. 3:6). And unlike the Old Covenant with its passing glory (2 Cor. 3:7,11), the New Covenant is characterized by the Hebrew Prophets as "everlasting" (Isa. 55:3, Jer. 32:40, Ezek. 16:60, 37:26). In Christ, the followers of Jesus are "new creations" (2 Cor. 5:17) enjoying the blessings of a "New Covenant" (2 Cor. 3:6), on a journey to a New Jerusalem (Rev. 21:2) and anticipating the day when God will make "all things new" (Rev. 21:5).

# About Obedience

In 1886 a young man was attending one of Dwight Moody's famous revival meetings in Brockton, Massachusetts. During the meeting he rose and said, "I'm not quite sure, but I am going to trust, and I am going to obey." Having received a letter about this man's testimony, J. H. Sammis, a Presbyterian minister, composed a refrain which provided the theme of the now classic hymn. "Trust and obey, for there's no other way to be happy in Jesus, but to trust and obey." This refrain captures in a few words a central theme of Paul's writings, indeed the message of the Bible.

Not only did Paul challenge Jews and Gentiles to trust in the Savior and Messiah, Jesus, but he called them to obedience. The Greek word for obedience (*hupakoe*) is derived from the words "under" (*hupo*) and "to hear" (*akouo*) and can be literally translated "to hear under." The noun "obedience" and the verb "to obey" means to listen attentively and respond with submission to the one in authority. Obedience is not always easy. Most people don't like to be told what to do. Yet obedience to authority is a biblical concept that believers are called to embrace.

First and foremost, all people are called "to obey" the gospel (2 Thess. 1:8), to hear and respond to the message of salvation through Jesus. Paul refers to a person's response to the gospel as "obedience of faith" (Rom. 16:26). Those who have believed in Jesus are called to obey Him. Paul told the Corinthians to "take every thought captive to the obedience of Christ" (2 Cor. 10:5). They are to "obey the truth" as taught and preached by Paul (Gal. 5:7). Paul also encouraged believers to obey church elders and those in spiritual leadership (1 Cor. 11:1; 15:15-16; 2 Tim. 2:25; Titus 2:15).

Paul also directed believers to obey authorities in civil leadership, including the kings, governors and tax collectors (Rom. 13:1-7; Titus 3:1). Paul called for servants to obey those who are your masters (Titus 2:9), "not by way of eye-service as men-pleasers, but as servants of Christ, doing the will of God from the heart" (Eph. 6:5-6). This would have application today in the employer-employee relationship. Workers are to obey the boss. If they can't do so, they should resign and find a more suitable job. This isn't always easy, for workers are dependent on their wages to provide for their families. When a worker's union enters the picture, the relationship between the employer and employee gets complicated. Which boss are workers called to obey, the company foreman or the union boss? I believe that the one who owns the business and pays the worker's salary is the one employees should obey.

There is also an order of authority within the family that Paul calls believers to recognize. Children are to obey their parents (Eph. 6:1,3; Col. 3:20). Paul appeals to the Hebrew Bible (Exodus 20:12) to support his claim that "this is right." And he confirms the Old Testament anticipation of a long and well-lived life for those who have learned from their childhood the importance of obedience. In my personal experience, I have found it to be true, that "there's no other way to be happy in Jesus than to trust and obey."

## About the Poor

People living in the first century didn't have social security, unemployment insurance, low income housing, food banks or any of the public assistance available today to help people in a time of financial crisis. What could the 1st century poor do in their time of need? Who could they look to for help when their pantry was empty and their children were hungry? We discover from the Book of Acts that the followers of Jesus reached out to help one another when they encountered persecution-induced poverty. Luke records that "there was not a needy person among them, for all who were owners of land or houses would sell them and bring the proceeds of the sales and lay them at the apostles' feet, and they would be distributed to each as any had need" (Acts 4:34-35). When a prophet announced the coming of a "great famine," the church at Antioch gathered a collection to provide financial relief for their impoverished brethren living in Judea. Paul and Barnabas were appointed to deliver that gift to the church in Jerusalem.

In his letter to the Galatians, Paul recounts his visit and how the leaders of the Jerusalem church recognized his divine commission to preach the gospel of God's grace to the Gentiles (Gal. 2:6-9). Having received "the right hand of fellowship" from James, Peter, and John, the church leaders asked Paul and Barnabas "to remember the poor" (Gal. 2:10). Paul commented saying, "this very thing I also was eager to do." And Paul was true to his word. Over and over again, we find Paul appealing to the churches to collect funds to assist the poor believers living in Jerusalem (Acts 24:17; Rom. 15:25-27; 1 Cor. 16:1-4). Sharing James' concern for the needs of orphans and widows (Jms. 1:27), Paul instructed Timothy to assist the widows at the church of Ephesus when they encountered financial distress (1 Tim. 5:3-16).

Martin Luther said, "After the preaching of the gospel, the office and charge of a true and faithful pastor is to be mindful of the poor." The question most Christians have is, "How can we wisely and responsibly help the poor and needy?" I have wrestled with this question myself. How should I respond to the person standing by a freeway entrance holding a sign reading, "Anything helps"? It might make me feel better to give them a few dollars, but have I really helped them? Will the money I have donated be spent on food and shelter or on alcohol and drugs? To help the poor responsibly, I give to charitable, Christian ministries which are prepared and equipped to provide food, shelter and clothing to needy people. Portland Rescue Mission and the Union Gospel Mission are examples of such ministries that are staffed and prepared to provide physical and spiritual help. In addition, believers should be sensitive to the Spirit's leading to respond to the needs of friends, family members and neighbors. Jesus said, "You always have the poor with you" (Matt. 26:11), so there will always be opportunities for us to follow Paul's example and Luther's admonition to be "mindful of the poor." Do you know someone who has recently lost their job or suffered a financial setback? What might you do to come alongside them and help?

## About Prayer

Paul was a man of prayer. He believed that God could and would change things through the prayers of His believing people. A good example of Paul's prayers is found in the first chapter of his letter to the Ephesians. Paul began by telling the Ephesian believers that he "never ceased" giving thanks to God for His work in their lives (Eph. 1:17). This is followed by his prayer requests for the Ephesians (1:18-23). Paul prayed that his readers would have a spiritually enlightened heart so that they would "know" (1) the hope of God's calling, (2) their value as God's special people, and (3) the greatness of God's power as demonstrated by the resurrection and exaltation of Jesus.

Paul's second prayer in his letter to the Ephesians begins in chapter three. Paul prayed on his knees, a position that reflects an attitude of reverence for God. His prayer requests (3:16-19) are that the Ephesians would (1) be spiritually strengthened by the Holy Spirit, (2) experience the indwelling ministry of Christ, (3) enjoy a greater comprehension of the multiple and magnificent dimensions of God, and (4) know and appreciate the incomprehensible love of God. Paul concluded his prayer for the Ephesians with a benediction highlighting God's abundant and amazing power to answer his prayer (Eph. 3:20-21). It is interesting and very significant that Paul focused his prayer on *spiritual* rather than physical needs. He didn't pray for someone who was sick, traveling or needed work. While these are legitimate needs and worthy prayer requests, Paul's greatest concern for the Ephesians was in regard to their spiritual lives. How different our spiritual lives might be if we prayed for one another like Paul prayed for the Ephesians?

Another of Paul's prayers is found in his letter to the Colossians who were faced with a heresy which undermined and diminished the truth of Christ and his redemptive work. Paul prayed for the believers that they would be "filled with the full-knowledge [*epignosis*] of His will" (Col. 1:9) so they could grow to spiritual maturity (Col. 1:9). Paul prayed specifically that the Colossians would (1) walk worthily of the Lord, (2) please God in all respects, (3) bear fruit in every good work, (4) grow in their knowledge of God, (5) gain spiritual strength, and (6) grow in joy and thankfulness to God the Father (Col. 1:9-12). Once again we see Paul focused on the spiritual lives of the Colossians rather than a multitude of their physical needs.

Paul not only prayed for others, he asked people to pray for him. He asked the Colossians to pray "that God will open up to us a door for the word so that we may speak forth the mystery of Christ, ... that I would make it clear in the way I ought to speak" (Col. 4:3-4). He asked the Thessalonians, "Brethren, pray for us that the word of the Lord will spread rapidly and be glorified, just as it did also with you" (2 Thess. 3:1). Paul asked the Romans, "Strive together with me in your prayers to God for me, that I may be rescued from those who are disobedient in Judea, and that my service for Jerusalem may prove acceptable to the saints" (Rom.15:31). Finally, Paul asked the Ephesians, "Pray on my behalf, that utterance may be given to me in the opening of my mouth, to make known with boldness the mystery of the gospel" (Eph. 6:19).

Paul believed so sincerely in what could be accomplished through believing prayer that he exhorted the Thessalonian believers to "pray without ceasing" (1 Thess. 5:17). Did Paul expect his readers to spend 24/7 on their knees in prayer? It is helpful to know that the Greek word translated "unceasing" was used in ancient times to describe a cough. When you have a cough, the *tendency* to cough is always present. Paul was encouraging the believers to make prayer such a part of their daily lives that when faced with a problem or an opportunity, the first thing that would come to mind would be, "This is a time for prayer." Paul knew that God could change circumstances and people through prayer.

# About Preaching

I have heard pastors say, "I am not going to preach to you this morning; I just want to share some thoughts." There are appropriate times to "share" one's thoughts, but this is not preaching. Paul was a strong believer in the power of the gospel presented through preaching. The New Testament word for preaching (*kataggello*) means to "announce" or "proclaim" with authority. This word was used in classical Greek of declaring war, announcing a religious festival and proclaiming a king's accession to the throne. Barclay comments that the word always carries with it "weight and authority" (William Barclay, *New Testament Words*, SCM Press, p. 162). This word is used 15 times in the New Testament to refer to the preaching or proclamation of God's truth *with authority*.

Paul and Barnabas "preached" (*kataggello*) the Word of God in the synagogues of Cyprus (Acts 13:5). Paul proclaimed the messiahship of Jesus in the synagogue at Thessalonica (Acts 17:3). What Paul proclaimed was not his private opinions, personal doubts or political views. What Paul proclaimed was the gospel (1 Cor. 9:14). Preaching can be accomplished in a variety of ways—sitting or standing, with a pulpit or without, with PowerPoint slides or printed outlines. But preaching must always bring into focus the person and work of Jesus Christ (Phil. 1:18). Paul wrote to the Colossians saying, "We proclaim Him, admonishing every man and teaching every man with all wisdom, so that we may present every man complete in Christ" (Col. 1:28).

Barclay concludes his study of *kataggello* ("to preach") with this insightful comment: "In the early preaching there was nothing apologetic, nothing diffident, nothing clouded with doubts and misted with uncertainties. It was preaching with authority; and the things preached with authority are still the basis of the message of the preacher today" (*New Testament Words*, SCM Press, p. 164). Paul's 1st century admonition to Timothy is still appropriate for 21st century pastors. He said, "Preach the Word" (1 Tim. 4:2).

# About Predestination

We have come to one of the most controversial topics in biblical theology. Christians have different opinions on the subject of predestination. But what we want to know is, "Did Paul believe in predestination?" What did the apostle teach on this subject?

In his letter to the Ephesians, Paul wrote, "He [God] predestined us to adoption as sons through Jesus Christ to Himself" (Eph. 1:5). A few verses later he added, "We have obtained an inheritance having been predestined according to His purposes who works all things after the counsel of His will" (Eph. 1:11). In Romans 8:29-30, Paul linked predestination with God's foreknowledge. He wrote, "For those whom He foreknew, He also predestined to be conformed to the image of His Son, ... and those whom He predestined, He also called, and those whom He called, he also justified, and those whom He justified, He also glorified" (Rom. 8:29-30). It seems clear from these texts that Paul believed in predestination. But what does this actually mean?

The Greek word translated "predestine" (*proorizo*) literally means "to mark out boundaries beforehand." In Romans 8:29-30 Paul sets forth a leak-proof succession of events that lead from God's divine foreknowledge of believers to their ultimate glorification with Christ in heaven. This is a divinely determined sequence which guarantees that God will get His believing people to their heavenly destination. Predestination certainly appears to be a biblical truth. But where does human freedom fit in?

If God has predestined our lives, do people have freedom of choice to make responsible decisions? I remember hearing a seminary professor say that human "freedom" is actually the *illusion* that we are free to do as we choose. According to this view, there is no freedom. All has been divinely determined. But how does this teaching integrate with what the Bible says about the necessity of making a decision to believe? Jesus invited people, "Come unto me, you who are weary and heavy-laden, and I will give you rest" (Matt. 11:28). He lamented His rejection by the people of Jerusalem saying, "How often I wanted to gather your children together, just as a hen gathers her brood under her wings, and you would not have it" (Lk. 13:34). If people are called or invited to make a decision, there must be human freedom to decide.

An illustration may help us understand how predestination works. Imagine that you have received the gift of a cruise from Seattle, Washington, through Puget Sound, to Anchorage, Alaska. You are thrilled by the opportunity to see the whales and sea life, and you accept the gift. You board the ship on Monday and by Friday you will arrive at the dock in Anchorage. You have complete freedom to walk the deck of the ship, enjoy the delicious food, rise and go to bed whenever it pleases you. But you can't change the course of the ship. It's going to Anchorage. That destination has been determined by the ship's captain. This is something like the biblical doctrine of predestination. God has integrated your life into his perfect, eternal plan. Within the boundaries which God has determined, you have freedom to make decisions about where to live, what job to take, who to marry and what kind of car to drive. But your destination has been sovereignly predetermined. This ship is taking you to heaven. And while He grants freedom for you to make decisions on the journey, God is going to get you safely there.

It is helpful to remember that predestination is a truth designed to give comfort and assurance to believers in the face of difficult and challenging times. This is not a doctrine that people need to understand in order to be saved. It may even leave us with questions about the mystery of God's workings. Nothing in Paul's teaching on predestination contradicts other biblical doctrines about God--His love, His justice and His grace.

# About Prophecy

When most people hear the word "prophecy," they usually think of the rapture, the tribulation and the Second Coming of Jesus. These are certainly prophetic, "last days" events. But the word prophecy is much broader. The Hebrew word for "prophet" means someone who speaks for another. Aaron was a "prophet" as he spoke for Moses to pharaoh (Exod. 7:1-2). The prophets of Israel were people who "spoke" for God, delivering His words to the people of Israel. There were prophets in Paul's day as well.  The famous prophetess, Pythia, spoke for the god Apollo at his temple in Delphi. She would sit on a three-legged stool in the temple and speak words which would be delivered to the people as a message from Apollo. In contrast with the prophetess Pythia, there were true prophets like Agabus who announced "by the Spirit" at Antioch that there would be a great famine throughout the Roman Empire (Acts 11:28). Luke mentions that there were "prophets and teachers" at the church at Antioch (Acts 13:1). Phillip the evangelist had four daughters who were prophetesses (Acts 21:9). Agabus announced by prophecy that

Paul would be arrested in Jerusalem (Acts 21:11). According to the Mosaic law, if someone announced a prophecy that didn't come true, they were to be regarded as a false prophet and subject to the death penalty (Deut. 18:20).

Biblical prophecy is identified by Paul as a spiritual gift (Rom. 12:6; 1 Cor. 12:10). The spiritual gift of prophecy is the divine enablement to speak for God by the ministry of the Holy Spirit. Like the other spiritual gifts listed by Paul in Romans 12 and 1 Corinthians 12, this gift was given by God "for the common good" (1 Cor. 12:7) to enable believers "to serve one another" (1 Pet. 4:10). Paul had a high regard for biblical prophecy and viewed the gift as having great potential to edify the church (1 Cor. 14:1,4).

Because of misuse of the speaking gifts in the church at Corinth, Paul provided the believers with some guidelines on how to use their gifts in such a way that the church would receive edification (1 Cor. 29-35). First, prophecy requires careful evaluation. Is the prophet's message consistent with God's Word and apostolic teaching? Second, interruptions are not permitted. If a prophet is speaking, others who wish to speak must be silent and wait their turn. Third, the prophetic gift must be used for teaching and edification. Fourth, since the Lord is not a God of confusion, prophets must be self-disciplined and under control. Fifth, female prophetesses are to use their prophetic gifts at places designed for prayer (1 Cor. 11:5-16), but not in the meeting of the church (1 Cor. 14:34-35). Paul's fifth regulation is problematic for many churches in our modern culture which affirm egalitarian roles for men and women. But Paul's instructions to the Corinthians are clear and are said to apply "to all the churches of the saints" (1 Cor. 14:33).

There is much debate about whether the gift of prophecy was for the 1st century only during the establishment of the church (Eph. 2:20), or is still a valid gift for the 21st century. Churches which recognize the validity of modern prophecy, should also recognize and adhere to Paul's regulations for the use of this gift.

## About Propitiation

The Bible reveals that God is infinitely holy (Lev.19:2, Isa. 6:3). Divine wrath is His holy and just response to what is contrary to His holiness. This truth is revealed in both the Old and New Testaments.

The prophet Nahum wrote, "The LORD is avenging and wrathful. The LORD takes vengeance on his adversaries. He reserves wrath for His enemies" (Nahum 1:2). Paul acknowledged this in his letter to the Romans, "For the wrath of God is revealed from heaven against all ungodliness and unrighteousness of men who suppress the truth in unrighteousness" (Rom. 1:18).

When the ark of the covenant was returned to Israel after being captured by the Philistines, the men of Beth-Shemesh took advantage of the opportunity to take a peek inside. As a result of violating the sanctity of the holy ark, God "struck the people with a great slaughter" (1 Sam. 6:19). As the people mourned the deaths of so many of their friends and family members, they cried out, "Who is able to stand before the LORD, this holy God" (1 Sam. 6:20). The answer to their question is, "No one." No person is able to stand in the presence of a holy, righteous God. All have sinned and fallen short of God's high and holy standard (Rom. 3:23). All of us are deserving of God's wrath.

Divine wrath is not a popular sermon topic. It is the scary side of God. His wrath is to be feared because we are sinful and stand condemned by our thoughts and actions before a holy and just judge. J. I. Packer helps us understand this attribute with his comment, "God's wrath in the Bible is never the capricious, self-indulgent, morally ignoble thing that human anger so often is. It is, instead, a right and necessary reaction to objective moral evil" (Knowing God, p. 151).

But this is why Paul's teaching on propitiation is so important. The word "propitiation" (hilasterion) means "to expiate, appease or atone for." Propitiation means that God's holy wrath on sin and sinners has been satisfied (1 Jn. 2:2, 4:10). The fire of His anger over sin has been quenched. How does this take place? On the top of the ark of the covenant was a lid where the blood of sacrifices was offered before God (Lev. 16:14). It is usually translated "the mercy seat," but a more accurate term is "the place of propitiation." When the blood of the sacrifice was sprinkled on the ark of the covenant, God's wrath was propitiated. But the Old Testament sacrifices had to be repeated year after year to deter God's wrath. His wrath on sin was never fully or finally satisfied until the coming of Israel's Messiah, Jesus (Heb. 2:17; 10:11-14). Paul explained to the Romans that the blood of Jesus is the "propitiation" for our sins (Rom. 3:25). His sacrifice was full and final. It never has to be repeated.

222

Paul's teaching on propitiation helps us answer the Israelites' question, "Who can stand before a holy God?" The death of Jesus satisfied His holiness, met His justice and averted His wrath. Propitiation enables believing sinners to be forgiven and reconciled with God through the atoning work of Jesus Christ. Joseph Scheumann observed, "In saving us from His own wrath, God has done what we could not do, and He has done what we didn't deserve" ("Five Truths about the Wrath of God," www.desiringGod.org). God's nature has not changed. He is still a God of wrath. But thankfully, God wrath is propitiated for all who believe in Jesus and welcome His atoning work.

## About Questionable Things

When I was growing up in the sixties, there were certain activities of which our church disapproved. These included drinking or selling alcohol, smoking, dancing and going to the movie theater. What struck me as a young person is that I could find nothing in Scripture which prohibited or condemned such activities. These are what we might call "the gray areas." There were "gray areas" in Paul's day as well. When a sheep or bull was sacrificed in a pagan temple, a portion of the meat would be served at a banquet and consumed by invited guests. Some of the meat from the sacrifice could also be sold in the public market. The Corinthian believers were wondering, "Should a follower of Jesus buy and eat meat which had been offered to a false god?" "When invited to the home of a friend, should a follower of Jesus eat meat which has been offered to an idol?" (1 Cor. 8:1-11:1)

The questions we have today are different, but Paul provided some helpful guidelines for the Corinthians which are still relevant for us in the 21st century. When making personal decisions in "the gray areas," the following questions can be helpful in guiding your conscience.

1. Is the activity forbidden by the civil authorities? Paul instructed believers to "be in subjection" to governing authorities and the laws that govern us. He said, "whoever resists authority has opposed the ordinance of God" (Rom. 13:1-2).

2. Does the activity have a good appearance? Paul told the Thessalonians to "abstain from every form [or appearance] of evil" (1 Thess. 5:22). If it looks bad, it probably is.

3. Is this activity commended by my conscience? Paul told the Romans that even unbelievers have a conscience which serves as "the work of the law written in their hearts" (Rom. 2:14-15). If your conscience tells you "No," it is wise to take this as from the Lord.

4. Is this activity profitable or useful? Paul wrote to the Corinthians, "All things are lawful for me, but not all things are profitable (1 Cor. 6:12). If an activity is not going to be helpful, why bother to get involved?

5. Could this activity control or enslave me? Paul wrote, "All things are lawful for me, but I will not be mastered by anything" (1 Cor. 6:12). Even the good things that we eat and drink or the medicines we take could become habitual and detrimental.

6. Might this activity harm my body? Paul questioned the Corinthians, "Or do you not know that your body is the temple of the Holy Spirit who is in you, whom you have from God, and that you are not your own?" (1 Cor. 6:19). If the activity could damage my body, it is probably wise to avoid it.

7. Could this activity cause a brother or sister in Christ to stumble? Paul concluded for himself, "If food causes my brother to stumble, I will never eat meat again, so that I will not cause my brother to stumble" (1 Cor. 8:13). Paul was willing to forego good activities that may cause temptation and hinder the spiritual life of another person.

8. Can this activity glorify God? Paul concluded his comments on the "gray areas," saying, "Whether, then, you eat or drink or whatever you do, do all to the glory of God" (1 Cor. 10:31). If your participation in the activity can magnify God's reputation in the eyes of other people, it is probably a good thing which God has created for His people to enjoy.

## About the Rapture

The Apostle Paul believed in the rapture, although he never used this particular word. The word "rapture" is actually derived from the

Latin *rapio*. The Greek word that Paul used to refer to this prophetic event is *harpazo*, "to catch up or snatch away." Paul used this word in 1 Thess. 4:17 to describe how after the dead in Christ are raised, the living believers will be "caught up" (or "raptured") to meet Christ in the air. After a glorious reunion with the believers who have gone before them, Paul prophesied, "So shall we always be with the Lord." Paul intended for his teaching about the rapture to be a comfort to believers who have lost loved ones (1 Thess. 4:18). Many religions include some teaching about afterlife. But Christians have a solid basis for their belief in life after death based on the resurrection of Jesus and the clear teaching of the Apostle Paul. God has planned a great reunion of the followers of Jesus. And that reunion will take place at the rapture of the church.

Paul's teaching about the rapture is clear from Scripture, but there is considerable debate about the timing of this prophetic event. Will it take place before, during or after the seven-year Tribulation predicted by Daniel and revealed in greater detail in the book of Revelation (Rev. 6-19)? Paul refers to this period as "the Day of the Lord" and describes how God will deal differently with believers and unbelievers in relationship to this future event (1 Thess. 5:1-11). A key to his teaching is to understand that divine wrath (*orge*) is a major characteristic of the Tribulation. This period of judgment is described as a day of "wrath." During this Tribulation period, unbelievers will cry out to the mountains and rocks, "Fall on us and hide us from the presence of Him who sits on the throne, and from the *wrath* of the Lamb, for the great day of their *wrath* has come and who is able to stand?" (Rev. 6:16-17). The Apostle John wrote of the last seven Tribulation judgments, "with them the *wrath* of God is finished" (Rev. 15:1).

This background is helpful when one considers Paul's teaching about the rapture in First Thessalonians. Paul looked expectantly for the coming of Christ "who delivers us from the *wrath* to come" (1 Thess. 1:10). Paul later declared that "God has not destined us for *wrath*, but for obtaining salvation through our Lord Jesus Christ" (5:9). The "salvation" referred to in this context is not soteriological, for the Thessalonians were already saved. As in Acts 7:25, the word "salvation" is used in this context to refer to physical deliverance. Paul made it clear to the Thessalonians that while unbelievers "will not escape" from God's coming wrath (1 Thess. 5:3), believers will be delivered (1 Thess. 5:9). Deliverance from the wrath of the Tribulation will be realized when believers are "caught up" (1 Thess. 4:17) from the earth to be with the Lord and with all of God's people forever!

## About Reconciliation

"Reconciliation" (*katallage*) denotes "a change on the part of one party, induced by an action on the part of another" (*Vine's Expository Dictionary of NT Words,* p. 934). Paul wrote to the Roman believers that, in the past, they had been hostile to God and were counted as His "enemies," but now they "have been reconciled to God through the death of His Son" (Rom. 5:10). Reconciliation means that hostilities have ceased. Those who were formerly enemies have become friends.

You may have read about the celebration and rejoicing that took place when it was announced that World War II had ended. Church bells rang. People danced in the streets. My mother recalled the fire trucks in her small town in Georgia giving rides to people up and down main street.

Paul must have felt a similar emotion over the truth that he and the Romans were no longer God's enemies. He wrote, "We also exult in God through our Lord Jesus Christ through whom we have received the reconciliation" (Rom. 5:11).

It is wonderful to be reconciled with God, but it is not a secret to keep to oneself. Paul explained to the Corinthians that God has entrusted the followers of Jesus with "the word of reconciliation" (2 Cor. 5:19). Proclaiming the gospel means announcing to the world that through Jesus' death on the cross, God is willing to "lay down his arms," accept our surrender and no longer regard us as His enemies. This is what Paul's ministry was all about. To unbelievers throughout the Roman world, Paul said, "We are ambassadors for Christ as though God were making an appeal through us; we beg you on behalf of Christ, be reconciled to God" (2 Cor. 5:20).

People around the world are hoping, wishing and searching for peace—peace in the Middle East, peace in Asia and peace in our nation's cities. More important than all this is personal peace with God which is now available for all who believe in Jesus. Paul wrote, "Therefore, having been justified by faith, we have peace with God through our Lord Jesus Christ" (Rom. 5:1).

# About Rejoicing

In spite of the hardships and suffering Paul experienced in his life and ministry, he was full of the joy of the Lord. During Paul's imprisonment in Rome, his circumstances limited his ministry. Other preachers were stepping up and taking Paul's opportunities. Paul might have complained, become unhappy or even envious. Yet even though he questioned the motives of some of these preachers, Paul was able to say, "In this I rejoice."

Many people have wondered about how someone can rejoice when their circumstances are unfavorable and difficult. They key is to recognize the difference between "joy" and "happiness." Happiness is a feeling that is dependent on circumstances. When things go well for us, we are "happy." But it is not possible to "be happy" all the time when we live in a fallen world with sickness, pain and disappointment. That's where joy takes over. Joy is deeply rooted in a relationship with God through Jesus.

The followers of Jesus can have joy knowing that their sins are forgiven and that they have been adopted into God's family. In spite of the trials we encounter here on earth, believers in Jesus are heading for a glorious, heavenly future. Happiness is dependent on circumstances, while joy is dependent on Jesus. That is why Paul could rejoice even though he may not have been happy about his imprisonment.

Paul set a good example for us by rejoicing during hard circumstances; and he encourages believers to do the same. He wrote to the Philippians, "I rejoice and share my joy with you. You too, rejoice in the same way, and share your joy with me." Paul wanted the Philippians to "rejoice in the Lord" (Phil. 3:1), recognizing His sovereignty over their circumstances and finding their ultimate joy in Him. In Philippians 4:4, Paul repeats the imperative by way of emphasis, "Rejoice in the Lord always; again I will say, rejoice." He repeated this command to the Thessalonians in one of the shortest verses in the Bible, "Rejoice always!"

By God's grace and through the power of the Holy Spirit, we can keep on rejoicing, knowing that God is good and that He cares for us no matter what the circumstances.

# About Revelation

God did not want to leave humanity in spiritual darkness, so He gave us divine revelation. Paul believed that God had revealed Himself to humanity in such a clear and irrefutable manner that there was no excuse for not believing in Him. The Greek verb "reveal" (*apokalupto*) means "to uncover or unveil." The noun, "revelation," refers to what has been uncovered or revealed. The word *apokalupsis* is actually the name of the last book of the Bible, "Revelation."

Paul believed that God had revealed Himself, both His existence and attributes, through creation. He explained to the believers at Rome, "For since the creation of the world His invisible attributes, His eternal power and divine nature, have been clearly seen, being understood through what has been made, so that they are without excuse" (Rom. 1:20). This *general* revelation "unveils" God's existence and makes all people accountable before Him. Beyond this general revelation, God has provided humanity with *special* revelation through His Word, the Bible. Paul frequently appealed to Scripture as the truth of God revealed in the Gospel. He declared to the Romans, "For I am not ashamed of the gospel,... For in it the righteousness of God is revealed" (Rom. 1:16-17, Hab. 2:4). In addition to the special revelation of Scripture, God has revealed Himself in the person of Jesus, Israel's Messiah. On Paul's way to Damascus to arrest Christians, God revealed the Messiah to him. When Paul heard the voice speaking to Him and asked, "Who are You, Lord?", he received the answer, "I am Jesus whom you are persecuting" (Acts 9:5; Gal. 1:16).

After his life-changing encounter with Jesus, God revealed to Paul something that had not been previously disclosed in the Hebrew Scriptures, the union of Jews and Gentiles in one body in Christ (Eph. 3:1-6). Paul referred to the prophecy of Agabus about the coming famine as "a revelation" of God's guidance (Gal. 2:2; also 1 Cor. 14:6,26). Paul believed that there would be additional revelation in the prophetic future—the revelation of the "lawless one" (2 Thess. 2:3,6,8), the revelation of Jesus Christ at His second coming (2 Thess. 1:7), the revelation of the true value of our Christian service (1 Cor. 3:13), and the revelation of the believer's future glory (Rom. 8:17-18).

# About Resurrection

The resurrection of Jesus, and the future resurrection of His followers, is one of the principal teachings of the Apostle Paul and biblical Christianity. I recall a television special which featured a theologian who said, "Whether or not Jesus actually rose from the grave is not essential to the Christian faith." Obviously, he had not been reading Paul! In the Apostle's sermon in the synagogue at Antioch, Paul preached that after Jesus had died and was laid in a tomb, "God raised Him from the dead" (Acts 13:30). Paul went on to explain that the resurrection of Jesus was in fulfillment of God's promise to raise Israel's Messiah as recorded by the Prophets (Ps. 2:7; 16:10, Isa. 55:3). Paul viewed the resurrection as an essential element of the "good news." Although some of his listeners scoffed at the idea (Acts 17:32), Paul never compromised his teaching or changed his view to accommodate his message to naturalistic thinking or cultural norms.

One of the problems in the Corinthian church was that some people were questioning the doctrine of the resurrection. These may have been young believers who were swayed by Greek philosophy which viewed death as liberation from the physical body and that resurrection would constitute a return to bondage. Or they may have been Jewish believers who had been influenced by the teachings of the Sadducees who denied life after death (Matt. 22:23-33; Josephus, *The Jewish War* 2.154-57). Paul responded to this false teaching in his letter to the Corinthians by establishing the fact of Jesus' resurrection (1 Cor. 15:1-11). He pointed out that not only was Jesus raised on the third day, but that he appeared to Peter, James, the eleven apostles and to more than five hundred of His followers at one time. Citing his own experience, Paul said, "He appeared to me also" (1 Cor. 15:8).

Having declared the certainty of Jesus' resurrection, Paul went on to explain to the Corinthians the logical consequences of denying this essential doctrine (1 Cor. 15:12-19). If there is no truth to the resurrection, (1) the Messiah would not be raised, (2) Paul's preaching would be pointless, (3) the Corinthian's faith would be void of reality, (4) the apostles would be false witnesses, (5) the Corinthians would still be unsaved, (6) the dead in Christ have perished, (7) the hope of believers is limited to this earthly life, and

(8) Christians are to be most pitied for having lived with a resurrection hope which will never be realized.

Having shown the consequences of denying the resurrection, Paul triumphantly affirmed this crucial truth. He wrote, "But now Christ has been raised from the dead (1 Cor. 15:20). Paul then explained to the Corinthians that because of the solidarity between Jesus and the believers, His resurrection must result in their own. Because Jesus is the "first fruit" of the resurrection (Lev. 23:10-11), His resurrection means that there are more to come. Because Jesus has been raised, God's program for resurrection has begun (Dan. 12:2). This resurrection program will include *all* who have placed their trust in Jesus, Israel's promised Messiah. Because of the resurrection, believers can be confident that their labors for Christ and His kingdom are not fruitless. Their hope in the Lord is *not* in vain (1 Cor. 15:58).

# About Rights

We hear a lot of talk these days about a person's "rights." Americans cherish the "rights" of free speech, freedom of assembly, freedom of the press and more. People are often encouraged to "assert their rights." Political activists often appeal to the courts to secure their "rights." Paul recognized that Christians have rights as well. But Paul sets an example for us as one who didn't demand his "rights."

The Greek word translated "rights" (*exousia*) denotes the freedom and authority to act. Paul explained to the Thessalonians that during his time of ministry among them, he labored night and day to avoid being a financial burden on the congregation of new believers. Although Paul had the "right" to receive financial support for his ministry, he didn't assert this right. Instead, he worked with his hands (see Acts 18:3) as a model and example to others (2 Thess. 3:8-9). In a similar context, Paul explained to the Corinthians that he had the "right" to refrain from working a secular job and receive financial support for his service to the church (1 Cor. 9:4-6). He even appealed to Scripture in support of this right (Deut. 25:4) and the instructions of Jesus that "those who proclaim the gospel [are] to get their living from the gospel" (1 Cor. 9:14). But Paul yielded his right to financial support to avoid any possible "hindrance to the gospel of Christ" (1 Cor. 9:12).

What we learn from the Apostle Paul's teaching on "rights" is that it is sometimes in the best interest of God's kingdom work to forego our rights in sacrificial service and loving concern for others. While believers have the freedom in Christ to assert their rights, doing so may be selfish and self-serving. Instead, Paul exhorted the Galatian believers, "through love, serve one another" (Gal. 5:13). Jesus is the ultimate example of one who yielded his rights and prerogatives out of sacrificial service to others (Jn. 13:13-15). It is not easy to yield our rights. But kingdom interests may sometimes require it.

# About Righteousness

Righteousness is the character or quality of being right. In the biblical sense, "righteousness" refers to one's "conformity to the Divine will in purpose, thought and action" (G. Abbott-Smith, *A Manual Greek Lexicon of the NT,* p. 116). The Bible teaches that God is righteous (Ezra 9:15; Ps. 116:5). This means that God's character always leads Him to do what is right and just. In contrast with God, people are unrighteous. Paul quoted a number of passages from the Hebrew Bible to prove this to his Roman readers, "There is none righteous, not even one" (Rom. 3:9-18). He summed up his point in Romans 3:23, "For all have sinned and fall short of the glory of God." So, the big question in Paul's day (and in ours as well) was, "How can unrighteous people have any kind of a relationship with a holy, righteous God?"

Many Jews of the first century believed that righteousness could be gained through prayer, piety and good works. But Paul was convinced that even our very best efforts and unselfishly motivated good works could never be sufficient to satisfy God and secure access into His holy presence. Since righteousness was unattainable by keeping the law or gaining sufficient merit, there had to be another way. What Paul taught in his proclamation of the gospel is that the righteousness of Christ is imparted to believing sinners on the basis of faith. Paul cited Abraham as a prime example of God's provision of righteousness through faith. Quoting from Genesis 15:6, Paul wrote, "Abraham believed God and it was credited to him as righteousness"

231

(Rom. 4:3). The same principle of "faith righteousness" applied to King David (Rom. 4:6-8) and extends to *all* ungodly people as well.

Since Jesus is perfectly righteous and people are totally sinners, God, though His grace, offers an exchange. For those who believe (or trust) in Jesus, God takes their sin and transfers it to Jesus (2 Cor. 5:21). Then God takes Christ's righteousness and transfers it to the sinner's account (Rom. 4:11). Jesus gets our sin, for which He was judged on the cross. We get His righteousness by grace and through faith. The Corinthians were a prime example of God's great exchange. Paul wrote, "Do you not know that the unrighteous cannot inherit the kingdom of God?" (1 Cor. 6:9). Then he listed the multitude of sins of which they themselves were guilty. Paul then concluded, "Such were some of you; but you were washed, but you were sanctified, but you were justified in the name of the Lord Jesus Christ" (1 Cor. 6:11). Righteousness is God's gift of grace, secured for us through the saving work of Jesus Christ. Have you received that gift?

## About Rulers

Emperors, kings, governors, magistrates, prefects, and judges ruled over the citizens of the Roman Empire as well as over the people of Israel. The word "ruler" (*achon*) refers to one who is "first" in authority and has the position of "chief." The word served as the title of the chief magistrates who ruled and governed Athens. It is not always easy living under someone else's authority. What did Paul have to say about those who rule?

Paul taught that the followers of Jesus must live "in subjection to the governing authorities" since they have been placed in their positions by God (Rom. 13:1). He added that to resist those whom God has placed in positions of authority is to oppose "the ordinance of God" (Rom. 13:2). Making practical application of this point, Paul further explained to the Romans that living in submission to those in authority includes paying taxes (Rom. 13:7). Both Peter and Paul called for believers to "honor" their rulers (Rom. 13:7; 1 Pet. 2:17). This includes the idea of respect as demonstrated by words and actions.

During Paul's hearing before the Jewish Sanhedrin, the high priest ordered someone standing nearby "to strike him on the mouth"

232

(Acts 23:2). When Paul rebuked the high priest, calling him "a whitewashed wall," a bystander questioned, "Do you revile God's high priest" (Acts 23:4). Paul then apologized saying, "I was not aware, brethren, that he was the high priest; for it is written, 'You shall not speak evil of a ruler of your people'" (Acts 23:5; Exod. 22:28).

Since kings and rulers are subject to human failings and sin, they need our prayers. Paul instructed Timothy to pray "for kings and all who are in authority" (1 Tim. 2:1-2). What should we pray for our leaders? First and foremost, we should pray for their salvation. Paul wrote that God desires "all people to be saved" (1 Tim. 2:4). We should also pray for their wisdom in leadership and decision-making, which may lead to a more "tranquil and quiet life" for us as citizens (1 Tim. 2:2). It is not easy to pray for people whose political views and policies you disagree with. But it is encouraging to remember that prayer can change things, including people.

# About Sanctification

In addition to being forgiven, redeemed and justified, Paul taught that believers are in the process of being sanctified. The word "to sanctify" (*hagiazo*) means "to set part." The word was used of the gold that adorned the temple and the gifts placed on the altar. These things were *set apart* from common use for a special purpose. A potter could make from the same lump of clay a cooking pot and a vessel for the temple. The vessel for the temple was "sanctified," set apart for a special, holy purpose. Sanctification is an important part of every believer's spiritual journey.

According to the teaching of Paul, there are three aspects of a believer's sanctification. The first is *positional* sanctification. This takes place when a person comes to faith in Jesus, is forgiven of their sins and is "set apart" as holy before God. Even though the Corinthian believers had many shortcomings and were struggling spiritually, Paul addressed them as "saints," literally "holy ones" (1 Cor. 1:2). Paul never referred to believers as "sinners." He always addressed them as "saints," because they had been set apart as holy before God (Rom. 1:7; 2 Cor. 1:1; Eph. 1:1). The second aspect of sanctification is *experiential*. This is the process of conforming a believer's experience in life to their position as "saints" in Christ. Paul prayed that the Thessalonians, who had been saved, would now be sanctified (1 Thess. 5:23). The third aspect of the sanctifying process is *ultimate* or final sanctification. This refers to that day when sanctification is complete and believers are presented as blameless before the Lord "having no spot or wrinkle" (Eph. 5:27).

As believers, we have become saints and we will in some future day be completely glorified. But Paul was very interested to encourage the present, experiential aspect of sanctification and devoted three chapters in Romans to this important subject. In Romans 5, Paul taught that there are two spiritual families—the family of Adam (sinners) and the family of Jesus (saints). In Romans 6-8 Paul encouraged the believers to live in light of their new family, not in light of their old ancestry.

Paul began explaining present sanctification by emphasizing a believer's identification with Christ and His death (Rom. 6:3). Paul used the image of baptism as a picture of a change of identity— separated from their old life by death and resurrected to new life in Christ (Rom. 6:3-5). Having considered these facts, Paul exhorted the believers to act accordingly. He said, "Even so consider yourselves to be dead to sin, but alive to God in Christ Jesus" (Rom. 6:11). The word "consider" (*logizomai*) means "to number or calculate." Paul was saying in essence, "Calculate what is true about you and live like the person you are, not the person you once were."

Paul proceeded in Romans 6:12-23 to explain that sanctification involves a decision resulting in action. Paul exhorted, "Stop yielding your body to the reign of sin, and present yourself to God for His service and righteousness" (Rom. 6:12-14). According to Paul, whatever a person submits to becomes their master. In the past, the Romans were slaves to sin, resulting in death. Now as believers, they must make a clean break from their old master, sin, and place themselves under the authority of Christ and His righteousness (Rom. 6:16-19).

In Romans 7, Paul dealt with the problem of a believer's relationship to the law which often seems to stimulate our "flesh" and lead to sin. Paul emphasized that while God's law is "holy, righteous and good" (Rom. 7:12-14), trying to live by the law results in an inner conflict with our "flesh." Our "flesh" refers to the physical desires of our human body, which are in conflict with our deepest and truest self, the new person we are in Christ. At the end of chapter 7, Paul cries out, "Wretched man that I am! Who will set me free from the body of this death?" The answer is found in the next chapter of Romans.

In Romans 8, Paul taught that sanctification in this life is accomplished by Christ's work and the Spirit's power. Paul begins by reminding believers of their justification through faith in the saving work of Jesus. This is the starting point for sanctification. Paul explained that what the law could not do, the indwelling Holy Spirit accomplishes by His power. Paul wrote that "the requirement [literally, "righteousness"] of the law is fulfilled in us, who do not walk according to the flesh but according to the Spirit" (Rom. 8:4). The process of sanctification in this life takes place as believers yield to God's will and conform to His Word by the enabling power of the Holy Spirit. By this process, our experience in this life is brought into greater conformity to our position as "saints" in Christ. Sanctification is a lifetime process with setbacks along the way. But the powerful and enabling work of the Holy Spirit will get the job done.

## About Satan

It may seem to be out of date and old fashioned to believe in Satan. The devil or Satan is often featured as a fanciful character in cartoons and humorous stories. But Paul believed in Satan and mentioned him (or the devil) 15 times in his writings. Every New Testament writer and 19 of the 26 New Testament books make reference to this evil, spirit being. Paul warned believers that Satan is a serious enemy of God and His people.

Paul didn't tell us anything about Satan's origin or beginnings. His name, *Satan,* appears in the Hebrew Bible (Job 2:1) and means "accuser" or "adversary." The term "devil" (*diabolos*), from the Greek word, "to accuse" or "malign," is another designation for this spiritual enemy. Sometime in past antiquity, Satan fell into condemnation, perhaps as a result of pride (1 Tim. 3:6). Since that time, he has been gathering a following to establish a counterfeit kingdom over which he intends to rule. Paul warned the Corinthians that Satan could "take advantage" of believers by his schemes and tempt them to follow him in sinning against the true and rightful King of the universe (1 Cor. 7:5; 2 Cor. 2:11). When and wherever Christians are at work advancing God's kingdom, Satan will be there too, seeking to hinder and thwart their ministry (1 Thess. 2:18). And while we often imagine

Satan as appearing dark and dangerous, Paul said that he "disguises himself as an angel of light" (2 Cor. 11:14) to give the impression of being worthy and inviting. It must have grieved Paul to know that some who had professed to be followers of Jesus had "turned aside to follow Satan" (1 Tim. 5:15).

Being aware of Satan's schemes, Paul warned the Ephesians not to "give the devil an opportunity" for easy access into their lives (Eph. 4:27). Paul explained to the Ephesians how God has provided spiritual armor to enable believers to "stand firm" against Satan, including the forces of darkness and spiritual wickedness (Eph. 6:11-12). Although the battle with Satan is real, our defense in Christ is stronger. Paul encouraged the Corinthians that there is a "way of escape" from every temptation we face. He wrote, "No temptation has overtaken you but such as is common to man; and God is faithful; who will not allow you to be tempted beyond what you are able, but with the temptation will provide a way of escape also, so that you will be able to endure it" (1 Cor. 10:13).

Although Satan's evil schemes and wicked pursuits will increase as the return of Jesus comes nearer (2 Thess. 2:9), Paul announced to the Romans that his fate is sealed. Paul wrote, "The God of peace will soon crush Satan under your feet" (Rom. 16:20). Although Satan is alive and well on planet earth, we have nothing to fear from this doomed enemy as we "stand strong in the Lord and the strength of His might" (Eph. 6:10).

## About Scripture

What is your ultimate authority? Many people look to science, philosophy or psychology to answer the ultimate questions of life. This was as true in antiquity as it is in the 21st century. The Apostle Paul took a different view. For Paul, Scripture was the ultimate authority because it constitutes the very words of God.

Paul's appreciation of the authority of Scripture is evidenced by how he used it in his preaching. In his sermon at Antioch (Acts 13:16-47), Paul appealed to the Hebrew Bible to demonstrate that Jesus' resurrection fulfilled messianic prophecy (Ps. 2:7, 16:10; Isa. 55:3; Hab. 1:5). He appealed to Scripture to prove that all people are sinners and need a Savior (Rom. 3:10-18). He quoted Genesis 15:6 to show that Abraham was declared righteous by faith (Rom. 4:1-5).

Paul quoted Scripture to explain Israel's unbelief (Acts 28:25-27; Rom. 11:7-10) and how Gentiles come to be included in the family of God (Rom. 9:24-26; Gal. 3:6-9). Paul repeatedly used the phrase, "Scripture says," to support the doctrines he taught.

In Paul's second letter to Timothy, he warned of the spiritual decline and anti-God attitude which would characterize the last days. He believed that the truth of divinely inspired Scripture was sufficient to guide us through such times. Paul declared, "All Scripture is inspired by God and profitable for teaching, for reproof, for correction, for training in righteousness" so that the people of God can be prepared for whatever challenges they may encounter (2 Tim. 3:16-17). The word translated "inspired" (*theopneustos*) literally means "God-breathed." Scripture is the "breathing out" of God's truth. It is alive with the life and vitality of God Himself (Heb. 4:12). Paul's words "all Scripture" include both the Old and New Testaments as evidenced by his appeal to both in 1 Timothy 5:18 (Deut. 25:4; Lk. 10:7). Since all Scripture is "God-breathed," then we can be assured that it is an accurate record of divine revelation and can be trusted in all that it teaches.

After recounting a number of Old Testament stories in his letter to the Corinthians, Paul wrote, "Now these things happened to them as an example, and they were written for our instruction" (1 Cor. 10:11). Paul further explained to Timothy that Scripture was given to instruct disciples, refute heresy, correct the confused and train believers in godly conduct (2 Tim. 3:16). The ultimate goal of Scripture is to make the followers of Jesus proficient for ministry and equipped to serve God (2 Tim. 3:17).

The original manuscripts of the New Testament are no longer available to us. But we do have ancient copies that date from as early as the 4th and 5th centuries. Most Christians are not trained to read ancient Greek manuscripts and must rely on translations. You might be wondering if these translations can be relied on as divinely inspired Scripture? Or does "Scripture" refer only to the original Hebrew or Greek manuscripts?

The quality of a Bible translation depends on the training of the translators, their textual decisions, and their translation theory. No translation is perfect. But imperfections in translation do not deny the true character of God's Word. A Ford automobile with a broken headlight is still a Ford. The president's speech is always the president's speech—even when clumsily translated into a foreign language. A Bible translation *is* the Word of God. The true character of God's inspired Word is not lost in translation.

# About the Second Coming

Paul believed that Jesus, Israel's Messiah, was coming again. My study of Paul's teaching on eschatology (the doctrine of "last things"), leads me to believe that the return of Jesus will take place in two stages. Jesus will return first at the Rapture to remove His followers from the earth. Then, after a period of wrath called the Tribulation, Jesus will return to the earth to destroy the "lawless one" (anti-Christ) and establish His earthly kingdom. There are four texts which reveal Paul's understanding of Jesus' Second Coming: 1 Thess. 4:13-18; 1 Thess. 5:1-11; 2 Thess. 1:3-13 and 2 Thess. 2:1-12. The Greek word Paul used for the Second Coming is *parousia*, translated "coming." This is the same word used by the disciples in their question which led to Jesus' teaching the Olivet Discourse, "What will be the sign of your coming (*parousia*) and of the end of the age?" (Matt. 24:3). Jesus used this word three times in answering the disciples question (Matt. 24:27,37,39).

At His Second Coming, Jesus will return from heaven where He has been preparing an eternal home for His followers (Jn. 14:3). He will be accompanied by His "mighty angels" (2 Thess. 1:7) who will gather believers from the four corners of the earth (Matt. 24:31). The coming of Jesus will be heralded by a loud "trumpet call" (1 Thess. 4:16, Matt. 24:31). The living saints will then be "caught up" in the clouds to meet the Lord in the air (1 Thess. 4:17).

The coming of Jesus for His people will be followed by what Paul calls "the day of the Lord" (1 Thess. 5:2). This day of eschatological judgment was a major theme developed by the Prophets (Joel 1:15, Zeph. 1:7; 2:14-16). This period of inescapable judgment will come unexpectedly, "like a thief in the night" (1 Thess. 5:2-3). Paul assured believers that they will not have to endure this future judgment since their salvation through Jesus has delivered them from God's wrath (1 Thess. 5:9).

Paul encouraged the believers in 2 Thessalonians that in spite of the persecution and afflictions they were enduring, "relief" was coming! Paul promised that persecution would cease "when the Lord Jesus shall be revealed from heaven…dealing out retribution to those who do not know God" (2 Thess. 1:7-8). Although they were given a chance to repent during the tribulation, the refusal of unbelievers to acknowledge the Messiah and Savior, leaves them with no other means of deliverance from God's coming wrath. "The penalty of eternal destruction, away from the presence of the Lord" (2 Thess. 1:9) is their sad and ultimate destiny.

The Second Coming of Jesus will also terminate the career of "the man of lawlessness…the son of destruction" (2 Thess. 2:3). Also known as anti-Christ, Paul describes him as exalting "himself above every so-called god or object of worship" (2 Thess. 2:4). Taking his seat in Israel's future temple, he will display himself "as being God" (2 Thess. 2:5). This anti-Christ, anti-God figure is associated with the activity of Satan, who will be making his last attempt to thwart God's kingdom rule and establish his own counterfeit empire. But the "man of lawlessness" will meet his doom with the coming (*parousia*) of Jesus, destroyed "with the breath of His mouth" (2 Thess. 2:8). The return of Jesus will be followed by the culmination of His kingdom rule in fulfillment of messianic prophecy (2 Sam. 7:16). For further discussion on the return of Jesus, see "About the Rapture."

# About Sin

We don't hear a lot of preaching about sin these days. Since most people don't like to think of themselves as sinners, sermons about sin don't usually receive positive accolades. But Paul wasn't hesitant to speak about this important subject. If it weren't for sin, there would be no need for a Savior.

The most common term in the New Testament for "sin" is *hamartia*, a word which Paul uses 60 times! The basic meaning of the verbal form of *harmartia* is "to miss the mark." When my son John (Navy veteran) and I go target practicing at the shooting range, my hits are some distance from the bull's eye. Due to his military training, John's shots are usually closer and sometimes dead center. But we both frequently "miss the mark." The failure to hit the bull's eye is what Paul calls "sin."

William Barkley points out that *harmatia* "does not describe a definite act of sin; it describes the state of sin, from which acts of sin come (*New Testament Words*, SCM Press, 1964, p. 119). According to the Apostle Paul, sin is not merely a sporadic event in human experience, but is a condition that characterizes all humanity. As he explained to the Romans, "All have sinned and fall short of the glory of God" (Rom. 3:23). He later adds that people without Jesus are "sold into bondage to sin" (Rom. 7:14). Sin is a powerful enemy which is said "to take us captive" (Rom. 7:23) and "to rule over" us (Rom. 5:21).

The universal prevalence of sin in our lives leaves us in a state of "failure" and spiritual "unrighteousness" in the sight of God. It is important to note that Paul doesn't distinguish between little sins and what might be thought of as really serious sins. Any bullet that fails to hit the bull's eye is a miss, no matter how close. The same is true of sin. Any act or attitude that falls short of God's standard of righteousness is sin. And Paul made it clear to the Corinthians that "the unrighteous [ie. "sinners"] will not inherit the kingdom of God" (1 Cor. 6:9). Sin creates a separation between us and God that no good deeds or human effort can bridge. The sobering and sad reality of human sin and failure is it that it leads to spiritual death (Rom. 6:23). This is bad news! In fact, this is the worst news we could ever hear.

But there is no need to linger on the bad news. God through His grace didn't leave humanity in a condition of sin for which there was no solution. Paul declared to the Romans, "For the wages of sin is death, but the free gift of God is eternal life in Christ Jesus our Lord." This is good news indeed! In fact, this is the best news anyone could ever hear. Through the saving work of Jesus, God has provided a cure for the condition of sin that leads to death. While sin results in unrighteousness, through faith in Jesus, our sins are washed away (Acts 22:16). Paul calls this "the washing of regeneration" (Titus 3:5). In another place he calls this "the forgiveness of sins" (Col. 1:14). Forgiveness means that sinners are released from the punishment that might have been inflicted upon them by the just standards of the law.

While Paul presents us with the tragic consequences of sin, he also presents us with sin's remedy which God has provided. In the spring of 2021 people around the world were lining up for a vaccine that would remedy COVID19. Have you taken God's remedy for sin? The "washing of regeneration" and the "forgiveness of sins" are available to you through faith in the saving and redeeming work of Jesus Christ.

# About Slavery

Slavery was universally taken for granted in the first century. It was practiced in Jewish, Roman and Greek cultures, although the institution varied, depending on the laws and traditions of each group. Jewish slaves had certain privileges and were under legal protection. Their term of forced service was limited to six years (Exod. 21:2) and they were not to be sent away empty handed (Deut. 15:13-15). As commanded by biblical law, the Jews were careful to avoid treating slaves with cruelty (cf. Exod. 21:7-11, Deut. 21:10-14). Slaves among non-Jewish peoples did not receive such consideration.

The Apostle Paul never argued for the legitimacy of slavery, nor did he condemn the institution. Rather than trying to overthrow the cultural institution of slavery, Paul sought to work within the system, requiring that slaves obey their masters (Eph. 6:5, Col. 3:22-24) and that masters not mistreat their slaves (Col. 4:1).

Slavery dehumanized people into property and was never a good thing. It is helpful to distinguish between the institution of slavery and the abuses to which the institution was subject. Kidner comments, "By accepting the system, even while humanizing it, allowed that society was not ready to do without it." He suggests that God's way "was the long process of spiritual nurture, education and sharpening the conscience rather than one of premature social engineering" (Derek Kidner, *Hard Sayings: The Challenge of Old Testament Morals* (Inter-Varsity Press, 1972, p. 33).

Paul was supportive of slave emancipation, as indicated by his words to Philemon, the master of the runaway, Onesimus. Paul asked Philemon to receive Onesimus back "no longer as a slave, but more than a slave, a beloved brother" (Philemon 16). Paul then added, "I know that you will do even more than what I say" (Philemon 21; 1 Cor. 7:21). However, Paul was more concerned for spiritual freedom than for release for slaves. He remarks in 1 Cor. 7:22 that a believing slave is "the Lord's freedman" and that a free believer is "Christ's slave."

Although President Abraham Lincoln issued the Emancipation Proclamation in 1863, the United States is still suffering from the effects of slavery and the racism which allowed for it. While God is always willing to forgive our sins and failures, the consequences of sin may be experienced for many generations (Exod. 20:5). Much of the conflict between races in America today can be traced back to the disregard for human equality at the time of our nation's founding.

## About Sovereignty

Paul believed that there is one King and Ruler over the universe, the Sovereign Lord of all. One of the greatest comforts when we encounter unexpected circumstances is to know that these events have not taken God by surprise. Like a hand in a glove, God directs the circumstances of our lives for our good and His ultimate glory. Paul believed in the sovereignty of God and this important doctrine is the uniting theme behind a number of the key words used in his teachings.

Like the word "trinity," the word "sovereignty" is not found in the New Testament. Yet it is a very biblical concept. David wrote in Psalm 103:19, "The LORD has established His throne in the heavens, and His *sovereignty* rules over all." The Hebrew word translated "sovereignty" (*malcuth*) refers to God's royal power and dominion.

Many statements by Paul reflect his belief in God's sovereignty, the exercise of His kingly rule. God's sovereignty is evidenced by the fact that He predestines or "marks out the boundaries" of our lives (Eph. 1:1,11), guiding our spiritual lives and bringing us to faith in Christ. The believer's salvation is "rooted in eternity past with the predestinating work of God" (Paul Enns, *Moody Handbook of Theology*, p. 106). God's sovereignty is also reflected in God's "foreknowledge." This Greek word (*proginosko*) speaks of God's intimate and personal knowledge of us *before* we came to know Him (Rom. 8:29). Paul wrote to the Romans, "For those whom He foreknew, He also predestined to become conformed to the image of His Son" (Rom. 8:29). The believer's election into the family of God (Eph. 1:4) also points to God's sovereignty over our lives. Paul taught that God is actively involved in "working all things after the counsel of His will" to secure the believer's salvation and eternal destiny (Eph. 1:11).

While election, predestination, and foreknowledge may seem somewhat remote from our personal, daily experiences, divine sovereignty means that God is also involved in and ruling over our day-to-day lives. Paul told the Romans, "And we know that God causes all things to work together for good, to those who love God, to those who are called according to His purpose" (Rom. 8:28). Paul could rejoice in his circumstances knowing that God was sovereignly working in his life to accomplish good (Phil. 1:12). Paul's knowledge of God's sovereignty led him to rejoice in the most challenging circumstances (Phil. 1:18; 2:17; Col. 1:24). Based on his own experience, Paul could write to the Thessalonian believers, "In everything give thanks; for this is God's will for you in Christ Jesus" (1 Thess. 5:18).

## About Spiritual Gifts

The Apostle Paul taught that God had given believers various gifts for the building up of the body of Christ. The words "spiritual gifts" doesn't actually occur in Paul's writings, but he uses the words "spiritual" (*pneumatikos*) and "gifts" (*charisma*) together in the context of describing God-given abilities for service, hence the expression "spiritual gifts." These gifts are "spiritual" in that they pertain to the ministry of the Holy Spirit. They are "gifts" in that they are freely and graciously given. A "spiritual gift" is a God-given ability for service in the body of Christ.

According to Paul, each believer has received one or more spiritual gifts. He wrote to the Corinthians, "But to each one is given the manifestation of the Spirit for the common good" (1 Cor. 12:7). Spiritual gifts are given, not to promote ourselves, but to serve one another in the body of Christ. Peter made this clear in his letter, "As each one has received a special gift, employ it in serving one another, as good stewards of the manifold grace of God" (1 Pet. 4:10). Paul told the Ephesians that the gifted individuals (apostles, prophets, evangelists, pastors and teachers) were given to the church "for the equipping of the saints for the work of service, to the building up of the body of Christ" (Eph. 4:12).

Paul explained that there is great variety among spiritual gifts, but they are all given by the same Holy Spirit (1 Cor. 12:4). He then proceeded in his letter to the Corinthians to list nine gifts which the

Holy Spirit has distributed "to each one individually just as He wills" (1 Cor. 12:8-11). In Paul's letter to the Romans, we find a different listing of spiritual gifts (Rom. 12:6-8). It is debated whether the list in Ephesians 4:11 refers to spiritual gifts or leadership offices given to the church by Christ. Since Paul's lists differ, it seems that his listings are suggestive rather than exhaustive. There may be other spiritual gifts which don't appear in Paul's catalog.

There is discussion among theologians regarding the difference between a spiritual gift and an innate ability. Since they were created in the image of our creative God, many musicians, artists and performers have innate artistic abilities. During the 1960's, the pop group, *The Beatles*, rose to prominence with their amazing ability to compose and sing popular songs. The Beatles had an innate, perhaps even a God-given, ability. But since this ability wasn't used in service for the body of Christ, it wouldn't qualify as a "spiritual gift" given by the Holy Spirit.

Many Christians have wondered how they can determine their spiritual gift. There are seminars and books which focus on this question. But it is really pretty simple. If you are seeking to discover your spiritual gift, begin by answering these three questions: (1) What do you like to do? (2) What do you do well? (3) Which of your ministries in the body of Christ are blessing and encouraging people? Often a pastor or spiritual mentor can help you answer these questions and point you toward opportunities to use your gift.

In Paul's teaching on spiritual gifts, he emphasized that each believer has been strategically placed in the body of Christ "just as He desired" (1 Cor. 12:18). Some members of the church may appear less important than others, but they are in fact vitally necessary. Where would the church be without nursery workers, janitors, and widows who give a small offering from their monthly Social Security check and pray for their pastor? Paul exhorted the Corinthians not to neglect the seemingly "less important" members of the body of Christ (1 Cor. 12:21). To avoid division and promote Christian fellowship, they should be honored and appreciated (1 Cor. 12:25-26). Seeking to apply this teaching at Western Seminary, we invited Ron Miller, the head of our maintenance department, to a faculty meeting where we expressed appreciation of Ron's ministry on campus and presented him with an *Honorary Doctorate of Maintenance!* He left the meeting wearing a cap and gown, and a big smile.

# About Spiritual Warfare

You may not have thought of it when you arose this morning, but you woke up on a battlefield, facing an enemy who is seeking your destruction. The battlefield is the unbelieving world which has come under Satan's dominion (Matt. 4:8-9; Jn. 12:31). Our enemy is the Evil One who hates God, opposes His kingship, and comes among God's flock as a thief "to steal and kill and destroy" (Jn. 10:10). So what can we do in the face of this deadly threat to our spiritual lives? Should we just hunker down and hope for the return of Jesus? Paul's answers this question in his letter to the Ephesians where he instructed the believers how to boldly defend themselves and achieve victory through the Lord.

Like a commander in the field of battle, Paul issued the Ephesians a "call to arms." He wrote, "Be strong in the Lord and the strength of His might" (Eph. 6:10). He made it clear that our strength to overcome the enemy is not in ourselves, but is "in the Lord" and "His might." Paul confirmed this in his letter to the Philippians, "I can do all things through Him who strengthens me" (Phil. 4:13). Paul identified our spiritual enemies as the "rulers," "powers," "forces of darkness and "spiritual wickedness" (Eph. 6:12). Paul is referring here to Satan and his spiritual allies—the unbelievers who oppose God and demonic forces which serve as agents of our Enemy. But in the face of spiritual conflict, Paul exhorted the believers to follow the example of General "Stonewall" Jackson who sat boldly on his horse to command his troops in the midst of battle. Paul said, "Stand firm" (Eph. 6:14). The word suggests the idea of standing your ground as victor when the outcome has been determined and the fight is over.

In order to defend ourselves and advance into enemy territory, God has provided believers with a complete suit of armor, as well as offensive weapons. In Ephesians 6:14-17, Paul used the imagery of a Roman soldier's armor to provide his readers with a vivid picture of our spiritual defenses and weapons. He knew this armor well from having traveled to Rome in the custody of a soldier (Acts 27:1) and having written his letters chained to a member of the Praetorian Guard (Eph. 6:20; Phil. 1:13).

As a thick, leather belt identified a soldier on active duty, so the "belt of truth" depicts a believer prepared with God's truth for spiritual engagement. The soldiers "breastplate" protected the vital organs of his upper body, front and back. The Christian's "breastplate of righteousness" refers to the righteousness of Christ which secures a believer's eternal destiny. Roman soldiers had special sandals with hobnails to give them good footing on the battlefield. The "shoes of preparation" refer to the believer's readiness to present the gospel to those who are wavering in their spiritual allegiance. The Roman infantry carried a large shield to deflect the spears and arrows of the enemy. The believer's "shield of faith" consists of our trust in Christ our Commander and Savior. As the soldier's helmet was designed to deflect blows and protect his head, so the believer's "helmet of salvation" provides eternal security and protection through Jesus.

Our spiritual warfare is not merely defensive. To advance God's kingdom in enemy territory, God has provided "the sword of the Spirit" which Paul identified as "the word of God." The particular word Paul used for "word" (*rema*) refers to the *spoken* words of God. This was the "sword" Jesus used when He quoted Scripture to refute the devil (Matt. 4:1-10). There is one more weapon in our spiritual arsenal to do spiritual battle in enemy territory. Paul concluded, "With all prayer and petition, pray at all times in the Spirit, … alert with all perseverance and petition for all the saints" (Eph. 18).

You may have never been in the army, but you are at war. And although the battle rages and the casualties are many, the outcome of the conflict is certain. "Thanks be to God who gives us the victory through our Lord Jesus Christ" (1 Cor. 15:57; Rev. 12:11).

## About Submission

Paul recognized that God, in His wisdom, has placed certain authority figures over Christians to lead and guide their behavior. These include civil or government leaders (Rom. 13:1-7), church leaders (Tit. 3:1), masters (employers by application, Eph. 6:5) and parents (Eph. 6:1). In his teaching on this subject, Paul calls believers "to submit" (*hupotasso*) to those in positions of authority. The Greek word translated "submit" is made up of two words, *hupo* ("under") and *tasso* ("to command"). Christian submission involves a recognition of the authorities God has placed over us and a willingness to obey them. Submission to authority is not easy, especially in a society which places a high value on individualism and self-determination. But submission to legitimate leaders and divinely appointed authorities is God's way of maintaining order in society and in our interactions with others.

One of the most challenging areas of submission to authority these days is in the home. Paul instructed wives to "be subject to their own husbands as to the Lord" (Eph. 5:22). This does not make the husband "commander-in-chief" to be mindlessly followed and obeyed. Rather, it means that a husband has the special responsibility of providing spiritual leadership for his wife and children. For the spiritual wellbeing of the family, wives are to recognize and support the leadership of their husband in the home. Husbands are called to "love your wives, just as also Christ loved the church and gave himself up for her" (Eph. 5:25). This means that the husband must carry out his family responsibilities and leadership through personal sacrifice and *agape* love. Unless the husband's leadership is in conflict with God's Word, he should be respected, followed, and supported with confidence in his biblically assigned role.

A student once asked me, "How do I make my wife submit to my leadership in the home?" I explained that biblical submission is something we do in obedience to Scripture, not something demanded by a person in leadership. The husband is called to love his wife with the kind of personal sacrifice that was demonstrated by Jesus in His love for the church. A husband is not called to *make* his wife acquiesce to his leadership. But most wives will gladly recognize the spiritual leadership of a loving husband who sacrifices himself for her.

# About Suffering

Paul suffered. Most people do. We suffer in a variety of ways during our spiritual journey to heaven. As followers of Jesus, we suffer rejection by the world and often by the people we love. We suffer from sickness and eventual death because while our souls have been redeemed, our physical bodies are still subject to the effects of sin's curse. How do we manage suffering when it comes our way? What did Paul teach about the universal experience of suffering?

As a persecutor of believers before coming to faith in Jesus, Paul himself was the cause of much suffering (Acts 8:3; Phil. 3:6). Once he became a follower of Jesus, the tables turned, and Paul experienced the same kind of suffering which he had caused others. Unbelieving Jews and leaders at Antioch "instigated a persecution against Paul and Barnabas, and drove them out of their district (Acts 13:50). Paul was stoned and dragged out of the city of Lystra (Acts 14:19), beaten and placed in stocks at Philippi (Acts 16:22-24). In a letter to the Corinthians, Paul provided details of the extensive suffering he had experienced as an apostle of Jesus (2 Cor. 11:23-27). But in spite of the painful and often humiliating experiences he had been through, Paul declared to Timothy, "I am not ashamed; for I know whom I have believed" (2 Tim. 2:9). Paul was willing to endure suffering for the sake of sharing the gospel (2 Tim. 2:10).

Paul knew that the suffering he had experienced would be shared by other followers of Jesus. He wrote to the Philippians, "For to you it has been granted for Christ's sake, not only to believe in Him, but also to suffer for His sake" (Phil. 1:29). In his letter to the Thessalonians Paul explained that the suffering they were enduring was an indicator that they were "considered worthy of the kingdom of God" (2 Thess. 1:5).

Paul used a number of different Greek words to describe believers' suffering. Adding the prefix *sun* ("with") to the term for general suffering (*pascho*), Paul describes shared or joint suffering. Because of our spiritual unity in the body of Christ, "If one member suffers, all the members suffer (*sunpascho*) with it" (1 Cor. 12:26). This word is also used by Paul to describe the suffering believers share with Christ (Rom. 8:17). Adding the prefix *pro* ("before") Paul refers to past suffering (1 Thess. 2:2). The Greek word *pathema* is used to describe suffering afflictions (Gal. 5:24; 2 Tim. 3:11). The Greek word *hupomeno* ("to abide" and "under") was used by Paul when he wrote Timothy about enduring suffering (2 Tim. 2:12). Adding the prefix *makro* ("long") to the Greek word for suffering, Paul extoled *agape* love as "long suffering" or "patient" (1 Cor. 13:4).

How should believers respond to their inevitable experiences of suffering? First, we shouldn't be surprised by it. Jesus promised that His followers would suffer (Jn. 15:18-25). Second, we should rejoice in what God is accomplishing through suffering. Paul wrote to the Romans, "We also exult in our tribulations, knowing that tribulation brings about perseverance; and perseverance, proven character; and proven character, hope" (Rom. 5:3-4). Third, we must remember that no experience of suffering can separate believers from the love of Christ (Rom. 8:35-39). Fourth, we can be confident that our present sufferings are as nothing when compared to the glorious future that awaits us. Paul wrote, "For I consider the sufferings of this present time are not worthy to be compared with the glory that is to be revealed to us" (Rom. 8:17-18). Suffering is painful. But God uses it to draw us to Himself, build our character, and prepare us for eternity where there will be *no* suffering.

## About Teaching

Paul was a teacher. During his early days in Jerusalem before coming to faith in Jesus, Israel's Messiah, Paul studied under Gamaliel, a respected rabbi and esteemed "teacher of the law" (Acts 5:34; 22:3). When Barnabas learned that the church at Antioch needed a teacher, he brought Paul from Tarsus and together they "met with the church and taught considerable numbers" (Acts 11:26).

Paul's preaching of the gospel at Pisidian Antioch (Acts 13:14-41) indicates that his sermons usually included a great deal of teaching about Israel's history, God's covenants, and the biblical prophecies of Messiah's coming. In addition to being an apostle, Paul identified himself both as "a preacher" and "a teacher" (1 Tim. 2:7; 2 Tim. 1:11). At Antioch, Paul did both (Acts 15:35). So, what is the difference between teaching and preaching? The Greek word "to teach" (*didasko*) has the basic idea of giving instructions. A "teacher" (*didaskalos*) is someone who gives instruction or imparts knowledge to others. Nicodemus, the prominent Pharisee who came to Jesus at night, is identified as "the teacher of Israel" (Jn. 3:10). A "preacher" (*kerux*) is someone who makes a proclamation. Noah is identified as a "preacher of righteousness" (2 Pet. 2:5). He proclaimed God's message about the impending flood and means of deliverance by entering the ark. I suggest that *teaching* provides information. *Preaching* calls people to respond to the information they have received. Paul's sermons included both teaching and preaching. My Bible class lectures deliver information. But I always encourage my students to *respond* by making personal application of the biblical principles they had learned.

Paul recognized that "teaching" was one of the gifts (*charisma*) that God gave believers to serve the church (Rom. 12:7). While there are many professional teachers in secular schools and universities, someone with the spiritual gift of teaching will use their gift to edify believers and build up Christ's church. The Apostle Paul clearly had this gift (1 Cor. 4:17). Being gifted or "skilled in teaching" (*didaktikos*) is one of the qualifications for the office of church elder (1 Tim. 3:2). The gift of teaching is not limited to men, for Paul encourages spiritually mature women to be "teachers of what is good" (Tit. 2:3). While Paul commended teaching what is good, he warned Timothy against those who teach a *heteros* ("different") doctrine, teaching that is contrary to the words of Jesus and the Word of God (1 Tim. 6:3).

If you are a teacher and are looking for someone to model your ministry after, look no further than Ezra, the scribe. "For Ezra had set his heart to *study* the law ("instruction") of the LORD and to *practice* it, and to *teach* His statutes and ordinances in Israel (Ezra 7:10). Ezra provides teachers with a timeless pattern for our ministry. First, we must study God's Word. Then we must personally apply the biblical principles in our own lives. Finally, we share with others the truths we have learned and applied. It has been my joy over a lifetime to study, apply and teach God's living and abiding Word.

# About Temptation

The Apostle Paul was quite familiar with the concept of temptation to sin. He had faced temptation many times and repeatedly succumbed to sin. He wrote Timothy saying, "Christ Jesus came into the world to save sinners, among whom I am foremost of all" (1 Tim. 1:15). What did Paul teach about temptation to sin?

The Greek word "to tempt" (*peirazo*) means "to try, test or prove." The noun form of this word (*peirasmos*) can refer to (1) *trials,* which may be intended to refine and develop character, or (2) *solicitation to do evil.* Paul used this word to refer to the "trial" of his bodily illness which he experienced during his ministry in Galatia (Gal. 4:14). Although God may send trials into our lives, He does not solicit us to do evil. Trials come from God. Temptation comes from our enemy, Satan (1 Cor. 7:5). In his letter to the Thessalonians, Paul used the present participle of *peirazo* to refer to Satan as "the tempter," indicating that temptation is our enemy's present and ongoing activity (1 Thess. 3:5).

Although the followers of Jesus will sometimes respond to temptation, taking the bait Satan offers, they can also say "no!" to Satan's solicitation to evil. After recounting the spiritual failures of the

Israelites during their forty years in the wilderness, Paul told the Corinthians that these stories "were written for our instruction" (1 Cor. 10:11). Then he added, "No temptation has overtaken you but such as is common to man; and God is faithful, who will not allow you to be tempted beyond what you are able, but with the temptation will provide the way of escape also, so that you will be able to endure it" (1 Cor. 10:13). This is especially good news for believers as they strive to live holy lives. We don't have to succumb to sin. Our faithful God will *always* provide "a way of escape" from the temptations Satan throws into our pathway! Conforming our lives to Christ is a lifetime endeavor, but even when we fail, God will never give up on us. His good work in our lives will continue until we enter heaven and are completely and finally glorified (Rom. 8:30). In that day, temptation and sin will be so far removed from us that they won't even be a memory!

## About Tongues

The Apostle Paul had the spiritual gift of speaking in tongues. In fact, he told the Corinthians, "I speak in tongues more than you all" (1 Cor. 14:18). The ability to speak in a language you haven't learned was given as a spiritual gift to the church on the Day of Pentecost (Acts 2:4). This gift was given by the Holy Spirit as a witness to Jewish people and for the edification of the body of Christ (Acts 2:5-6; 1 Cor. 12:7). The gift of tongues enabled people to speak in known and understood languages (Acts 2:6,11), not merely ecstatic utterances which they had not studied or learned.

Several observations are helpful as we consider Paul's teaching about the gift of tongues. First, not everyone in the early church had this gift (1 Cor. 12:30). Second, tongues were given as a temporal gift. Paul declared, "Tongues will cease" (1 Cor. 13:8). Third, tongues are not unique to Christian experience. Tongues were used in ancient times by Gnostics to deliver the oracle in Apollo's temple at Delphi. Tongues are used today in Eastern religions, in the practice of Yoga, by Mormons, and African animists.

While Paul valued the gift of tongues when accompanied by translation, he believed that prophecy was superior. He explained to the Corinthians that tongues *without* interpretation are unintelligible and do not serve to edify the church (1 Cor. 14:2-17). Paul insisted that the gift of prophecy was potentially more edifying since a prophetic word could be readily understood without the need for interpretation (1 Cor. 14:19).

Paul believed that anyone with the gift of tongues should understand the biblical purpose of this unusual gift (1 Cor. 14:20-22). Paul quoted from Isaiah 28:11-12 to show that tongues were a sign of God's judgment on the people of Israel who had rejected His Word. Isaiah told the Judeans that when they heard "strange tongues" being spoken by strangers, God's judgment was upon them. The "strange tongues" were the words of the Assyrians who were God's instrument of judgment on the unbelieving and disobedient Judeans. Paul's point was that tongues do not serve as God's greeting to a believing congregation, but serve as His rebuke to an unbelieving nation (Zane Hodges, "The Purpose of Tongues," *Bibliotheca Sacra*, July 1963, pp. 226-33). The sign rejected would lead to judgment. The sign of tongues accepted would lead to repentance and deliverance from judgment.

While Paul emphasized the superiority of prophecy over tongues, he did not forbid the use of this gift (1 Cor. 14:39). But to avoid confusion in the assembly of believers, Paul provided the Corinthians with some regulations for using the gift (1 Cor. 14:26-27). First, the guiding principle for the use of speaking gifts, whether tongues or prophecy, is that they must be used for the edification of the body. Second, no more than two or three should speak at one meeting. Third, there must be no interruption of the one who is speaking. Fourth, if no one is available to interpret, the person with the gift of tongues "must keep silent in the church."

Paul believed that tongues were a temporary gift. He explained to the Corinthians that tongues will someday cease (1 Cor. 13:8-10). Paul associated this cessation of tongues with the coming of "the perfect" (*to teleion*). The key question for us is, "What is the 'perfect'?" Some have argued that the "perfect" refers to the completed canon of Scripture. Others have suggested that the "perfect" refers to the Second Coming of Jesus. A third view suggests that the "perfect" refers to the maturity of the body of Christ. This third approach seems broad enough to embrace the relative maturity implied in Paul's illustration (13:11) as well as the absolute maturity depicted in verse 12. The word *teleios* ("mature") pictures the church growing collectively as a body, beginning with its birth and progressing through different stages during the present age.

252

According to Robert Thomas, the church will reach complete maturity at the return of Christ ("Tongues Will Cease," *Journal of the Evangelical Theological Society*, Spring 1974, pp. 81-89).

The question, "When will tongues cease?" is bound with the question, "When will the church be mature?" Certainly, the church will be mature at the return of Christ (13:11). It may also be considered mature when a time of continuing revelation is no longer necessary. At such a time, the gifts of knowledge, tongues and prophecy will no longer be needed to provide or verify special revelation.

# About Traditions

A tradition is something that is handed down from one generation to the next. The Laney family has a tradition of joining hands at the table as we give thanks to God for the food He has provided for us to enjoy. Paul had some "traditions" that he had received and wanted to "pass on" to disciples in the churches he had established.

In the first century Jewish context, a tradition (*paradosis*) was a custom or teaching handed down by the rabbis. The Pharisees and scribes accused Jesus' disciples of breaking "the tradition of the elders" when they didn't follow the custom of ritual handwashing before eating (Matt. 15:2). Traditions like this were the oral teachings of Judaism which were believed to have been given to Israel when they received the written law from God at Mt. Sinai. Jesus responded by telling the Jewish leaders that they gave more credence to their oral traditions than the written Word of God (Matt. 15:3-6).

Before coming to faith in Israel's Messiah, Paul had been "extremely zealous" for Israel's ancestral traditions (Gal. 1:14). But he came to recognize that these ceremonial rules and regulations constituted "the tradition of men" rather than the teaching of Jesus (Col. 2:8).

On the other hand, Paul commended the Corinthians for holding "firmly to the traditions" which he had delivered to them (1 Cor. 11:2). In this context, Paul used the word "traditions" to refer to the orthodox doctrine which he had received and taught as an apostle of Jesus Christ. He wrote to the Thessalonian believers, "So then, brethren, stand firm and hold to the traditions which you were taught, whether by word of mouth or by letter from us" (2 Thess. 2:15). One of these "traditions" came directly from Jesus. Paul told the Corinthians, "For I received from the Lord that which I also delivered to you, that the Lord Jesus in the night in which He was betrayed took bread and when He had given thanks, He broke it and said, 'This is My body, which is for you; do this in remembrance of Me'" (1 Cor. 11:23-24). Paul's summary of the gospel in 1 Corinthians 15 was prefaced by his acknowledgment that this teaching comes as an authoritative, apostolic tradition. Paul wrote, "For I delivered to you as of first importance what I also received…" (1 Cor. 15:3). According to Paul, authoritative tradition includes conduct, as well as doctrine. He warned the Thessalonians about how to deal with unruly believers who are not living "according to the tradition which you received from us" (2 Thess. 3:6).

Churches in the 21st century embrace many traditions which are based on Scripture. Other traditions are based on the experiences of believers living in different times and cultures. Some Christians baptize "in the name of Jesus." Others immerse new believers "in the name of the Father, Son and Holy Spirit." Some churches observe the Lord's Supper once a month. Others observe communion weekly. Some churches fill communion cups with grape juice while others use wine. We look to Scripture as the biblical basis for Christian doctrine and traditions. And we seek to respect and appreciate denominational differences and traditions that don't violate the clear teaching of Scripture.

## About Tribulation

Many Christians who read the word "tribulation" think immediately of the eschatological period referred to by the Apostle John as "the great tribulation" (Rev. 7:14). But the Greek word for "tribulation" (*thlipsis*) is broader than that. The root meaning of the Greek word is "pressure," and can be translated as "tribulation," "affliction" or "distress." Jesus announced that His followers, living in an unbelieving world, would experience "tribulation" (Jn. 16:33). Paul understood and confirmed that promise.

After being stoned and dragged out of the city of Lystra, Paul encouraged the disciples to continue in the faith saying, "Through many tribulations we must enter the kingdom of God" (Acts 14:22).

Paul commended the Thessalonians for their enduring faith in the midst of their persecutions and afflictions (2 Thess. 1:4) and promised that God would give "relief to you who are afflicted" when the Lord returns from heaven with His mighty angels (2 Thess. 1:7). This suggests that "tribulations" or "afflictions" are going to be with us for a while!

Paul wanted the Corinthians to know that God comforts us in all our afflictions (2 Cor. 1:4). He further explained that the purpose of our receiving God's comfort is so that we will be able "to comfort those who are in any affliction with the comfort with which we ourselves are comforted by God" (2 Cor. 1:4). In other words, while tribulations or afflictions are not pleasant, God uses these experiences to expand our ministry. The best comforters are those who have experienced God's comfort in the midst of their own suffering. Having survived a personal ordeal, they are well prepared to comfort others who are going through similar circumstances.

One of my former students had his right arm severed as the result of an accident in the bakery where he worked. I'll never forget his return to my class in a shirt with an empty sleeve. Yet through his personal loss, Tom gained a ministry of comforting other young people who had lost a limb. When he walked into their hospital room, the patient knew that he had experienced what they had suffered. Tom lost an arm, but gained a ministry of counsel and encouragement that would have been impossible for someone with two well attached arms.

Paul warned that sometimes "tribulation" enters our lives because of sin (Rom. 2:9). These afflictions can be avoided by steering clear of temptation. But when we humbly confess our sins and are restored to fellowship with Christ, even those troubles can be used to build our character (Rom. 5:3). The good news about *thlipsis* is that no matter what the cause or how we experience it, tribulation will never be able "to separate us from the love of God, which is in Christ Jesus our Lord" (Rom. 8:39).

## About Virgins

Paul believed in the institution of marriage and encouraged it among his disciples. But he also recognized that the single life was also a good option for the followers of Jesus. In fact, Paul wrote to the Corinthians that a single person may even be "happier" than someone who marries (1 Cor. 7:40). In 1 Corinthians 7, Paul explains why.

In 1 Corinthians 7:1, Paul began responding to questions which had been raised by the believers at Corinth. After answering several questions about marriage and divorce, Paul addressed the subject of the unmarried (1 Cor. 7:25; "Now concerning virgins"). The principle that forms the basis of Paul's instructions is that believers should remain in the marital state in which they were called to Christ. The married should stay married, and single people should remain single (1 Cor. 7:26-27). But then he added, "But if you [a man] marry, you have not sinned; and if a virgin [woman] marries, she has not sinned" (1 Cor. 7:28). Paul makes it clear that deciding to marry is not an act of sin. Whew! I'm sure glad he settled that question!

Continuing his comments on virgins, Paul offered three advantages for those who remain unmarried (1 Cor. 7:28-35). First, the single life is less complicated in these uncertain and troubled times. Second, the single life helps people focus on what is eternal rather than things that are transitory. Third, the single life provides a greater opportunity to devote oneself to serving Christ.

I am glad that the Lord led me to Nancy with whom I have enjoyed 49 wonderful years of shared ministry and family life. Marriage has been "good" for me. But Paul made it clear that in certain times and situations, the single life is "better" (1 Cor. 7:38). God's people need to recognize and celebrate the *blessed* state of singleness along with the *happy* state of matrimony.

## About Widows

The Bible reflects God's particular concern for the most vulnerable members of society, especially the widows and orphans (Exod. 22:22; Deut. 27:19; Ps. 68:5; Isa. 10:1-3; Jer. 22:3). The Apostle Paul shared this concern and wanted to make sure that the widows in believing congregations were being cared for. In his first letter to Timothy, who was giving pastoral leadership to the church at Ephesus, Paul provided specific instructions regarding the care of widows.

Paul instructed Timothy that the care of widows is a family responsibility. He wrote, "If any widow has children or grandchildren, they must first learn to practice piety in regard to their own family and to make some return to their parents; for this is acceptable in the sight of God" (1 Tim. 5:4). He directed some strong words against those who might be tempted to neglect this responsibility. Paul wrote, "But if anyone does not provide for his own, and especially for those of his household, he has denied the faith and is worse than an unbeliever" (1 Tim. 5:8).

After the passing of Nancy's dad, we had the privilege of caring for her widowed mother for over twenty years before she joined him in heaven. Nancy's mom was able to meet her own financial needs, but there were emotional, physical, and spiritual needs that we were able to help her with. What a privilege and a joy it was to have her visit our home, help her with taxes, and take her to doctor appointments as she declined. For widows without a family to help with their needs, Paul directed the church to reach with our compassion, love and personal assistance.

While Paul had a high regard for the single life, he encouraged younger widows to remarry (1 Tim. 5:14). Young widows were likely to have children and would be more interested in raising a family. If possible, a young widow should remarry and be cared for by her husband. But older widows could qualify to receive financial and other forms of assistance from the church.

Paul provided Timothy with a list of qualifications for widows who might receive church support (1 Tim. 5:5-10). To be placed on the list, a widow must be (1) completely alone, with no family available to assist, (2) a Christian woman, (3) a woman of prayer, (4) a woman who is "above reproach," (5) over sixty years of age, (6) the wife of one man, and (7) known for her good works. The reference to her having "washed the saints' feet" (1 Tim. 5:10) reflects her humble service to others in the body of Christ (Jn. 13:14-15).

These qualifications may be helpful for church leaders today as they consider the kind of assistance they are able to offer widows in their congregations. Even if a widow (or a divorced woman) doesn't meet all these qualifications, Paul encourages us to follow the example of Jesus and "do good to all people, and especially those of the household of faith" (Acts 10:36; Gal. 6:10). Helping widows in your church is one way to follow the example of Jesus in doing good.

# About Wisdom

Wisdom is a theme that is developed throughout Scripture. In fact, the books of Job, Proverbs, Ecclesiastes, the Song of Songs and several psalms are regarded as Wisdom Literature. Biblical wisdom (*sophia*) is more than knowledge. There are people who have lots of knowledge, but are not very good at applying what they know. Wisdom is the ability to use knowledge in a practical and successful way. Paul referred to the God of Israel as "the only wise God" (Rom. 16:27), and He is the ultimate source of wisdom for believers (Jms. 1:5). Paul told the Colossians that in Jesus Christ "is hidden all the treasures of wisdom and knowledge" (Col. 2:3).

In Paul's letter to the Corinthians, he contrasted "the wisdom of the world" with "the wisdom of God" (1 Cor. 1:20-25). The unbelieving world attempts to find wisdom apart from God and His Word. Rejecting the ultimate source of wisdom, they remain in their ignorance and folly. Paul questioned his readers, "Where is the wise man?" (1 Cor. 1:20). The answer he expected from this rhetorical question is, "There are none." The world's so-called "wisdom" is actually foolishness in the sight of God. Worldly, human wisdom is vain and fruitless, for it can never lead to salvation or give someone comprehension of the plan of God. Human reason, secular philosophy and religious traditions may have "the appearance of wisdom" (Col. 2:8,23), but self-made religion has no ability to deliver us from sin's power or penalty.

According to Paul, God's wisdom is captured and summarized in the message of "Christ crucified" (1 Cor. 1:23). While this message appears foolish in the eyes of the world, the redemptive work of Jesus Christ reflects the power of God and the wisdom of God (1 Cor. 1:24). Paul wanted to make sure that the message he preached was not based on human wisdom or persuasive rhetoric, but on the power and wisdom of God as displayed in the gospel. God continues to display His wisdom through the church (Eph. 3:10) as the gospel is proclaimed.

# About Women in Ministry

The subject being considered here is the most controversial issue I have had to deal with over my forty years of teaching at

Western Seminary. I have studied this topic extensively and taught what I believe the Bible teaches on the role of women in ministry. Some students have agreed with me. Others have disagreed. All I ask is that we read and study what Paul taught on this subject. It is OK if we come to different conclusions so long as we have studied the key texts and sought to honor Christ by our careful exegesis and application of Paul's teaching.

In 1 Timothy 2-3 Paul wrote Timothy about how believers should conduct themselves "in the household of God, which is the church of the living God" (1 Tim. 3:15). The meeting of the church is a gathered congregation where elders lead, the Word is preached, and the ordinances are observed. Within *this* specific context, Paul wrote, "I do not allow a woman to teach or exercise authority over a man, but to remain quiet" (1 Tim. 2:12). Then, in listing the qualifications for the "office of overseer," another term for "elder" (Acts 20:17,28), Paul wrote that these church leaders must be "the husband of one wife" (1 Tim. 3:2). I conclude from these two statements that the authoritative teaching of the Word of God in the meeting of the church is to be done by men who serve in the office of elder/overseer. There is considerable debate as to whether this is what Paul meant to say and whether this teaching has any application for the 21st century. While it is important to consider other views, I keep returning to the words of Paul for further study and reflection. I have concluded that this is what Paul intended to say and his instruction has application for the meeting of the church today.

That being said, you may be wondering what Christian women *can* do to serve Christ today. There are many opportunities for women to serve, teach, and lead outside the parameters of Paul's specific regulations for the meeting of the church (1 Tim. 3:15). Christian women can evangelize, teach, provide health care, do counseling, lead organizations, write books, translate Scripture, exercise hospitality, serve on the staff of a church, a conference center, a Christian ministry, a mission organization, a Bible school or seminary, and minister as a hospital or military chaplain. This list is only suggestive of the *many* opportunities God has provided for Christian women to serve the body of Christ and advance God's kingdom.

You may disagree with my comments and conclusions. That's OK. It is not going to make a difference in eternity. There is room in the body of Christ for different views on this subject. The main thing to remember is that women are spiritually gifted and have been given a great variety of opportunities to minister in the body of Christ. It has been my privilege to have many gifted women in my seminary classes who are actively serving Christ's church and doing God's kingdom work today.

## About Worship

The Apostle Paul was not just an evangelist, a missionary and a teacher. He was a man who was deeply devoted to Jesus and sought to worship God in spirit and in truth. He believed that when people were confronted with the truth of God's Word, they should "fall on their face and worship" (1 Cor. 14:25). The Greek word translated "worship" (*proskuneo*) is the combination of two words: *pros* ("towards") and *kuneo* ("to kiss"). To worship is literally, "to kiss towards" God and reflects an attitude of reverence, affection and adoration towards our one true Sovereign Lord.

Lydia, who came to faith and was baptized by Paul at Philippi, was described as a "worshiper of God" (Acts 16:14), as was Titius Justus at Corinth (Acts 18:7). When the Jews brought charges against Paul at Corinth, he was accused of persuading men "to worship God contrary to the law" (Acts 18:13). Paul included himself when he wrote to the Philippians and described believers as those who "worship in the Spirit of God and glory in Christ" (Phil. 3:3).

Although Paul never defined what it means "to worship," it is clear from Scripture that believers can worship God through songs, hymns, praise, sacrificial giving, humble service for Christ and His followers, thanksgiving, prayer, preaching and public proclamation of God's attributes, ways, claims and worthiness. Paul interjected worship into his letter to Timothy when he wrote, "Now to the King eternal, immortal, invisible, the only God, be honor and glory forever and ever. Amen" (1 Tim. 1:17). The study of God's Word should always lead us to worship. I pray that your study of Paul's life and teaching would serve this same purpose, leading you to worship Jesus, our Messiah, Savior and King.

# Appendix
## Chronology of the Apostolic Age

The Book of Acts covers the period from the ascension of Jesus (May 14, AD 33) through Paul's first imprisonment in Rome (AD 60-62). Secular history has pinpointed some events in Acts upon which one might build a chronology: the death of Herod Agrippa (12:20-23; AD 44), the expulsion of the Jews from Rome by Claudius (18:2; AD 49), the proconsulship of Gallio (18:12; AD 51/52), and the procuratorship of Festus (24:27; AD 59). By synchronizing these historically fixed dates with the events in Acts, Dr. Harold Hoehner has made a valuable contribution to the study of Acts in his "Chronology of the Apostolic Age" (Dallas: Th.D. dissertation, 1965; revised April 1972).

The following chart presents a summary of the dates determined by Hoehner's chronological research. All dates are *anno Domini* (AD), "In the year of the Lord."

| The Event | The Scripture | The Date |
|---|---|---|
| Crucifixion of Jesus | Matt. 28:33-66 | April 3, AD33 |
| Ascension of Jesus | Acts 1 | May 14, 33 |
| Pentecost | Acts 2 | May 24, 33 |
| Stephen martyred | Acts 6:8-7:60 | April 35 |
| **Saul meets Jesus** | Acts 9:1-7 | Summer 35 |
| Saul in Arabia | Acts 9:8-25; Gal. 1:16-17 | Summer 35-37 |
| 1st Jerusalem visit | Acts 9:26-29; Gal. 1:18-20 | Summer 37 |
| Saul to Tarsus | Acts 9:30; Gal. 1:21 | Fall 37 |
| Peter goes to Gentiles | Acts 10:1-11:18 | 40-41 |
| Saul to Antioch | Acts 11:25-26 | Spring 43 |
| Prediction of famine | Acts 11:27-28 | Spring 44 |
| Famine Relief Visit | Acts 11:30; Gal. 2:1-10 | Fall 47 |
| Saul in Antioch | Acts 12:25-13:1 | Fall 47-Spring 48 |
| **Paul's 1st Journey** | Acts 13-14 | Apr. 48-Sept. 49 |
| Peter in Antioch | Gal. 2:11-16 | Fall 49 |
| Letter to the Galatians | | Fall 49 |
| Jerusalem Council | Acts 15 | Fall 49 |
| Paul in Antioch | Acts 12:25-13:1 | Winter 49/50 |
| **Paul's 2nd Journey** | Acts 15:36-18:22 | Apr. 50-Sept. 52 |

| | | |
|---|---|---|
| 1st Thessalonians | | Early summer 51 |
| 2nd Thessalonians | | Summer 51 |
| Jerusalem visit | Acts 18:22 | Fall 52 |
| Return to Antioch | Acts 18:22 | Nov. 52 |
| Winter in Antioch | Acts 18:23 | Winter 52/53 |
| **Paul's 3rd Journey** | Acts 18:23-21:16 | Spring 53-May 57 |
| Departure from Antioch | Acts 18:23 | Spring 53 |
| Arrival at Ephesus | Acts 19:1 | Spring 53 |
| 1 Corinthians written | | Spring 56 |
| Departs from Ephesus | Acts 20:1 | May 56 |
| Arrival in Macedonia | Acts 20:2 | June 56 |
| 2 Corinthians written | | Fall 56 |
| Departs Macedonia | Acts 20:2 | Nov. 56 |
| Arrival in Corinth | Acts 20:2 | Nov. 56 |
| Romans written | | Winter 56/57 |
| Departs Corinth | Acts 20:3 | February 57 |
| Return to Judea | Acts 20:6-21:8 | March-May 57 |
| Stay in Caesarea | Acts 21:8-14 | May 57 |
| Caesarea to Jerusalem | Acts 21:15 | Late May 57 |
| Meeting with James | Acts 21:13-23 | Late May 57 |
| Arrest in Jerusalem | Acts 21:26-24:22 | Early June 57 |
| Taken to Caesarea | Acts 23:33 | Early June 57 |
| Trial before Felix | Acts 24-26 | June 57 |
| Caesarean Imprisonment | Acts 24:27 | June 57-Aug. 59 |
| Trial before Festus | Acts 25:7-12 | July 59 |
| Trial before Agrippa | Acts 26 | Early August 59 |
| **Paul's Voyage to Rome** | Acts 27:1-28:29 | Aug. 59-Feb. 60 |
| Departs from Caesarea | Acts 27:1 | Mid-August 59 |
| Shipwreck on Malta | Acts 27:39-44 | Late October 59 |
| Departs from Malta | Acts 28:11 | Early February 60 |
| Arrival in Rome | Acts 28:16 | Late February 60 |
| Roman Imprisonment | Acts 28:30-31 | Feb. 60-Mar. 62 |
| Ephesians written | | Fall 60 |
| Philippians written | | Early spring 62 |
| Colossians & Philemon written | | Early spring 62 |

| Paul's Travels after Acts | | Spring 62-67 |
|---|---|---|
| Paul in Ephesus & Colossae | 1 Tim. 1:3; Philemon 22 | Spring-Fall 62 |
| Paul in Macedonia | 1 Tim. 1:3; Phil. 1:15, 2:24 | Summer 62-winter 62/63 |
| 1 Timothy written | 1 Tim. 3:14-15 | Fall 62 |
| Paul in Asia Minor | 1 Tim. 3:14 | Spring 63-spring 64 |
| Paul in Spain | Rom. 15:24 | Spring 64-spring 66 |
| Paul in Crete | Titus 1:5 | Early summer 66 |
| Paul in Asia Minor | 2 Tim. 4:13,20 | Summer-Fall 66 |
| Titus written | Titus 1:1-4 | Summer 66 |
| Paul in Nicopolis | Titus 3:12 | Winter 66/67 |
| Paul in Macedonia & Greece | Titus 3:12; 2 Tim. 4:20 | Spring-Fall 67 |
| Paul arrested and brought to Rome | 2 Tim. 1:8,6; 2:9 | Fall 67 |
| 2 Timothy written | 2 Tim. 1:1-2 | Fall 67 |
| Paul's death in Rome | 2 Tim. 4:6-8 | Spring 68 |
| Destruction of Jerusalem | | Fall AD 70 |

# Bibliography for Further Study on Paul

Beitzel, Barry J., General Editor. *Lexham Geographic Commentary on Acts through Revelation*. Bellingham, WA. Lexham Press, 2019.

Beck, John A. *The Basic Bible Atlas*. Grand Rapids: Baker Books, 2020.

Bruce, F. F. *Paul: Apostle of the Heart Set Free*. Grand Rapids, MI. Wm. B. Eerdmans, 1977.

Longenecker, Richard N. *Paul, Apostle of Liberty*. Grand Rapids, MI. Wm. B. Eerdmans, 1964, 2015.

Rasmussen, Carl G. *Essential Bible Atlas*. Grand Rapids, MI. Zondervan, 2013.

Schreiner, Thomas. *Paul: Apostle of God's Glory in Christ*. Downers Grove, IL. InterVarsity Press, 2006.

Paul H. Wright. *Understanding the New Testament: An Introductory Atlas*. Jerusalem: Carta, 2004; *Holman Illustrated Guide to Biblical Geography*. Nashville, TN. Holman, 2020.

Young, Brad. *Paul: The Jewish Theologian*. Grand Rapids, MI. Baker Publishing, 1977.

## Books by the Author

*The Divorce Myth*. Bethany House Publishers, 1981.
*First and Second Samuel*. Moody Publishers, 1981.
*Ezra-Nehemiah*. Moody Publishers, 1982.
*Zechariah*. Moody Publishers, 1984.
*Your Guide to Church Discipline*. Bethany House,1985.
*Concise Bible Atlas*. Baker, 1988.
*New Bible Companion*. Tyndale House, 1990.
*Commentary on the Gospel of John*. Moody Publishers, 1992.
*Answers to Tough Questions.* Kregel, 1997.
*Messiah's Coming Temple*. Kregel, 1997.
*God.* Word Publishing. 1999.
*Essential Bible Background: What You Should Know Before You Read the Bible.* CreateSpace, 2016.
*Your Psalm of Praise.* Kindle e-book, 2017.
*Biblical Wisdom: Your Key to Success.* CreateSpace, 2018.
*Discipleship: Training from the Master Disciple Maker.* CreateSpace, 2018.
*The Story of Israel.* Kindle Direct Publishing, 2019.
*The Story of Jesus.* Kindle Direct Publishing, 2020.

Made in the USA
Columbia, SC
11 April 2021